STUDIES IN HIGHER EDUCATION

Edited by
Philip G. Altbach

Monan Professor of Higher Education
Lynch School of Education, Boston College

A ROUTLEDGE SERIES

Studies in Higher Education

Philip G. Altbach, *General Editor*

THE CHANGING LANDSCAPE OF THE ACADEMIC PROFESSION
The Culture of Faculty at For-Profit Colleges and Universities

Vicente M. Lechuga

Routledge
Taylor & Francis Group
NEW YORK AND LONDON

Published in 2006 by
Routledge
Taylor & Francis Group
711 Third Avenue
New York
NY 10017

Published in Great Britain by
Routledge
Taylor & Francis Group
2 Park Square
Milton Park, Abingdon
Oxon OX14 4RN

10 9 8 7 6 5 4 3 2 1

International Standard Book Number-13: 978-0-415-97699-2 (Hardcover)
International Standard Book Number-13: 978-0-415-64649-9 (Papercover)
Library of Congress Card Number 2005026751

Library of Congress Cataloging-in-Publication Data

Lechuga, Vicente M.
    The changing landscape of the academic profession : the culture of faculty at for-profit colleges and universities / Vicente M. Lechuga.
        p. cm. -- (Studies in higher education)
    Includes bibliographical references and index.
    ISBN 0-415-97699-5
    1. For-profit universities and colleges--United States--Faculty. 2. College teachers--United States--Attitudes. I. Title. II. Series.

LB2331.72.L45 2006
378'.04--dc22   2005026751

Taylor & Francis Group
is the Academic Division of Informa plc.

Visit the Taylor & Francis Web site at
http://www.taylorandfrancis.com

and the Routledge Web site at
http://www.routledge-ny.com

To my dear wife Diana, for all of her love and support

Contents

List of Tables

Acknowledgments

I would like to thank all of the faculty members who agreed to participate in the study for allowing me to explore their work lives. I was impressed by their commitment to students and education. They are all dedicated educators, many of whom chose to pursue a teaching career despite having the knowledge and skills to be employed in their respective, and higher paying, fields. I would like to thank the four institutions represented in the study, along with their senior administrators, who agreed to allow a relative stranger critically examine their organizations.

I am grateful to my dissertation advisor, Bill Tierney, who was instrumental in assisting me to shape this study. He has been a wonderful mentor and will continue to be a valued friend and colleague. Guilbert Hentschke provided valuable input throughout my graduate career, and challenged me to think about the for-profit higher education industry in new and innovative ways. Dean Campbell, Karri Holley, Kristan Venegas and my colleagues from the Center for Higher Education Policy Analysis also provided valuable support, feedback, and constructive criticism on the original manuscript.

Although I am considered the author of this text, there are a number of individuals that must be acknowledged for the encouragement and support they provided as I wrote what was to become this book. I am indebted to my brother Patrick who has become a wonderful friend over the years, and who stepped in at a moments notice to assist me with completing my research. I am grateful to Jaime Lester, who provided invaluable feedback and was a constant source of personal and professional support. My life-long friend Jaime Cabrera, whom I consider a brother, would give me the shirt off of his back if he thought it would help sell more books.

In addition, I would also like to acknowledge my mother and father Magdalena and Vicente R. Lechuga who, even though they were never given the opportunity to complete high school, are wise beyond their years. The dedication they show to their children made it possible for my siblings and I to obtain a college education. Merle and Sarah Jaque and the rest of the Jaque and Lechuga families also provided constant encouragement and moral support throughout the years. Lastly, I would like to thank my wife Diana Jaque. My dissertation and the resulting book would not have been possible without her constant encouragement, moral support, as well as her extraordinary research and editing abilities. This book is as much her endeavor of love as it is mine, and I will always be grateful to her for that.

Part I
The Changing Landscape of Higher Education

Higher education institutions are unique organizations in that they comprise one of the largest industries in the nation, but operate in ways that are foreign to most corporations (Birnbaum, 1988). Baldridge (1980) describes colleges and universities as complex institutions with fragmented professional staffs that deal with non-routine problems using a wide range of skills. Higher education institutions are comprised by variety of stakeholders; each constituency is involved, to some extent, in the governance process. Decision-making authority is decentralized and is determined by rank or status (Clark, 1963). For example, deans have considerable authority due to their rank and standing within the organization. Status within the institution also is determined by one's prominence within a discipline.

Colleges and universities are dominated by highly trained faculty members who require considerable autonomy and freedom from supervision in their work (Baldridge, Curtis, Ecker, & Riley, 1977). By and large, faculty members possess extensive knowledge and expertise within a given specialty or field, which accords them substantial decision-making authority within the institution. Rosovsky (1990) describes faculty members, as well as administrators and students, as 'owners' of the institution. Faculty involvement in governance activities is tied to academic freedom through the university's unique mission of both creating and disseminating knowledge. Academic freedom is a construct of the tenure system; tenure is the mechanism that protects this freedom.

Higher education institutions are characterized by decentralized decision-making structures; governance activities are shared. Decisions are made through informal interaction among peers, and through formal collective action of the faculty (Clark, 1963). Colleges and universities display elements of "independent" and "captured" firms (Baldridge et al., 1977). In other words, they are autonomous organizations, having considerable freedom to operate with moderate oversight from external entities, yet are economically dependent and highly vulnerable to the external environment (Tierney, 1998).

Over the last decade, higher education has witnessed the entry of a new breed of postsecondary education providers. For-profit postsecondary education institutions have reshaped the traditional views of the function and purpose of higher education. These institutions provide a small but rapidly growing segment of the student population with the knowledge and skills required to compete in the current job market. As new technologies continue to emerge, education is increasingly important to employees seeking to upgrade their skills and to employers in search of individuals who possess the necessary expertise and training to help their organizations succeed. Given the increasing monetary returns associated with additional postsecondary schooling, education is no longer an option individuals exercise at a particular point in life. It is an ongoing, life-long process necessary to remain viable in an increasingly competitive job market.

This text and the study from which it was derived are intended to provide the reader with a foundation from which to understand two interconnecting phenomena. The first relates to the rapid rise and success of for-profit colleges and universities. The second and most important aspect of the text examines the work lives and working conditions of faculty members at for-profit institutions; arguably the most visible of all employees. I begin the text by presenting the distinctive elements that define institutions of higher education (IHEs) as organizations, and offer a context from which to view the constantly changing landscape of higher education. Additionally, I discuss the rise of for-profit postsecondary education in the US along with the underlying principles that define the academic profession. The bulk of the study consists of four case studies that explored various aspects of faculty work life. This is followed by an analysis of the data and the study implications. I also have provided below, a set of definitions that aid the discussion for the remainder of this book.

DEFINITION OF TERMS

Traditional Higher Education Institutions—The term "traditional" refers to the prototypical two- or four-year college or university, which is either a public or private, regionally accredited institution that awards associate, bachelor, master, and/or doctoral degrees.

For-Profit Higher Education Institutions—To alleviate any confusion that may arise, the term "for-profit institution" is narrowly defined here as proprietary institutions that award associates, bachelors, masters, and/or doctoral degrees in addition to certificates. Additionally, the institutions represented in this study were nationally and/or regionally accredited. I did not include unaccredited institutions and institutions that offer certificates only in this study. Corporate universities that offer courses and training to their employees are also excluded.

Contingent Faculty—The term "contingent" refers to faculty members who are appointed off the tenure-track on either a part-time or full-time basis. The term includes adjuncts, which are generally compensated on a per-course or hourly basis, as well as full-time non-tenure-track faculty members who receive a salary. Many contingent faculty members are reappointed to the same position for a number of years, therefore the term "contingent" does not imply employment on a temporary basis—although this is an important aspect of these appointments (Benjamin, 2003).

Chapter One
The Contours of Higher Education

Traditional colleges and universities are complex institutions that differ in many respects from organizations in business and industry. Traditional IHE are unique in their function and purpose, organized to create and disseminate knowledge. They ostensibly regard knowledge as an intangible, or "invisible substance" (Clark, 1983, p. 7) that is neither intended to be a product nor a service; it is the means by which to promote citizenship and democracy (Tierney and Lechuga, in-press). Higher education institutions also are paradoxical in nature; they are hierarchical organizations, yet are designed to provide individuals with autonomy and decision-making authority. Duderstadt (2000) describes the traditional 4-year university as a residential institution with a classroom-based curriculum consisting of about 120 credits. The traditional undergraduate experience consists of academic programs that are enhanced by extracurricular activities; the development of the 'individual' is part of the educational process. Students range age in from 18-24 years of age, and attend school full-time. Graduate education at traditional IHEs is designed around academic disciplines, with professional schools dominating the landscape, and professors engaging in research and publishing alongside their students.

In recent years, enrollments of non-traditional aged students at many non-profit colleges and universities have increased. For example in 1999, NCES (National Center for Education Statistics) shows that 43% of higher education students were over the age of 25, and 25% of students attending degree-granting institutions in the 1999-00 academic year were over the age of 30 (NCES, 2000b). Many of these students typically do not partake in the conventional college experience, i.e. living on campus, attending full-time, etc. As the median age of the college student population increases so, too, will the enrollments of older students (Munitz, 2000). Yet regardless of their student populations and due to their unique missions and goals, traditional colleges and universities operate in ways that deviate from large corporations.

DISTINCTIVE ELEMENTS

Traditional higher education institutions are unique as a result of the inter-related roles, structures, authority of individuals and constituencies throughout the institution (Birnbaum, 1984). There are distinctive elements that separate colleges and universities from other types of organizations (Baldridge, et al. 1977; Birnbaum, 1988). Cohen and March (1974) intro-duced the theory of organized anarchy as relating to traditional higher edu-cation institutions. In an organized anarchy, the organization is "a collection of choices looking for problems, issues and feelings looking for decisions ..., solutions looking for issues..., and decision-makers looking for work" (Cohen and March, 1974, p.81). From afar the organization tends to look as though it is in chaos. Yet, there is an inherent structure within the chaos.

Cohen and March (1974) outline four fundamental ambiguities fac-ing leaders of higher education institutions; ambiguity of purpose; ambigu-ity of power; ambiguity of experience and; ambiguity of success. These essential characteristics are fundamental to understand organized anarchy; they explain the distinctive organizational nature of traditional IHEs. Baldridge et al. (1977) expands on these ambiguities by presenting five spe-cific elements that describe the unique characteristics of colleges and uni-versities: (1) goal ambiguity, (2) client service, (3) problematic technology, (4) professionalism, and (5) environmental vulnerability.

Traditional colleges and universities are marked by *ambiguous goals*; they create and disseminate knowledge, they educate the public, produce citizens, provide services to the local community, etc. They accomplish these goals using problematic or *unclear technologies*. Generally speaking, organizations use standardized practices when manufacturing a specific product, yet, professors use different teaching methods and research tech-niques that cannot be standardized. IHEs *serve clients* with specific needs on a temporary basis and are vulnerable to the external *environment*. Although students flow in and out of the institution, they demand a voice and contribute to the institutional decision-making process. Faculty mem-bers are skilled professionals that perform a range of tasks that require spe-cialized training. Fluid participation is a component of a *professional organization*; faculty members expect to be included in decision-making activities and at the same time demand to work autonomously without strict supervision (Clark, 1963).

LOOSELY COUPLED SYSTEMS.

Scholars have described colleges and universities as 'loosely coupled' systems (Birnbaum, 1988; Cohen and March, 1974; Weick, 1979). Birnbaum (1988) defines 'coupling' as the interaction between various subsystems and elements within a system. The degree to which systems are coupled depends upon the strength of the variables and number of activities they have in common (Glassman in Weick, 1979). In a traditional higher education setting, coupling can refer to the interaction or interconnectedness between the faculty and administration, the governing board and the president, and the office of admission and the business department.

Colleges and universities can be characterized as having a set of 'sensing mechanisms' that allow each academic department to adapt to change as well as isolate problematic areas of the system without affecting the rest of the institution. Glassman (1973) argues that loosely coupled systems allow parts of an organization to persist by permitting individual subsystems to react to changes swiftly. That is to say that a business department can adapt to the changes and needs in the business field by adding new courses or creating new programs without greatly affecting the institution as a whole. The loosely coupled operational structure of today's colleges and universities is not characteristic of the earliest postsecondary institutions. Colleges and universities have evolved since the establishment of higher education in the US during the 17th Century. Throughout the history of American higher education, changes in the academy have resulted in changes to the academic profession.

THE CHANGING LANDSCAPE OF HIGHER EDUCATION

The evolution of postsecondary institutions has shaped the type of responsibilities associated with the professorate. The earliest colleges such as Harvard, William and Mary, and Yale originally were religiously affiliated, residential institutions. The role of the faculty member was to teach the religious doctrine and to prepare an educated clergy (Nuss, 1996). The late 18th and early 19th Centuries gave rise to the development of numerous small religious institutions and, later, the liberal arts colleges.

Following the Civil war, the 1862 Morrill Act aided the expansion of public higher education institutions, such as the University of Michigan and University of California, whose missions were to educate the sons and daughters from ordinary families (Clark, 1987a). Land-grant universities were established as charitable, non-profit, tax exempt institutions that solidified the idea of higher education as a public good (Pusser & Turner, 2004). Alongside the development of the university was the emergence of normal schools, public institutions established for teacher education. Normal schools gave way to teachers colleges; many are known today as state colleges. The relatively recent development of the community college increased the number of postsecondary degree-granting colleges and universities in the US to over 4,100 (NCES, 2001). The vast array of postsecondary educational institutions—and faculty expectations associated with each institutional type—make it difficult to clearly define the academic profession.

Higher education is in a state of flux yet again. Birnbaum (1984) asserts, "neither organizational nor institutional characteristics of colleges and universities should be thought of as 'given'. In fact, these characteristics evolve in response to the changing social, economic, and political environments in which institutions function" (p.1). As the academic profession evolves so, too, do the types of opportunities that are available to future academics. The proliferation of part-time and full-time non-tenure-track faculty members over the past twenty years is a well-documented phenomenon (Leatherman, 1997; Foster and Foster, 1998; Schnieder, 1999; Baldwin and Chronister, 2001; Leslie and Gappa, 2002). During the twenty year period between 1975-1995, part-time faculty appointments increased by 103%; non-tenure-track appointments increased by 93% (Benjamin, 2003). An increased reliance on non-tenure-track, or contingent, faculty is partially attributed to the fiscal and financial constraints many institutions have and will continue to face due to declining state appropriations and budget cuts to higher education (National Association of State Universities and Land Grant Colleges, American Association of State Colleges and Universities, 2002; Selingo, 2003; Symonds, 2003). Moreover, new postsecondary educational providers are redefining the academy by treating education as a commodity, offering programs that focus specifically on job training, and exclusively employing contingent faculty members.

A NEW UNIVERSITY

Higher education has witnessed the tremendous growth of the for-profit, higher education market over the last decade. In 1988-89, the number of 2-year for-profit institutions represented 19% of all 2-year postsecondary institutions in the US, and the number of 4-year for-profit institutions represented only 3% of all 4-year IHEs. A decade later in 1998-99, 2-year for-profit institutions represented 28% of all 2-year colleges and universities, corresponding to a 78% increase. There was also a dramatic increase in the proportion of 4-year for-profit institutions during the same decade. In 1998-99, data from the Education Commission of the States (ECS) show that the proportion of 4-year for-profit institutions rose from 3% to 8% of all 4-year IHEs, representing an increase of 266% (ECS, 2001). By the 2002-03 academic year, 4-year for-profit institutions represented 11% of all 4-year and above institutions and 19% of all degree-granting institutions in the US (NCES, 2003b). For-profit higher education providers will continue to grow, most notably by expanding into international markets (Farrell, 2004).

For-profit, postsecondary education providers encompass a wide range of organizations. Corporate universities, such as Motorola University and University of Toyota, provide training and professional development opportunities to their employees, i.e., education is an auxiliary, not core, mission of these organizations. Vocational and trade schools offer certificates and diplomas in diverse fields ranging from automotive repair to information technology. Many for-profit colleges and universities offer degree programs ranging from the associate degree level thru the masters and doctoral levels, in addition to diplomas and certificates. These institutions are the focus of this study.

For-profit education is not a novel concept to the education arena. Kirp (2003) asserts that American proprietary schools date back to the 17th century, teaching illiterate adults to read, write, and do arithmetic. In the 19th century, the Industrial Revolution brought with it the need to train individuals for specific trades; proprietary institutions provided much of the training. By the 20th century, proprietary education gave way to publicly supported higher education institutions. However, the 1972 reauthorization of the Higher Education Act provided students with federal financial aid to attend proprietary schools. In the 1980s, trade schools were held in poor regard. They operated with few constraints with respect to the recruitment and training of students, and most offered less than 2-year diploma programs (Bailey, Badway & Gumport, 2001). High default rates and fraudulent recruiting practices led to tighter restrictions and regulation of the for-profit postsecondary industry. By the early 1990s, Congress made it tougher for for-profit IHEs to receive federal financial aid dollars by decreasing institutional dependence on federal funds and mandating an increased percentage of outside funding sources.

Over the last decade, a new breed of proprietary institution entered the market. These institutions are nationally and/or regionally accredited, offering degree programs that mirror those at traditional non-profit colleges and universities. Much of what is known about this new type of for-profit institution is based on anecdotal evidence rather than empirical research. Ruch (2000), an experienced administrator in both traditional and for-profit institutions, characterizes for-profit IHEs in much the same way one would describe traditional colleges and universities, with some exceptions. Donors become investors, endowments become private invest-ment capital and corporate management practices replace shared gover-nance. These institutions exhibit other characteristics akin to traditional IHEs (Goldstein, 2000). They display similar hierarchical structures, with presidents atop the organizational chart, subsequently followed by vice presidents, deans, and staff members. They serve the public by educating students to enter the workforce. And faculty members comprise a large proportion of the institution's personnel.

Enrollments at for-profit colleges and universities represent only a small percentage of total enrollments at all institutions in the US, 4.7% for Fall 2001 (NCES, 2003). Nevertheless, for-profit institutions are a prominent fixture in higher education today and will likely become a permanent fixture in the future. A significant factor that distinguishes for-profit IHEs from traditional colleges and universities is the belief that education is considered a private, rather than a public, good (Pusser & Doane, 2001). In particular, for-profit IHEs do not rely on public subsidies to operate. They shift the burden of pay-ing for a postsecondary education to the individual. Moreover, these institu-tions focus on enhancing an individual's employment opportunities by providing the education and skills required to compete in the job market.

Unlike traditional non-profit institutions, for-profit institutions are man-aged by individuals with corporate experience (Ruch, 2000). Their organiza-tional models combine the economies of scale found at large public universities with corporate sector marketing and organizational practices (Pusser & Turner, 2004). Degree programs are designed to follow the current trends in the job market and fulfill employers' needs. This approach to educa-tion stimulates institutional growth and reduces the financial risk to the insti-tution by offering students the types of programs and training that are currently in demand. A basic component of the for-profit education business model includes employing an overwhelming majority of contingent faculty members. With few exceptions, these institutions do not offer tenure. Full-time faculty members comprise only a small percentage of the faculty. The unique characteristics that define these institutions likely result in work envi-ronments that depart from the norms of traditional institutions.

For-profit IHEs challenge traditional notions of the academy such as shared governance, tenure, and academic freedom, creating distinctive institutional cultures. This study will provide an increased understanding of faculty culture at for-profit institutions by examining the working environ-ments of faculty members. The intent of the study is neither to bemoan nor celebrate the rise in prominence of for-profit colleges and universities. Rather, the aim is to provide a lens from which to consider faculty work and faculty culture at this distinctive type of higher education institution.

THE ACADEMIC PROFESSION

Since the inception of Harvard in 1636, the American academic profession has taken on numerous forms. The clerics who served as resident tutors in the early years of Harvard College did not dominate the institution, nor did they have control over what would be taught and who would teach it. These faculty members were empowered to act *in loco parentis*. That is to say that faculty were empowered (and expected) to act as surrogate parents.

With the development of graduate education at the turn of the century, institutional authority slowly began to shift away from trustees to presidents and administrators (Clark, 1987b). As specialized research and advanced training began to dominate higher education institutions, the production of knowledge and the training of graduate students—future professors—became a key responsibility of the professorate. Moreover, faculty ties to their respective disciplines became increasingly fervent, as evidenced by the rise in prominence and power of disciplinary associations (Clark, 1996).

Until recently, basic assumptions about the professorate could be made with some certainty (Finkelstein, 1984). Following the end of World War II, formal academic life in the US consisted of several facets categorized under teaching related activities, service to the academic community, and research and publishing (Finkelstein, 1984). Traditional colleges and universities continue to favor this multi-faceted vision of faculty work life. Yet, faculty members' priorities with regard to these various duties are a reflection of the norms and values of the institutions that employ them. At the nation's most prestigious universities, for example, faculty members spend the majority of their time focusing on the latter. At less prestigious regional colleges, faculty may focus more of their efforts on the teaching rather than the research component of the profession. Moreover, many community college faculty members are not required to perform research or to publish. They instead spend the majority of their time focusing on their teaching and service to their institution.

Given that faculty work life reflects an institution's values and culture, it cannot be explored without considering the institutional context and culture in which faculty work takes place. In other words, the social settings in which faculty work occurs shape the academic profession (Clark, 1987b). Bolman and Deal (1997) assert that culture is a combination of product and process within the organization. Hence, faculty work is a key process in the organizational culture of colleges and universities. The primary faculty responsibilities—teaching, research, and service—are entrenched values of the academy that contribute to faculty culture at most traditional higher education institutions (Campbell, 2003). These deep-rooted values of faculty work manifest themselves in the fundamental principles that define the profession and the academy.

A NEW FACULTY

Faculty members at traditional IHEs live and work in a number of conflicting cultures, including that of the academic profession, the institution, and their discipline (Austin, 1990). Until recently, a basic assumption of faculty work life is that typical faculty members are appointed to full-time, tenure-track positions. Certain aspects of the professorate are tied to this basic notion and are assumed to be inherent to the profession. More specifically, full-time tenure-track faculty members have the right to participate in the institution's governance and decision-making processes and have the protection of academic freedom, which is guaranteed by the tenure system.

However, such images of the professorate do not necessarily reflect academic life for a growing number of faculty members. Part-time faculty members provide an increasing amount of the instructional services at traditional colleges and universities; these faculty members make up over 43% of the professoriate (NCES, 1998). Individuals appointed to part-time positions, by definition, are non-tenure-track faculty members. Part-time faculty generally earn no benefits and are paid a fraction of what their full-time tenured and tenure-track counterparts earn, comparatively.

Additionally, the American Association of University Professors (AAUP) asserts that more than 50% of all new appointments in higher education are non-tenure-track hires, also known as off-track hires (AAUP, 2003). Such faculty appointments were virtually unheard of thirty years ago; they accounted for only 3.3% of all full-time positions in 1969 (AAUP, 2003). Although numerous debates continue as to whether higher education institutions damage the principles of the academy by relying on an increasing number of contingent faculty, little empirical research on the topic exists.

Colleges and universities hire part-time and full-time off-track faculty as a money-saving tactic that allows administrators to keep full-time, tenured and tenure-track faculty salaries competitive while maintaining low levels of tuition for students. Traditional institutions continue to hire increasing numbers of part-time faculty due to institutional budget cuts resulting from decreasing state appropriations to higher education. The main controversy regarding contingent faculty centers on the idea that the nature of this type of appointment undermines the basic tenets of the academy, i.e. shared governance, tenure, etc. With the advent of for-profit postsecondary institutions, debates regarding a growing dependence on contingent faculty persist as their numbers continue to increase. It is unclear how this new faculty work-force will affect the future of the academy. This study intends to provide insight into the issues that confront contingent faculty at for-profit IHEs, and explore the challenges, roles, and responsibilities associated with faculty work at these institutions.

At issue are the roles and responsibilities of this new, and financially viable, faculty workforce. A major assertion is that the increasing number of contingent faculty threatens the fundamental values of the academy and has a dramatic effect on the practice of shared governance, collegiality, and the role of the faculty in developing curricula. Contingent faculty are vulnerable to subjective hiring and firing; such decisions often are made based on enroll-ment figures and other arbitrary factors (Buck, 2001). Since off-track faculty members are not eligible for tenure, these appointments result in the loss of academic freedom and strengthen the role of the administration.

As contingent employees, their provisional status may limit their capac-ity to deliver course material in the way they see fit. A statement issued by the American Association of University Professors regarding contingent faculty members asserts that, "contingent faculty members have minimal influence in the governance and decision-making process." It also states:

> The excessive use of, and inadequate compensation and professional support for, such contingent faculty exploits these colleagues and undermines academic freedom, academic quality, and professional standards... Improving the professional status of the growing number of non-tenure-track faculty members is unpopular with most adminis-trations... (AAUP, 2003)

While the number of part-time and non-tenure-track appointments continues to increase, researchers ponder the benefits and detriments of employing contingent faculty (Baldwin & Chronister, 2001; Breneman, 1997). The economic benefits of employing contingent faculty result in an increased number of credit hours of instruction per dollar invested, and allow institutions to accommodate larger enrollments with a limited budget. However, an increased reliance on non-tenure-track faculty affects the nature of academic work. By and large, full-time tenure-track faculty members at traditional institutions are responsible not only for teaching, but for research and scholarship activities. Critics of off-track appoint-ments are concerned that faculty who do not perform research cannot be as effective in the classroom as research-oriented faculty members.

For-profit colleges and universities are at the forefront in the develop-ment of this new faculty workforce, who likely have a different set of values and beliefs pertaining to the academic profession, faculty roles, and responsibilities. Although the for-profit higher education market continues to expand, little is known about faculty work life at these institutions. What is known is that faculty at for-profit IHEs do not perform research and are not required to write and publish, resulting in work environments that depart from the norms of traditional IHEs. To a large extent, for-profit IHEs ostensibly create unique institutional cultures that are partially the result of the roles faculty play. By coupling these factors with the rapid expansion of the for-profit postsecondary market, one can begin to comprehend how changes taking place in the academic profession will affect the academy as a whole.

THE IMPENDING FUTURE?

The rise of for-profit postsecondary education in the US can be attributed to the ability of these institutions to provide marketable job training skills to their students. Moreover, for-profit IHEs appeal to investors because they offer a quality product while keeping costs low—in part by employing contingent faculty—yielding sizable returns to investors. As for-profit IHEs continue to expand their reach, their *modus operandi* is expected to attract attention from traditional colleges and universities (Farrell, 2004). Recent trends point toward continued growth in the for-profit sector, bringing with it a rising number of part-time and full-time contingent faculty members. The influence that this burgeoning workforce will have on the future of the academic profession is unknown. Taken as a whole, the aforementioned factors raise questions regarding the goals of higher education and the consequences of employing contingent faculty.

As previously stated my intent is not to lament or applaud the increased prominence of for-profit higher colleges and universities. Rather, my goal here is to provide an understanding of the culture of faculty members teaching at for-profit institutions. Ultimately, this study offers a basis from which to view for-profit colleges and universities by exploring faculty roles and responsibilities. The underlying assumption of the study is based on the belief that two key factors influence faculty work and faculty culture at for-profit higher education institutions—the nature of the institution as a profit-making entity, and faculty members' status as contingent employees.

Although the notion of providing education to generate a profit elicits strong opinions from various individuals in higher education, little is known about for-profit colleges and universities and their faculty. An exploration of the faculty, the roles they play and the nature of their work, provides a glimpse into this fastest growing sector of higher education (ECS, 2001). The nature of for-profit institutions as profit-seeking entities results in institutional goals that diverge from those of traditional IHEs. The cultural framework, as will be discussed in detail in Chapter Three, fosters an understanding of the dynamics of contingent faculty at for-profit institutions. More specifically, the framework reveals how an organization's mission and goals influence its culture, and focuses on how faculty at for-profit IHEs define themselves and their roles within the institution. In essence, the conceptual framework explores the attitudes, perceptions, and beliefs of faculty members at for-profit colleges and universities.

CONCEPTUAL FRAMEWORK

The conceptual approach this study employs provides insight into this emerging class of academicians by focusing on how faculty at for-profit IHEs define themselves and their roles within the institution. I utilize a cultural framework that investigates for-profit colleges and universities as interpretive entities. The study provides a foundation from which to consider for-profit degree-granting institutions by exploring the attitudes, perceptions, and beliefs of their most visible employees, the faculty. In using a cultural approach, four questions arise:

(1) *What are the shared beliefs and assumptions that characterize the dynamics of faculty work at for-profit institutions?*

(2) *What is the impact of organizational, disciplinary, academic, and individual cultural forces on faculty work at for-profit colleges and universities?*

(3) *What influence do forces external to the academy have on faculty work life at for-profit IHEs?*

(4) *What can the academic community learn from for-profit institutions that may help to reshape faculty work life at traditional colleges and universities?*

In using a cultural framework, the investigation examines the factors that establish and create the faculty culture of for-profit institutions. This study considers a number of elements that influence the actions and behaviors of the actors within the institution. It considers how these actions are reflective of the institution's mission, i.e. how faculty members define the nature of their work. Ultimately, the aim of the study is to provide a foundation from which to understand the future role of contingent faculty members in higher education.

This qualitative study is designed to explore faculty experiences at for-profit institutions and employs an interpretive approach to studying faculty members work environments. Through in-depth interviews, I examine faculty culture by interpreting events, accounts, actions, and experiences to develop an innate understanding of faculty work life within the context of the cultures that define their profession; i.e. the disciplinary culture, the institutional culture, the academic culture, etc. The interpretive approach also allows for an examination of how faculty members conceptualize and organize their work activities and how they interact with students and colleagues (Austin, 1990).

This book is organized into ten chapters. In the following chapter, I detail the relevant literature used for the study. I discuss organizational culture and faculty culture, and highlight significant literature on non-tenure-track faculty. I also explore for-profit degree-granting institutions and the factors that contribute to their recent success. Chapter Three reviews the methodology I employed, including data collection methods and data analysis techniques. Chapters Four–Seven explore the experiences of 52 faculty members from four for-profit institutions, each chapter representing a single case study. Of note, I utilize pseudonyms when discussing each institution. Pacific-Atlantic University, for example, is one of several campuses that comprise a large multi-campus university with locations across the country. It offers a wide range of academic programs at the associates thru masters level. Miller College also is a multi-campus institution. However, it is regional in its scope with campuses located throughout the Midwest. Moreover, unlike Pacific-Atlantic University, it is privately owned and operated whereas shares of Pacific-Atlantic University can be bought and sold on the stock market. The distinction between privately held and public traded institutions will be discussed in detail in Chapter Two. As its name suggests, Distance Learning University is an on-line distance education-only institution whose focus is on graduate education. Only recently has it begun to offer 4-year undergraduate degree programs. The fourth and final institution is Southeastern College. It is a single-campus for-profit institution that offers academic degree programs with a business focus, most leading to an associates degree. Chapter Eight offers a cross-institutional analysis of the case study data. The broad themes that span across all institutions represented in the study are explored within the context of the for-profit higher education industry as a whole. Chapter Nine provides an analysis of the data focusing on the important difference between faculty work life, roles, and responsibilities between traditional vs. for-profit institutions. The final chapter re-conceptualizes faculty culture from the perspective of for-profit higher education institutions, and provides a basis from which to understand the purpose and function of these institutions. I also offer a new component to the cultural framework that illustrates how the close ties between for-profit institutions, employers, and the market affect the nature of faculty work.

The lack of empirical research on for-profit IHEs makes a study of this nature timely and essential. The hope is that this study will contribute to the modest, but growing, body of research-oriented literature on for-profit colleges and universities. For-profit colleges and universities are beginning to establish themselves as a permanent part of the higher education community. Those in academe can no longer choose to ignore their presence. Instead, those within the traditional higher education community can only benefit from an increased understanding of the principles that guide the operation of for-profit IHEs.

Chapter Two

Mapping the For-Profit Terrain

For-profit colleges and universities are a prominent force in higher education today. They have created a new educational paradigm that sets aside many of the fundamental principles of the academy. Moreover, for-profit IHEs have sparked debates regarding the merits of education driven by profit and have raised concerns over the purpose of education as a private, rather than a public good. These institutions provide a small but rapidly growing segment of the student population with the knowledge and skills required to compete in the current job market.

For-profit higher education providers constitute a substantial proportion of our postsecondary institutions. Recent data from the National Center for Education Statistics (NCES) show that of the 6,600 Title IV eligible postsecondary institutions in the US, 38% are proprietary; nearly one-third (32%) of all proprietary institutions are degree-granting colleges and universities (NCES, 2001). The remaining 68% are non-degree-granting career colleges providing vocational training and certificate programs. Enrollments at for-profit degree-granting institutions increased 52% between 1995 and 2000 (NCES, 2001). However, it is important to take into account that for-profit degree-granting institutions make up less than one fifth of all degree-granting institutions. To be specific, of the 4,200 degree-granting institutions in the US, for-profit degree-granting institutions constitute about 800 or 19% of all degree-granting institutions (NCES, 2003b).

In the 1999–00 academic year, proprietary institutions along with public community colleges enrolled a majority of students seeking an education below the baccalaureate level (NCES, 2000b). Although proprietary institutions enroll only 5% of all college students, enrollments at these institutions are growing at least three times faster than at traditional institutions (Blumenstyk, 2003).

For-profit IHEs exhibit many of the same characteristics of traditional non-profit institutions—such as offering academic programs that lead to bachelors, masters, and doctorate degrees. They also exhibit numerous differences that distinguish them from their non-profit counterparts. While there are numerous areas that can be examined with regard to for-profit institutions, it would be impractical to explore the various issues in the course of this study. Therefore, the study will not center on the role of institutional boards, resource development, budgets and marketing, and financial performance, among others. However, it is necessary to offer an in-depth understanding of the for-profit higher education sector to provide a context from which to consider faculty work life.

In what follows, I provide a foundation from which to view the growth in prominence of for-profit postsecondary education. The discussion of for-profit colleges and universities begins with an examination of several factors that contribute to their success, including the growing non-traditional student population. I address their function within the postsecondary education market, how that function differs from that of traditional institutions, and consider how the institutional missions of for-profit IHEs are aligned to the job market. This chapter also will address many of the relevant issues regarding for-profit colleges and universities today.

I utilize a cultural framework to examine for-profit IHEs and the faculty they employ. The framework, which will be explored in detail in the latter part of this chapter, allows for an in-depth investigation of for-profit institutions by focusing on faculty members' perspectives of their roles within the institution. Before moving into an examination of the conceptual framework, I discuss several points of controversy associated with faculty work at for-profit higher education institutions including the absence of a shared governance system, faculty involvement in curriculum development, and the concept of treating students as customers.

THE FLOURISHING MARKET OF FOR-PROFIT HIGHER EDUCATION

In 1999 annual expenditures in the higher education market totaled approximately $230 billion, making it attractive to investors (Goldstein, 2000). While traditional IHEs continued to face declining income streams and struggled to remain financially viable, for-profit colleges and universities posted record gains for 2003; the top ten publicly traded for-profit higher education companies saw revenues increase by more than 30% (Farrell, 2004). For-profit higher education institutions appeal to investors because of their ability to offer a quality product while keeping costs low, yielding sizable returns to investors.

For-profit institutions can be categorized in several ways. This study classifies for-profit IHEs as fitting into one of two categories—privately held or publicly traded institutions. Publicly traded for-profit IHEs sell shares of their stock on the open market; privately held institutions, by definition, do not. In Chapter III, I further elaborate on the taxonomy used to classify for-profit colleges and universities.

There are several elements that account for the recent rise of for-profit higher education. In the following section, I highlight three important areas that provide insight into the growth of the for-profit postsecondary education market: technological innovations, changes in the workplace environment, and the increase of the non-traditional/adult student population. Each of theses element has contributed to the increased prominence of for-profit higher education institutions.

The Emergence of Technology

Higher education has been overwhelmingly affected by technological innovations such as the Internet. The success of for-profit IHEs is due, in part, to their ability to link technology with education (Goldstein, 2000). For-profit IHEs use technological innovations to expand their coverage, enter new markets, ease capacity constraints, and improve the educational experience (Collis, 2000). Cook and Fennell (2001) argue that non-profit higher education institutions lose their share of students to for-profit colleges because they are ill prepared to deal with rapid changes in the higher education arena, such as new technologies. De Alva (1999/2000) offers data from a 1998 poll of 50 state governors that affirms the public's interest in obtaining an education at any time and in any place through the use of technology, i.e. through asynchronous distance learning.

Higher education institutions will continue to face increasing competition from one another as educational technology continues to improve. Investing in and utilizing technology in the classroom may be problematic for many traditional institutions due to high cost issues. For-profit IHEs are conscious of the economics behind investments in new technology. Although new investments often require a large initial expenditure, the low marginal costs of technologies, such as computer-aided teaching, coupled with the economies of scale of such an investment subsequently will reduce the overall cost of educating students (Newman & Couturier, 2001). The nature of for-profit IHEs as businesses allows them to adapt quickly to changes in technology.

Technological innovations also have changed the workplace environment. Munitz (2000) asserts that the increased use of technology prompts employees to pursue additional education. He also posits that technological innovations impinge on the feasibility of having a single career throughout one's lifetime. With the emergence of a globalized market economy, today's workforce has little expectation for permanent employment with a single company (Sperling & Tucker, 1998; Munitz, 2000). Rather, individuals are challenged with the prospect of numerous careers over their lifetime. As a result, education is no longer an option individuals exercise at a particular point in life. It is an ongoing, life-long process necessary to remain viable in an increasingly competitive job market.

Until recently, traditional institutions were responsible for training the majority students in information technology and computer sciences (Newman & Couturier, 2001). Of late, major corporations such as Microsoft and IBM have created instructional programs to train the personnel needed to operate their systems. Many of these companies contract with postsecondary institutions, such as for-profit and/or corporate education specialists, to provide the requisite training to their employees. Corporate training and education providers are not the focus of this study. However, recent technological innovations in the workplace have increased the demand for new skill sets and additional training; traditional IHEs previously provided this type of instruction. For-profit IHEs have responded quickly to fill that need and are among the leading providers of training in computer and information technologies (Collison, 1998).

Changes in Job Requirements

There has been an increase in the percentage of skilled workers as new technologies and a reliance on human capital, as opposed to physical or financial capital, continue to shape the current job market (De Alva, 1999/2000; Munitz, 2000). When job requirements become tightly linked to new technologies, the certification of skills becomes increasingly important to employees and employers. For-profit education providers respond to this workforce trend by emphasizing the certification of competencies and by focusing on the acquisition and demonstration of knowledge and skills (De Alva, 1999/2000). As our knowledge base accumulates and new technologies emerge, the acquisition of information creates a distinct advantage to those in the workforce who are able to obtain additional schooling.

Moreover, many employers express dissatisfaction with graduates from traditional universities and assert that today's graduates possess neither the knowledge nor the skill sets to survive in a competitive environment (Schrage, 1988). Employers feel that traditional IHEs are unable to provide students with the proper skills and practical training. Gardner

(1999) describes the skills that individuals are required to possess to enter the workforce; individuals must be flexible, highly literate, and have the ability to shift roles or even their line of work should their current position be phased out. The ability to learn and utilize technology is becoming a critical and necessary component to enter and remain viable in today's workforce. The rise of for-profit higher education also may signal the public's discontent with the quality and training traditional institutions provide their students (Schrage, 1988; Winston, 1999).

Catering to Non-traditional Students

In a recent report issued by the National Center for Education Statistics (NCES, 2002), the traditional undergraduate student is characterized as someone who "earns a high school diploma, enrolls full time immediately after finishing high school, depends on parents for financial support, and either does not work during the school year or works part time" (p. 1). The report continues by stating that this 'traditional' type of undergraduate student is now considered to be the exception rather than the rule. The report goes on to state:

> Today's undergraduate population is different than it was a generation ago. In addition to being 72 percent larger in 1999 than in 1970 (with fall enrollment growing from 7.4 to 12.7 million), proportionately more students are enrolled part time (39% vs. 28 %) and at 2-year colleges (44% vs. 31 %), and women have replaced men as the majority (representing 56 %of the total instead of 42 %). There are proportionately more older students on campus as well: 39 % of all postsecondary students were 25 years or older in 1999, compared with 28 % in 1970. (p.1)

The success of for-profit education institutions also is attributed to their ability to cater to the non-traditional student population. In 1999, 43% of higher education students were over the age of 25 (Collis, 2000); 25% of students attending degree-granting institutions in the 1999–00 academic year were over the age of 30 (NCES, 2000b). The majority of students enrolled at for-profit institutions are older adults. For example, 70% of students enrolled at for-profit degree-granting institutions are at least 24 years of age, and 50% are over 30 years old (NCES, 1999). When compared to students attending traditional institutions, higher proportions of students at for-profit IHEs are married, financially independent, and work more than 35 hours a week. Although the traditional-age student population is growing, enrollments of older and employed students will continue to increase (Munitz, 2000). This growing student population is interested in specialized training for technical and professional careers (Sperling & Tucker, 1997).

Soley (1998) argues that although community colleges and most state universities are a cheaper alternative, students continue to enroll at for-profit institutions for their convenient and flexible schedules. Since the majority of non-traditional students are employed, they cannot enroll full-time, and cannot attend during the day. Unlike many traditional universities, for-profit institutions allow non-traditional students to enroll in a degree program without sacrificing time away from work and family (Blumenstyk, 2003).

The majority of for-profit institutions offer evening courses and/or distance learning opportunities that fit into the schedules of working adults. The ability to deliver asynchronous learning is increasingly becoming important to the non-traditional student population. The total percentage of students enrolled in online distance-learning programs was .6% in 1997–98 and is expected to grow to 5.3% in academic year 2004–05, nearly an 800% increase (Gallagher & Newman, 2002). Adult learners are also willing to pay the larger price tag that accompanies a for-profit education because of the customer service approach to education (Traub, 1997). Morey (2001) asserts that in addition to the convenient schedules, small class sizes coupled with the ability to prepare students for the job market—as well as or better than traditional universities—fuels the growth of the for-profit higher education market.

Older part-time students prefer a different type of relationship with their institution and will forgo a 'brand name' degree program in favor of a more convenient education that is able to meet their needs (Morey, 2001). As well, employers and students feel that there is no difference between the type of education received at a for-profit institution versus an education from a traditional institution (ECS, 2000b). For-profit IHEs benefit from this indifference; it contributes to their success and implies tremendous growth potential. An educational experience that individuals can integrate into their job is not only practical, but appealing as well.

One important factor that has contributed to the rise of the for-profit higher education market relates to the notion that our current market economy is one that supports the kind of educational innovations for which for-profit IHEs are known. More specifically, for-profits have the ability to train individuals to fill job market needs quickly and competently using new educational technologies and innovative degree programs that cater to the needs of employers. Breneman, Pusser, and Turner (2000) assert that the demand for training by older non-traditional students, those catered to by for-profit IHEs, is sensitive to shifts in labor market conditions as well as educational costs. That is to say, adults will seek to educate themselves for 'in-demand' jobs at institutions that cater to their needs.

For example, for-profit IHEs have taken advantage of the shortage of licensed nurses in California by creating academic programs that help fill that need. Many of these programs are offered at night and on weekends, and cater to adult learners. More importantly is the idea that the market does not differentiate between licensed nurses graduating from non-profit or for-profit institutions. Graduates will find employment because employers are more interested in filling their openings than in the institution a given individual attended. The shortage of trained teachers provides an additional example of how the labor market, in this case school districts, seeks qualified individuals capable of filling their needs, regardless of whether the individual attended a traditional or for-profit institution.

In this section, I provided an analysis regarding the recent rise of for-profit higher education. For-profit IHEs serve a growing population of non-traditional students with the type of education many traditional institutions cannot or do not provide. The convenient and customer-oriented approach also fits the needs of adult learners. The increased use of technology in the workplace forces many employees to seek additional schooling. These trends point towards continuing prosperity in the for-profit higher education market. I now turn to a detailed discussion about how their function and their alignment of mission to goals differ from those at traditional colleges and universities. I then move into a discussion of controversial issues pertaining to for-profit higher education.

PURPOSE AND FUNCTION OF FOR-PROFIT HIGHER EDUCATION

Traditional institutions contend their focus is on furnishing students with critical and analytical skills, as well as providing marketable skills to enter the workforce. Pusser & Doane (2001) argue that traditional institutions also are committed to enhancing the labor-market outcomes of their students by providing them with an education that focuses on the development of the student. Community colleges develop programs that train students for specific professions such as culinary arts and automotive repair. Nevertheless, traditional IHEs espouse the importance of creating citizens rather than teaching job training skills (ECS, 2001). For-profit institutions operate in a different domain than that of traditional IHEs. For-profit colleges and universities serve students with specific educational needs, which often are aligned with the needs of the job market.

It is in this way that the goals of for-profit IHEs differ from that of traditional institutions. For-profit institutions do not focus their efforts on the development of the student outside the academic arena. In addition, the institutions take into account specific learning objectives when designing curricula and measure learning outcomes. As one newspaper reporter and observer of the for-profit higher education market commented:

> The nation's for-profit higher education companies have been around for years, and they are nothing like a typical football-obsessed college. Students who enroll in these institutions care about one thing: classes. They are in their mid-30's. They don't want frat parties. They want better jobs. These schools read the want ads closely, and they respond by offering courses in subjects such as finance, management, nursing, and information technology.–Danielle Sessa, April 2, 2001 (Newman & Couturier, 2001, p.13)

The Education Commission of the States (ECS) undertook a three-year study to examine for-profit education from the viewpoints of owners, managers, faculty members, and students. Students chose to attend a for-profit college because it met their academic and personal needs. Many had attended traditional institutions and were dissatisfied with the educational experience, but the career-oriented, hands-on learning that takes place at for-profit institutions provided them with the incentive to complete a program of study (ECS, 2001). Nevertheless, critics of for-profit IHEs contend that profit motives are not compatible with the academic values of traditional non-profit institutions (ECS, 2001).

Proprietary institutions, including career colleges and for-profit degree-granting IHEs, also enroll large percentages of minority students. Minority students make up 48% of the student population at for-profit IHEs, which constitutes a greater proportion of minority students than at private non-profit and public institutions (NCES, 2000c). Miller (2000) contends that for-profit IHEs serve the public good by providing access to postsecondary education to students who previously lacked access; they educate disadvantaged students, including students of color. In 1998, the top producer of minority baccalaureates in computer and information science, and in engineering-related technologies was a for-profit university; the second and third top producers were also for-profit institutions (Collison, 1998). Ward (2000) acknowledges that for-profit IHEs serve a student population previously underserved by traditional institutions and at the same time recognizes the importance for traditional institutions to adapt adequately to the changing environment of higher education. One can argue that in addition to providing requisite skills to compete in the current job market; a major function of for-profit IHEs is to serve the underserved student population.

POINTS OF CONTROVERSY

Profit Motive vs. Quality

The success of for-profit universities gives rise to questions regarding the nature of education driven by profit motives. The notion that colleges and universities can generate profits while providing a quality education is a new, if not controversial idea that challenges the principles of conventional academia. Breneman et al. (2000) asserts that students are vulnerable to an information asymmetry. At the onset, customers know considerably less than the 'producers' about the content and delivery of the product, i.e. the quality of the education. In other words, students are unable to assess the quality of an educational program until they are enrolled, making it difficult for them to seek monetary damages if an institution has not delivered a quality product. Many for-profit IHEs require students to sign an arbitration clause that obligates them to settle any disputes, especially those regarding educational quality, through binding arbitration (Farrell, 2003b). The possibility that profit-seeking institutions would exploit this information asymmetry to increase profits—by investing less on course design and curriculum development, hiring unqualified instructors, etc.—is a controversial issue. For-profit IHEs run a risk by exploiting the education asymmetry. Since employers ultimately judge the quality of the students, profits ultimately would decrease if institutions produce an inferior education.

Ruch (2000) argues that non-traditional students are more mature, knowledgeable, and capable of determining educational quality. Ruch (2000) asserts that adult students demand a challenging curriculum with substantive courses in exchange for their time and money. Furthermore, accreditation is an important asset to for-profit IHEs. For-profits are aware of the importance of accreditation in sending a message to potential students about the quality of education they provide (Breneman et al., 2000). Although accreditation poses a major barrier to entry for for-profit postsecondary institutions, students are not eligible to apply for federal financial aid funds if an institution is not accredited by an association that has met the approval of the U.S. Department of Education.

In 2000, the Education Commission of the States conducted a study regarding regional accreditors' perception of for-profit institutions (ECS, 2000). The study involved interviews with seven regional accrediting agencies.

Among the findings, the study revealed that the overall approach for accrediting proprietary institutions is no different than the approach used to accredit non-profit institutions; most accrediting agencies do not have separate standards of quality that pertain to for-profit institutions (ECS, 2000a). Garber and Steiger (1996) assert that the competition for-profit IHEs bring to the education market raises the overall quality of our nation's higher education system.

Student as Customer

A distinctive characteristic of for-profit institutions is the customer service approach they provide to students (ECS, 2001). For-profits regard the education they provide as a consumer product—students are purchasers who expect a quality product in exchange for their time and money (Ruch, 2000). The arguments against treating students as customers stem from the belief that to consider education a product reduces its overall quality. In other words, critics contend that by viewing education as a product and students as customers who purchase the product, for-profit IHEs disregard educational quality to give their customers what they ultimately pay for—a certificate or degree. The profit motive lends credence to the argument that education linked to profit-motives reduces educational quality.

Ruch (2000) argues that viewing students as customers has little to do with compromising quality and is a matter of being responsive to their needs, i.e. listening to their concerns, addressing problems, answering questions, etc. He asserts that today's students are increasingly demanding in terms of their wants and needs, and contends that traditional institutions also have customers—the alumni, parents, and students. In an era of increased accountability, both parents and students are growing increasingly alarmed over rising college costs while legislators are pushing for standardized measures of educational quality at traditional colleges and universities (Farrell, 2003b; Morgan 2002). The high cost of attending college has created a student population that is more customer-oriented; students want a valuable product for the prices they are asked to pay (Ehrenberg, 2002). Moreover, parents want assurances that their daughters and sons will receive a solid educational foundation and will be employable after graduation (Kolb, 1995).

Chaffee (1998) echoes those arguments by challenging traditional IHEs to consider the people they serve as their customers, i.e. parents, students, alumni, and the public. Defining the customer allows an institution to focus their mission and goals to reflect the customers' needs. However, Chaffee's arguments aim to affect institutional change by asking traditional IHEs to restructure and redefine their role and scope so that they become more responsive to the public's needs. Nevertheless, the argument that traditional colleges and universities have customers still conflicts with the altruistic beliefs that permeate from within traditional colleges and universities.

Curriculum Development

One of the most controversial issues regarding for-profit IHEs pertains to course design and curriculum development. Traditional institutions allow the faculty to have authority over the curriculum. Conversely, at a number of for-profit IHEs, Ruch (2000) asserts that courses are designed by curriculum specialists at a central office, rather than by individual faculty members. Ruch argues that faculty members have input into the process, as do the marketing, admissions, and finance departments. This curriculum development process concerns academics at traditional IHEs because final approval of courses and programs rests outside the faculty realm and often is tied to a business decision.

Pusser and Doane (2001) argue that the model of curriculum development utilized by many for-profit institutions may not be an appropriate method of designing degree programs. In the world of business and industry, the strategy of 'giving people what they want' is widely recognized. For-profit institutions do not attempt to oppose or change market demands by imposing their beliefs regarding the educational needs of students. They offer a limited number of degree programs, which can be replicated easily by other campuses, and are designed to fit employers' needs. They align their educational programs to market trends. Faculty members are required to deliver a structured curriculum designed to achieve specific and measurable outcomes, often bereft of general education requirements (ECS, 2000a).

Wolfe (1998) contends that many traditional universities abandoned the liberal arts curriculum years before the proliferation of for-profit institutions and argues that traditional IHEs pioneered the negative aspects that characterize for-profit institutions, i.e. a reliance on adjunct professors, night classes, trimesters, and an emphasis on practical skills. However, a recent study by Education Commission of the States (2000a) revealed that a major barrier to accreditation was the insufficient number of general education courses offered at for-profit IHEs. Other curricular issues that were of particular concern include the length of academic programs, appropriate numbers of full-time faculty, and the inability to transfer coursework to traditional institutions. According to Wolfe (1998), issues regarding the lack of faculty control over the curriculum will continue to be referenced as a trait that damages the quality of higher education.

Academic Freedom

No value is more fundamental to traditional universities than academic freedom. The American Association of University Professors' (AAUP) *Statement on Institutional Governance* (2001) codified the role of faculty in academic decision-making. Its purpose was to clarify the roles of governing boards, administrators, and faculty members in the process of institutional decision-making, with each constituency having primary authority over specific areas. Faculty members have a fundamental responsibility over areas of curriculum, instruction, research, and promotion and tenure. The tenets of academic freedom are intrinsically linked to faculty participation in governance activities such as curriculum development. Yet as previously discussed, final authority over the curriculum at for-profits rests with executive administrators.

Sperling and Tucker (1997) argue that for-profit institutions do not infringe upon faculty members' academic freedom. Faculty members are free to discuss issues and express their opinions provided that they follow the curricular guidelines and that their students achieve the desired learning outcomes. However, the principles of academic freedom are based on the assumption that faculty are granted autonomy based on their specialized knowledge and expertise, therefore should be free to decide what is best for their students. Ruch (2000) describes it this way: "The result of the for-profit environment is that everyone's work is supervised by someone else" (p. 128). He argues that the three components that define academic freedom in the AAUP's statement are the freedom to do research and publish, the freedom to discuss any issue without fear of reprisal, and the freedom to write and speak as citizens, and maintains that for-profit universities do not infringe upon any of these fundamental components. He also fails to address any issues relating to the lack of tenure as it relates to a faculty members' right to participate in decision-making activities.

Shared Governance

Shared governance is a hallmark of traditional IHEs. Faculty members participate in governance based on the assumption that their specialized training allows them to determine acceptable practices within their field. Many for-profit IHEs employ only a small number of full-time faculty. They rely on a majority of part-time faculty to provide instructional services. The lack of full-time faculty creates an environment in which administrators make the majority of decisions. A report issued by Education Commission of the States (2000a) maintains that the lack of a faculty governing body at for-profit institutions, such as a faculty senate, is seen as problematic by some accrediting agencies.

Ironically, many faculty members at traditional IHEs have become less interested in participating in governance activities, especially since the rewards for participation do not encourage them to sacrifice time away from their research and teaching duties (Miller & Seagren, 1993). Shared governance, as a structure, is meaningless unless there is true participation by faculty and other constituencies. Individuals affiliated with traditional IHEs, who support the shared decision-making process, posit that in the rapidly changing environment of higher education current governance structures and processes are deficient; they are unable to keep pace with change. Existing decision-making methods create obstacles to informed, effective, and timely decisions (Longin, 2002; Morphew, 1999). Although this may be the case, critics of for-profit postsecondary institutions point to the lack of faculty involvement in governance as a factor that diminishes the quality of the higher education system (Goldstein, 2000).

Dever (1999) asserts that governance structures at traditional IHEs are more complex than the processes found in the corporate world. Results from his study show that corporate executives demonstrated more independent, 'take-charge' strategies; a style that can adapt to rapid changes. The corporate decision-making approach can be problematic in a higher education setting. The Education Commission of the States' (2000a) recent study regarding accreditors' perceptions of the role and impact of for-profit institutions found that the lack of independence between corporate governing boards and CEOs was a chief concern of the regional accrediting bodies. Two accrediting agencies reported having to educate for-profit administrators about shared governance.

I have spoken about the broad missions of both traditional and for-profit colleges and universities. Upon close examination, one can compare differences that exist between specific institutional missions. For example, a traditional research university may contain as part of its mission a research agenda that focuses on issues related to Pacific Rim countries. Conversely, a local state college may espouse educating members of the local community rather than focusing on specific research goals. The mission of the University of Phoenix is to "educate working adults to develop the knowledge and skills that will enable them to achieve their personal goals, improve their productivity of their organizations, and provide leadership and service to their communities" (Breneman, 2003, p.2). The point here is to say that faculty work will vary by institutional mission, resulting in variations of faculty priorities across different types of colleges and universities. Faculty work life is a product of an institution's set of priorities and espoused values, which contribute to the development of faculty culture. As mentioned in Chapter I, the purpose of this study is to provide an increased understanding of faculty culture at for-profit institutions by examining the work lives of faculty members via an in-depth analysis of their values, perceptions, beliefs, and attitudes. My intent is to provide a framework from which to consider the role of the faculty at for-profit colleges and universities by exploring faculty roles and responsibilities.

FACULTY CULTURE

Faculty work at traditional colleges and universities typically is characterized by three major functions—teaching, research, and service to the university. The priority faculty place on each of these components is a function of the mission of the university and the value the institution places on each responsibility. For example, faculty members working at prominent research-oriented universities such as Stanford and Yale will spend a large percentage of their time focusing on their research endeavors. Faculty work life at less prominent state colleges may consist of heavier teaching loads, with less emphasis placed on research and publishing. Faculty members at community colleges are expected to spend a majority of their time on classroom instruction and service-related activities to the college; there is little or no expectation of research and publishing at these institutions. Institutional mission influences faculty members' duties and responsibilities which, in turn, shape the development of faculty culture.

In the following section, I provide an overview of faculty culture and discuss its use as a conceptual framework. I explore faculty culture by examining the various subcultures that comprise it. I address faculty commitment and areas of conflict between subcultures, then move to a discussion of organizational culture to provide a context from which to view faculty culture.

Towards a Definition of Faculty Culture

The term 'culture' has been defined as "the collective, mutually shaping patterns of norms, values, practices, beliefs, and assumptions that guide the behavior of individuals and groups" (Kuh & Whitt, 1988, pp.12–13). An interpretive framework, as used in this study, views culture as a constant interpretation of actions and behaviors by individuals within the group. Utilizing this definition of culture, Austin (1990) states that faculty members "live and work in at least four (and often more) cultures. As 'interpretive frameworks,' these cultures affect how faculty interact with students, conceptualize and organize their work, participate in institutional decision-making, and balance disciplinary and institutional responsibilities" (1990, p.61).

Faculty culture explores the various conditions in which faculty undertake their work responsibilities; it situates faculty work via the numerous subcultures in which faculty reside. Austin (1990) identifies four subcultures that contribute to the development of faculty culture; the culture of the *academic profession;* the culture of the *discipline;* the culture of the *academy* as an organization; and the culture of *institutional types.* I will turn to a detailed discussion of each subculture later in this chapter. Nevertheless, it is important to note that each subculture contributes to the overall conditions in which faculty members live and work. In other words, the subcultures, taken as a whole, create the whole of faculty culture.

Tierney and Rhoads (1993) explore faculty culture as a foundation from which to examine the socialization process of faculty members. They argue that the formal and informal roles that faculty members play within an institution provide a view of academic communities as cultures. The culture of an institution shapes the roles of its faculty, and in turn, faculty roles are a product of the institutional culture. Put another way, faculty behavior within an institutional setting forms the basis of faculty culture. Tierney and Rhoads (1993) assert that faculty culture is "a complex interplay of symbolic meanings predicted on five sociological forces: national, professional, disciplinary, individual, and institutional" (p.9). Each subculture adds an additional layer of density from which to examine faculty culture. Table 1 outlines faculty culture as a set of subcultures that, when taken as a whole, come together to form faculty culture.

Table 1: Faculty Culture as a Collective of Subcultures

Subculture	Characterize by...
National Culture	The cultural norms, customs, and beliefs of a particular country and its citizens, i.e. US, China, Mexico, etc.
Culture of the Academic Profession	The conventional view of the academic profession such as teaching, research, and service, as well as ideals of the professorate such as academic freedom, collegiality, and autonomy.
Culture of the Discipline	Academic departments, and/or individuals with similar schools of thought, research interests, using similar bodies of literature.
Culture of the Individual	An individual's personal qualities, life experiences, beliefs, etc.
Culture of the Institution	The norms of the institution, its policies, methods of decision-making, and its formal and informal rules.

Faculty Culture as a Framework

Exploring faculty culture is a challenge due to the multiple layers of complexity from which to view faculty members. Utilizing a cultural lens provides a method from which to analyze faculty members by using several different frames of reference—from a broad (national) view of culture to a more focused (individualistic) view. This process can be further complicated because the multiple frames of reference are not clearly delineated. It is difficult to assess where one layer ends and the other begins; subcultures overlap and intersect with one other. For example, instilled within the culture of the profession is the notion that individuals are expected to be involved with professional associations and attend annual meetings. The culture of a research-oriented institution communicates to its faculty that participation at annual meetings is important by covering all of their professional travel expenses. Hence, the decision to attend annual meetings can be characterized as adhering to both the culture of the profession and the institution.

An additional challenge in using faculty culture as a contextual framework relates to the context from which the framework was developed. Current notions of faculty culture (Austin, 1990; Becher, 1987; Clark, 1987b; Tierney & Rhoads, 1993) are constructed under the assumption that faculty members are full-time, tenure-track employees at a traditional nonprofit college and university. For example, the culture of the academic profession does not take into account differences in faculty status, i.e., part-time, at-will, or off-track employment categories. Similarly, the research component of faculty work provides the basis from which to analyze disciplinary cultures. However, how do faculty members view the culture of their discipline when research does not constitute part of their faculty responsibilities?

Faculty culture also is constructed with conventional practices of traditional IHEs in mind. For instance, implicit in traditional colleges and universities is the notion of collegiality. Shared decision-making activities are a result of collegial relationships between faculty members as well as administrators. Moreover, traditional IHEs by nature are not profit-seeking entities. Although comparisons have been made between traditional non-profit colleges and universities and profit-seeking corporations in the realm of business and industry (Chaffee, 1998; Collis, 2000; Hebel, 2004; Newman & Couturier, 2001; Ruch, 2000), revenue generation coexists with the creation and dissemination of knowledge as major functions of traditional IHEs. For-profit colleges and universities are first and foremost businesses. Their purpose is to generate profits for their investors while imparting practical knowledge and skills to their students. Knowledge production is not a function of these institutions because it increases operating costs and decreases profits.

Austin (1990) includes the culture of institutional type as one of the subcultures of faculty culture. More specifically, she addresses institutional mission and goals, governance structures, and leadership styles, among others, as important elements that contribute to faculty culture. Universities that focus on the production of knowledge recruit research-oriented faculty who are experts in highly specialized fields, whereas universities with stronger teaching missions recruit faculty with extensive classroom experience. Implicit in the discussion of the culture of institutional type is the assumption that the institutions are not seeking profits; profit motive is irrelevant when referring to institutional type. However, the profit-seeking motive of for-profit IHEs contributes to the culture of the institution and its faculty. In utilizing faculty culture as a contextual framework, I show that both the profit motive and faculty employment status add an additional layer of complexity to faculty work life and faculty culture. These elements contribute to the existing subcultures that comprise the whole of faculty culture and also serve to inform this study.

FACULTY SUBCULTURES

Culture within a National Context

National systems of higher education differ across countries. Moreover, national customs and cultural assumptions also differ. Clark (1983) provides a cross-national perspective of higher education systems, detailing how higher education is organized and governed around the world. He posits that although there are basic features of higher education systems that remain constant—knowledge-bearing groups are an essential component of higher education and tasks are organized around knowledge areas—there remain fundamental differences in how higher education is organized and who is able to participate. For example, how do citizens regard higher education in a given country? Is it a right or a privilege, a public good or private commodity? To what extent is the structure of a higher education system linked to the national economy, state and/or local governments, the needs of citizens and the labor market? My intent is not to provide answers to these questions. Rather, the questions help to illustrate that higher education is inextricably linked to national culture.

Similarly, proper etiquette and modes of behavior differ from country to country. Tierney and Rhoads (1993) advance the notion that individuals often will think of another person's behavior as unique because it often contradicts societal and cultural norms. Such differences play an important role in determining the culture of higher education institutions, which in turn contribute to the culture of the faculty. For example:

> In Central America, the concept of a faculty member is often of an indi-
> vidual who devotes part of his or her time to teaching students, but the
> individual holds another job as well. The idea that a professor is sup-
> posed to devote a significant portion of time to research is often absent.
> Similarly, concepts such as tenure, academic freedom, and institutional
> autonomy are dramatically different from such concepts in the United
> States. (p. 10)

One can draw a similar parallel between conflicting views of the role of higher education within the worlds of business and industry and that of the academy. One constituency may view higher education primarily as a training ground for students to enter the work force, while the other may view higher education as providing students with practical skills as well as offering a foundation from which to build good citizenship. Both views not only are valid but also will affect faculty members' roles and responsibili-ties, and influence faculty culture at a national level.

Culture of the Academic Profession

Traditional views of the academy are rooted in fundamental concepts that bridge faculty across institutional lines. One such value views education as serving the public good through the pursuit of 'truth,' the discovery of knowl-edge, and its dissemination via publications, presentations, and classroom instruction. Faculty members are afforded a great deal of autonomy in pursu-ing this work. Hamilton (2000) argues that faculty members are granted autonomy due to their standing within the community. Specifically, he intro-duces the idea of a social compact between the public and members of the 'learned' professions, such as lawyers, doctors, and professors. Members of these professions agree to maintain high standards in order to serve the public good. In return, the public allows them to remain autonomous and to regulate themselves through peer review. This 'public trust' stems from the belief that members of the learned professions are instilled with values and ethics due to their extensive education and training; these values and ethics are reinforced through professional associations. Professional autonomy is the product of the social compact between the public and the group.

Academic freedom plays an essential role in maintaining faculty autonomy. As a fundamental tenet of the academy, academic freedom provides faculty considerable autonomy in their research and teaching. The assumption behind academic freedom is that society benefits when faculty are able to search for truth without external constraints. Thus, they can report their findings regardless of what those findings state. Similarly, tenure, another value espoused by the academy, is at the heart of academic freedom. It protects academic freedom and allows for the free inquiry of ideas and the unfettered pursuit of knowledge without fear of reprisal from administrators and other external constituencies.

Collegiality is considered a cornerstone of the academy and is a unique characteristic of traditional colleges and universities. It "is held up as the ideal framework for faculty interactions and institutional decision-making" (Austin, 1990, p.62). While tenure protects academic freedom and sustains faculty autonomy, it also provides a foundation for the practice of shared governance. Academic freedom is intrinsically linked to faculty participation in governance activities. Faculty members participate in the decision-making process based on the assumption that their specialized knowledge and experience allows them to determine acceptable practices within their field.

Culture of the Discipline

A discussion of faculty culture would not be complete without exploring the concept of disciplinary cultures. Defining a discipline can prove to be a difficult task; it involves one's view of knowledge construction (Becher, 1989). Clark (1987a) emphasizes that disciplines are "the primary units of membership and identification within the academic profession" (p.7). Academic disciplines can be categorized in two ways: 1) by structural knowledge or 2) by knowledge areas (Becher, 1987). The former manifests itself via structural qualities such as departments or schools, i.e. school of engineering, school of architecture, chemistry department. With regard to the latter, disciplines are constructed by individuals with similar bodies of ideas, areas of inquiry, values, and norms. In other words, faculty members who share a similar knowledge base, but are members of different departments, are considered members of the same discipline, i.e. an economist in an education department and an economist in the business school.

Academic disciplines cross international boundaries so "a French physicist would share [a] sense of affiliation with a Chinese physicist, for they share the culture of the discipline" (Tierney & Rhoads, 1993, p.13). Still, disciplines are not homogeneous cultures. Becher (1990) posits that when closely examined, a discipline is made up of smaller, constantly changing sub-disciplines or specializations that all relate to the larger discipline. Chemistry, for instance, encompasses a variety of specializations such as hydrocarbon chemistry/energy, molecular dynamics, and catalysis. Additionally, these chemistry specialties also may be classified as either organic-materials or inorganic-biological. Each specialty area has its own unique language, theories, professional associations, and journals. Yet, all specializations have fundamental features that relate back to the general discipline of chemistry. Geography provides an example of a discipline that spans across different schools of thought; physical geography is considered a natural science while human geography falls into the category of social science.

With the proliferation of interdisciplinary research one can observe disciplinary specialties overlap with one another when individuals from different disciplines pursue similar research interests or areas of inquiry. For example, an anthropology professor and a professor of education may have more in common with each other than they do with other professors in their own departments because both professors study similar phenomena and are very familiar with the other's discipline, i.e. theories, concepts, and frameworks. Research areas rather than structural boundaries determine the foundation of a discipline. A psychologist whose specialty is psychology and the law may find him or herself better suited to teach in a law school rather than in a psychology department. In some cases, the interdisciplinary research area forms a new sub discipline; biomedical engineering focuses both on biological sciences and engineering applications but is now considered its own specialty area and even its own discipline.

There also may be conflicts or boundary disputes over how to interpret research outcomes or phenomena (Becher, 1989, 1990). For instance, a sociologist and an economist who both specialize in areas related to post-secondary education will observe a specific phenomena, such as declining enrollments or high attrition rates, using different frames of reference resulting in different explanations of the same phenomenon. This is not to say that one viewpoint is more valid than the other. Rather, different perspectives on the same research phenomena underscore how disciplinary specialties from different schools of thought are inextricably linked. Moreover, disputes over the division of intellectual labor—what discipline is best suited to perform research in given area of inquiry—occur when disciplinary specialties overlap with one another.

Faculty research areas provide the basis from which to examine disciplinary cultures. Implicit in the notion of disciplinary culture is the act of research, which is a primary component of faculty work life at many traditional higher education institutions. One of the major differences between faculty work life at traditional versus for-profit IHEs is the 'knowledge creation' component. For-profit institutions are not in business to generate knowledge. Consequently, research and publishing are not considered part of a faculty member's responsibilities. In examining disciplinary cultures at for-profit IHEs, one must first understand how faculty members view themselves in relation to their work before considering the impact of disciplinary culture on faculty work life.

Culture and the Individual

Disciplinary culture provides a means by which faculty can identify themselves in relation to their work, their field, and their research interests. The culture of the individual provides an additional lens from which to examine the concept of faculty culture. Individual differences significantly influence the development of faculty culture (Tierney & Rhoads, 1993). Research on the political attitudes of professors show that faculty in the social sciences were at the extreme left, engineers and other applied scientists were at the far right, while faculty in the physical and biological sciences took up the middle ground (Ladd & Lipset, 1975 in Becher, 1987). Political views can have an affect how a faculty member goes about their work, i.e. the topics they research and content of the courses they teach.

Tierney and Rhoads (1993) argue that differences related to race, class, gender, and sexual orientation impact how faculty members are socialized into a discipline or institution. Moreover, these characteristics highlight significant individual differences among faculty members and contribute to the development of faculty culture. Individuals within each social group will experience faculty work life in distinctive ways. In other words, men will experience the workplace different than women; gay and lesbian professors will experience the academy different than heterosexual professors.

Freedman (1979) found that individual differences exist among faculty who are employed at different types of institutions, paying specific attention to institutional size. Faculty members who taught at medium-sized state colleges were very student-centered. They enjoyed working with and teaching their students because many of the students came from backgrounds similar to their own. The faculty members "wanted to provide for students what college gave them—upward mobility and a greater awareness of the world" (p.89). Freedman (1979) also found that faculty members at private liberal arts institutions enjoyed teaching, yet many of them derived a great deal of satisfaction from the academic culture itself, i.e. the freedom to pursue their own interests with the autonomy that the profession provides. The point here is to illustrate that individual differences affect how faculty members perceive their roles and responsibilities. Faculty members' perspectives and intrinsic qualities will influence how they experience their working environment. The importance an individual places on ideals such as academic freedom, faculty autonomy, and shared governance influences how he or she views the role of for-profit institutions—a topic of discussion in subsequent chapters. As well, a faculty member's point of view about the merits of 'education for profit' shapes the individual's perspective regarding the significance of for-profit colleges and universities and the role they play.

AREAS OF TENSION

The subcultures that have been examined interconnect with and influence one another producing areas of conflict and tension. For example, the culture of a specific institution may communicate to faculty members that they are rewarded for their teaching abilities and service to the institution. A faculty member may find him or herself at odds with the culture of the institution because they have been socialized as researchers during their doctoral training and have a strong commitment towards their discipline. As a result, they are unable to succeed at an institution that requires them to take on heavy teaching loads and a good deal of committee work. Similarly, the culture of the academy may view certain areas of inquiry as soft or trite, whereas the culture of the discipline will view these same areas of inquiry as vital areas of inquiry. Many scholars would place little significance on research pertaining to for-profit higher education, while others may consider it valid or necessary.

Tierney and Rhoads (1993) identified an area of tension resulting from culture differences at traditional institutions: *local vs. cosmopolitan* commitment. This refers to a faculty member's level of commitment to the institution, and can be applied to for-profit IHEs. Faculty members with a stronger commitment to their discipline are described as locals, whereas faculty who are more loyal to their institution rather than to their discipline are cosmopolitans. Two factors are at play here with regard to faculty work life and for-profit institutions; one is the level of commitment that faculty have to their institution given their at-will status and two, how that commitment affects the roles and responsibilities of faculty members. Since a majority of faculty members who teach at for-profit IHEs are contingent employees one would expect that the commitment to their profession is stronger than their ties to the institutions in which they teach. This will, no doubt, have an affect on the culture of the institution and its faculty. My point is not to argue whether a local commitment is more valid than a cosmopolitan. Rather, I offer these examples to illustrate the differences that exist within the domain of faculty culture at for-profit IHEs due to employment status. Such areas of conflict can result in faculty who are less productive and less committed to their work, but can also help to inform faculty culture.

ACADEMIC INSTITUTIONS AND INSTITUTIONAL CULTURE

Arguably, faculty members comprise the core of any higher education institutions and the culture of a group of individuals, such as faculty, helps shape the institutional culture. Moreover, the various subcultures previously described are enacted within the culture of the institution (Tierney & Rhoads, 1993). The culture of a college or university—its policies, methods of decision-making, and its formal and informal rules—influences the culture of a specific group of individuals. Colleges and universities, like other types of organizations, exist as social constructions of reality. An institution's culture is constantly being created and interpreted by individuals within it. In this context, one should not disregard the culture of the institution; it provides a context from which to examine the culture of its members. As such, it is important to consider the culture of colleges and universities as a basis for understanding the culture of its faculty. In doing so, my aim is to provide a context from which to view faculty culture at for-profit IHEs.

Colleges and universities are influenced by external forces i.e. social, economic, and political. For-profit IHEs maintain particularly strong ties with the external environment, more specifically with employers and the job market. However internal forces, such as an institution's historical roots, core values, and the contributions of single individuals, also shape its culture. An institution's culture develops from the complex interplay between external influences and its significant internal characteristics (Kuh & Whitt, 1988). Culture concerns itself with managing meaning to foster an understanding of an institution's environment (Dill, 1982); it has been defined in various ways. Masland (1991) refers to organizational culture as "the shared values, beliefs, and ideologies which are unique to a campus" (p. 119). Additionally, Martin (1985) describes culture as "a set of commonly held attitudes, values, and beliefs that guide the behavior of an organization's members" (p. 148). Deal and Kennedy (1982) define organizational culture as "a core set of assumptions, understandings, and implicit rules that govern day-to-day behavior in the workplace" (p. 4). Although this study primarily focuses on faculty culture, it is important not to overlook the culture of colleges and universities in examining faculty culture. The culture of an institution provides the venue for subcultures to develop, and offers a foundation from which to examine the institution's faculty members.

Tierney (1988) provides a framework to examine the institutional culture of colleges and universities. Culture is reflected in the shared assumptions

of individual members within an organization. Shared assumptions are identified through stories, language (vernacular), institutional norms, and ideologies. These assumptions are reflected in a group's activities, how the activities
are accomplished, and the individuals that participate in the activities (Tierney, 1988). A researcher, for instance, derives a meaning of culture from an
acute awareness of other researchers within the organization and their perceptions and beliefs regarding the importance of research activities.

Understanding the culture of a group requires one to have insight into
the group's shared assumptions and to have an awareness of the cultural
dynamic that exists within the group. Culture helps define faculty work; it
shapes and defines the boundaries for acceptable behavior (Masland,
1991). Insight into a for-profit institution's culture provides a medium by
which to understand faculty work life in context to their working environment. Tierney and Rhoads (1993) contend that culture is shaped by social
forces, which, in turn, shape faculty work life. Thus, analyzing faculty culture at for-profit institutions requires the researcher not only to look at
structures and processes, but also to examine the actor's interpretation of
the institution and their working environments (Tierney, 1988).

Basic assumptions of academic culture differ at traditional and for-
profit IHEs. The culture of traditional colleges and universities supports
important foundations of the academic profession, including professional
autonomy and academic freedom. There are basic assumptions inherent
within the principle of academic freedom which include the notion that a
higher education institution is comprised of a "community of scholars who
work together to govern the institution" (Austin, 1990, p.62). For-profit
colleges and universities create their own distinctive cultures. One can formulate basic assumptions about for-profit IHEs. By definition, they aim to
generate profits. In doing so, for-profit institutions organize themselves for
efficient operation. They are accountable not only to their students, but to
their investors as well. For-profits use market-based decision-making in
their pursuit of profit-building. In other words, they base strategic decisions
on market trends and the needs of their customers. These institutions seek
knowledge for competitive advantage. Knowledge is considered proprietary
and is not shared with other institutions. Moreover, Millett (1962, in Bleak,
2004) argues that traditional colleges and universities are collegial in
nature, whereas corporations are managerial. That is to say that shared
decision-making is not commonplace at for-profit IHEs.

In addition, the culture of for-profit colleges and universities supports
the use of a large majority of contingent faculty, both part-time and full-
time. Consequently, these faculty members have considerably less autonomy and decision-making authority than their counterparts at traditional

IHEs. The main controversy regarding contingent faculty centers on the idea that the nature of this type of appointment undermines the basic tenets of the academy. The increasing use of contingent faculty is an emergent trend that may compromise the traditional values of colleges and universities. For-profit IHEs exacerbate these concerns by employing mostly contingent faculty.

CONTINGENT FACULTY MEMBERS

The American Association of University Professors (2003) provides a definition of contingent faculty that I utilize in this study. The term 'contingent' refers both to part-time and full-time faculty members, who are appointed off the tenure-track, i.e. are not eligible to receive tenure. By definition, part-time faculty positions are contingent appointments while full-time faculty can be appointed either as tenure-track or as off-track faculty members. The term "off-track" is used synonymously with non-tenure-track to refer to contingent faculty members.

There has been a rapid transition in higher education pertaining to the use of contingent appointments (Baldwin & Chronister, 2001). There are numerous explanations that account for their growing use, including increased competition from other institutions, and the changing demographics of college students. Baldwin and Chronister (2001) argue that, "Virtually all higher education institutions, even the best endowed, have encountered constraints on their resources as they have tried to respond to seemingly insatiable demands for knowledge and education. Simply put, no institution can operate the way it used to. Adjustments must be made to cut costs and reorder priorities." (p. 1)

An important aspect of this study examines the effects of contingent status on faculty work life. For-profit colleges and universities hire part-time and full-time faculty members. As will be discussed in subsequent chapters, the proportion of part-time to full-time faculty members varies by institution. Two of the institutions in this study hire primarily full-time faculty. The remaining two institutions hire full-time faculty members, but the majority of their instructional staff is comprised of part-time instructors. The part-time faculty members participating in the study are employed as full-time practitioners in their respective fields and have varying amounts of classroom teaching experience, which is typical for part-time faculty members at for-profit IHEs. Such circumstances greatly affect faculty members' attitudes, beliefs, and assumptions about the role they play within the scope of their institution. In what follows, I summarize the relevant literature on contingent faculty, both part-time and full-time. Due to the lack of research on for-profit institutions, the literature pertaining to contingent faculty members focuses on faculty issues at traditional colleges and universities.

Part-time Faculty

The typical image of part-time faculty members is that of a dissatisfied group who string together a number of simultaneous part-time positions to earn a living. Although partially true, it is important not to over-generalize how part-time faculty members are regarded. Typically, they are employed in full-time positions in other professions (Leslie & Gappa, 2002, Foster & Foster, 1998). Researchers found that the widespread assumptions of part-time faculty as under-qualified, nomadic individuals who are inattentive to their responsibilities are not valid (Leslie & Gappa, 2002). Many part-time faculty members have teaching experience and hold graduate degrees. A number of part-timers are retired professors who wish to maintain a connection to higher education; others simply enjoy sharing their professional knowledge and experience with inquisitive minds.

Part-time faculty members play a significant role in providing instructional services to postsecondary institutions. An increasing number of part-time faculty members are providing instructional services to traditional colleges and universities. This is not to say that part-time faculty members are not qualified instructors. In fact, research shows that part-time faculty members are just as effective in the classroom as compared to their full-time counterparts (Gappa & Leslie, 1993). Since the early 1970s, the proportion of part-time faculty has doubled. Part-time faculty now make up close to half of all instructional staff at traditional colleges and universities (Schuster, 2003). Moreover, research has shown that few college administrators direct their efforts toward integrating part-time faculty into their institutions (Roueche, Roueche, and Milliron, 1996). Traditional IHEs hire part-time faculty as a money-saving tactic that allows administrators to keep full-time, tenured, and tenure-track faculty salaries competitive while maintaining low levels of tuition for students. Traditional institutions continue to hire increasing numbers of part-time faculty due to institutional budget cuts resulting from decreasing state appropriations to higher education.

For-profit institutions are redefining faculty work and the role faculty members play within the institution. Unlike faculty members at traditional institutions who are considered an integral part of the governance process, most faculty members at for-profit institutions play a minimal role in the decision-making process with the majority of the decision-making authority resting with the administration. Yet, research shows that traditional institutions also are pushing for more administrative control. Rhoades (1996) conducted a study that sought to understand the reorganization process of faculty members, and the issues that surround administrators' push for greater managerial control over academic personnel. His study suggests that institutions hire part-time faculty as a means of retaining greater administrative control and flexibility over instructional staff. For example, Rhoades examined 183 faculty contracts in which part-time faculty are mentioned and found that conditions of appointment and release were not specified in 140 of the contracts.

Full-time Contingent Faculty

While relatively little research exists regarding part-time faculty in higher education, there is even less literature with regard to full-time, contingent faculty members. Full-time off-track faculty members are conventional faculty members in many ways; they are required to teach courses and participate in university service activities. Yet, they are ineligible for tenure and are appointed to contracted positions that are renewed every few years. Arguments persist regarding the merits of creating of a new echelon of faculty who are on a different career track than their tenure-track counterparts and who are, in essence, appointed to probationary positions which are subject to renewal (Baldwin & Chronister, 2001; Schuster, 2003).

There has been a steady increase in the number of full-time faculty who are being appointed to off-track positions (Schuster, 2003). The number of full-time non-tenure-track appointments is growing at a faster rate than the number of part-time appointments. Full-time off-track faculty appointments were virtually unheard of 30 years ago. In 1969, they accounted for only 3.3% of all full-time positions, but the number of full-time off-track faculty grew by 22.7% between 1992 and 1998 (AAUP, 2003). These types of appointments were still rare in the 1980s. By 1998, full-time non-tenure-track appointments comprised 28.1% of all higher education faculty posts (AAUP, 2003). Recent data also show that 54% of all full-time appointments made between 1993–1997 were made off the tenure track (Schuster, 2003).

Although some off-track faculty members replicate the work of tenure-track faculty, off-track faculty members are hired primarily to teach. They have heavier teaching loads than tenure-track faculty and, in general, are not required to perform research. A recent study showed that more than 70% of full-time off-track faculty members reported that their primary activity was teaching, while only 11% described their primary focus as administrative in nature (Baldwin & Chronister, 2001). However, the same study found that full-time term-appointment faculty assumed administrative, and other duties that tenured and tenure-track faculty did not want, including coordinating student internships and advising international students. Finkelstein and Schuster (in press) conducted a study to examine how the work roles of full-time off-track faculty differ from those of regular faculty. They found that faculty members appointed to non-tenure track positions perform specific roles within the institutions; they spend more time teaching, less time in service activities, and were twice as likely to spend no time interacting with students informally than regular faculty.

Nonetheless, when viewed in the context of this study, the duties of part-time and full-time contingent faculty members at traditional IHEs are somewhat similar to those required of faculty at for-profit IHEs. Part-time faculty at for-profit institutions are hired primarily to teach; full-time faculty tend to have both teaching and administrative responsibilities. Additionally, full-time faculty at both institutional types spend little time on research activities; any time that is spent on research is done on their own time. In spite of the similarities and differences between faculty roles and responsibilities, questions regarding the quality of education students receive at for-profit colleges and universities remain. At issue is the relationship between education and profit and how the latter affects the former.

MEETING SOCIETY'S NEEDS?

Access to lifelong learning is a critical component of success to an increasingly diverse society and workforce (Myers, Park, & Hacegaba, 2000). As new technologies continue to emerge, education is becoming of increasing import to employees seeking to upgrade their skills and employers seeking individuals that possess the education and skills to help their organizations prosper. Technological innovations and the increasing financial returns associated with additional postsecondary schooling have created conditions in which individuals choose to continuously re-educate themselves to remain viable in an increasingly competitive job market.

For-profit postsecondary education providers are conscious of and responsive to the increasing demand for higher education. These institutions, as we know them today, are a relatively new entrant into the higher education market. Their business model allows them to adapt to the educational needs of students and create new curricula quicker and more cost effective than traditional IHEs. Many of the students they attract are not interested in a traditional postsecondary education. For-profit IHEs are reaching into an untapped market of non-traditional students and are providing them with the education and training they seek.

Arthur Levine (2000), Dean of Teachers College at Columbia University, offered nine "inevitable changes" regarding the future of higher education. Among his predictions he noted that the number of higher education providers would increase and become more diverse in the near future. The most successful institutions would be those who are able to respond quickly to rapid changes while offering a quality product. For-profit IHEs have proven they are able to adapt to the rapidly changing environment of the higher education market. They also have succeeded in their efforts to combine education and technological innovations. Yet, questions remain regarding the quality of the education they provide.

Levine (2000) also speculated that the focus of higher education would shift from a teaching to a learning centered model with an emphasis on learning outcomes. Traditional IHEs are coming under increased public scrutiny. Calls for accountability will likely force them to begin measuring educational quality by developing learning outcomes—a standard practice at for-profit IHEs. Levine (2000) maintains that although research, like athletics, generates revenues for traditional higher education institutions, teaching is the most profitable and stable task. For-profit institutions are teaching centered institutions. Consequently, traditional colleges and universities that focus on the realm of teaching will face competition from for-profit IHEs. In any event many authors agree that, for better or worse, for-profit institutions will occupy a permanent place in the higher education landscape.

Chapter Three
A Case Study Approach to Faculty Culture

Faculty members live and work in environments that differ from those in the realm of business and industry. The 'product' they produce—knowledge—is intangible and difficult to quantify. The method of delivery is neither standardized nor consistent. Faculty members are free from direct supervision. The autonomous relationship they have with their 'employer,' their institution and, in the case of public universities, the state provides them with independence (and solitude) to complete their work in a manner in which they see fit. Faculty work life is a product of the work place environment. Traditional colleges and universities view faculty members as experts in their field who need little supervision. Their knowledge and expertise allows them to participate in governing their institutions. In essence, faculty work life is unique. Professionals in the corporate realm have very different employment conditions, most noticeably the lack of autonomy.

Until now, faculty work life at for-profit colleges and universities has not been explored in detail. Assumptions are made about faculty work conditions at these institutions, yet most assertions are developed using anecdotal evidence, opinion and conjecture. What we do know is that for-profit IHEs operate using structures and processes that depart from traditional colleges and universities. An obvious example relates to the at-will or contingent status of faculty members. Given what we do know about for-profit institutions, how do the working conditions of faculty members contribute to the development of faculty culture and what are the implications of the culture of faculty on the development of this new breed of faculty members? The purpose of this study is to gain insight into the issues confronting faculty members at for-profit IHEs by examining faculty culture. The intention is to explore the challenges, roles, and responsibilities associated with faculty work at these institutions. A qualitative approach to understanding for-profit IHEs and their faculty is appropriate and useful in that it allows the researcher to interpret culture using multifaceted and interactive methods.

Qualitative research has been defined as a process that examines a little-known phenomenon or an innovative system (Marshall and Rossman, 1999). An examination of faculty members' experiences at for-profit institutions requires one to understand the institution as a whole—as an innovative system—and the social actors that make up the organization—as a little-known phenomenon. Unlike quantitative methods, qualitative research allows the researcher to produce an understanding of social settings using flexible data gathering tools that are sensitive to the social context rather than being removed from a social setting (Mason, 1996). Qualitative methods are not constrained or limited by fixed questions and predetermined analysis. The social actors, in this case faculty members, furnish the evidence and are part of the research; they provide their own interpretations of their environment. Each of them make meaning of their world based on personal experiences. In other words, the evidence I present is based on what the participants provided; my job as a researcher is to understand how the participants create meaning. Moreover, I interpret events, accounts, actions, and experiences to develop an innate understanding of the social setting as a basis for examining faculty culture.

Implicit in this approach is the belief that the social actors, i.e. the faculty, are continuously interpreting the social environment under examination, i.e. the institution that employs them. My job is to understand the everyday experiences of participants and provide social science explanations to those experiences. An essential component of the study is to create an understanding of how faculty members at for-profit colleges and universities define their work in relation to the various subcultures that comprise faculty culture. An examination of faculty culture at for-profit institutions requires an understanding of the institution and the roles of the social actors that make up the organization.

TIMELINE

This study was a 12-month undertaking that began in December of 2003 and ended in November of 2004. I began by collecting background information about several potential institutions via the Internet. I sent initial email invitations to faculty members from each institution. I used email addresses obtained through and located on institutional websites. I offer these details here to provide a context from which I will examine, in a subsequent chapter, a crucial difference between performing research on non-profit vs. for-profit colleges and universities. Complications arose during this initial invitation stage, which will discussed in detail in Chapter Eight. Needless to say, gaining entry into for-profit IHEs to conduct research is a difficult undertaking (Pusser, 2005).

Data collection took place between February and June 2004; a total of 52 participants were interviewed. Throughout the interview process, I also collected data in the form of documents such as syllabi, course outlines, employee handbooks, and reports. Documents were collected via the Internet, through faculty participants and administrators, and through other individuals associated with each institution. What follows is an examination of the research methodology and data gathering methods used in this study. I begin by defining the traditional case study approach before moving into a discussion of what I refer to as a modified-case study method utilized in this study. I discuss the criteria used to select institutions and study participants before moving to a discussion of two methodological tools used to gather data—the qualitative interview process and document analysis. Each data gathering technique plays an important role in exploring faculty culture. I discuss the data analysis process used to organize and evaluate data, and then illustrate how one can ensure trustworthiness of the data through the use of triangulation.

CASE STUDIES

Case studies are useful when there is a need to understand complex social settings. The case study, as a methodological approach, is used "when the investigator has little control over events, and when the focus [of the study] is on a contemporary phenomenon within some real-life context" (Yin, 1984, p.13). In exploring faculty culture the researcher has little control over the actions, behaviors, and events of the study participants. Case studies permit one to understand how individuals situate themselves within their environment, and to examine how they identify with that environment. As such, the case study approach is an appropriate method to study faculty culture as it naturally exists, in an uncontrolled or unmanipulated setting.

Case studies are useful in capturing individual differences to produce cases that are "rich in information—rich in the sense that a great deal can be learned from a few exemplars of the phenomenon in question" (Patton, 1987, p. 19). They are also helpful for understanding how faculty define themselves and their work within their own institutions. Yet, it is important to keep in mind that outcomes are institutionally specific and may not provide a broad understanding of faculty culture.

MODIFIED-CASE STUDY APPROACH

This research project does not utilize a traditional case study approach as defined in the social science research literature (Marshall & Rossman, 1999; Mason, 1996; Patton, 1987; Yin, 1984). In other words, I do not pursue an understanding of specific issues of central importance to each institution. Rather, I develop four cases that explore issues relating to three broad areas, using predetermined themes; 1) the parameters of faculty work; 2) the parameters of decision-making; 3) the parameters of employment. Each case study also presents a fourth characteristic, one that is unique to each institution and its faculty. In addition, I develop several overarching themes that span across the institutions represented in the study. I chose this approach to foster a broader understanding of the distinctive issues that faculty members face at two types of for-profit IHEs—privately held vs. publicly traded—and to simultaneously highlight issues specific to each of the four institutions. The modified case study approach provides an accurate description of faculty culture at each institution yet also offers a broader understanding of faculty culture at for-profit IHEs by incorporating data from faculty participants across institutions.

SELECTION CRITERIA

A clear sampling strategy provides accuracy and soundness to any qualitative study. A study of faculty members at for-profit institutions requires that I identify characteristics that provide a clear picture of who to include. Faculty members participating in this study, for example, were part- and full-time faculty, who taught in pre-determined degree programs. It is also necessary to include individuals with a wide spectrum of beliefs (Tierney, 1991). The sampling strategy was flexible enough to allow me to test specific themes that developed during the research process. For instance, after several interviews it became evident that low faculty morale due to the absence of a faculty governing body was a serious issue that could not be overlooked. It was necessary for me to go outside the pre-determined interviewee characteristics to understand the factors that contributed to this condition. Thus, I sought faculty members whose efforts to create a faculty senate were thwarted by the administration.

INSTITUTIONAL SELECTION CRITERIA

I adapted specific institutional criteria to identify potential for-profit institutions. Since the for-profit higher education market encompasses a wide array of institutional types, it was necessary to identify two fundamental institutional classifications that could serve as the basis for this study. The colleges and universities that participated in this study represent higher education institutions that offer degrees; three of the institutions offer certificate programs in addition to degrees. In addition, each institution offers courses online and in-person, but the degree to which the institutions utilize distance education varies.

Accreditation

While most for-profit colleges and universities are served primarily by national accrediting agencies, only 67 institutions are accredited by regional accrediting associations (Kinser, 2003). Regional accreditation is considered more prestigious than national accreditation. Institutions such as Stanford, Harvard, and the University of Chicago are regionally accredited by such entities as the Western Association of Schools and Colleges, the New England Association of Schools and Colleges, and the North Central Association Higher Learning Commission, respectively. Three of the four institutions represented in this study are regionally accredited. National accrediting bodies, such as the Accrediting Council for Independent Colleges and Schools (ACICS), serve numerous public and private, non-profit and for-profit institutions; the fourth institution represented in the study is accredited nationally by the Accrediting Commission of Career Schools and Colleges of Technology (ACCSCT).

The first step in identifying potential institutions for this study was to limit the study to for-profit IHEs that were listed in the *2000 Higher Education Directory* or HED (Rodenhouse, 2000). HED lists only degree-granting institutions, defined by the directory as institutions that are legally authorized to offer programs of study that lead towards a degree. To be listed in HED the institutions must be accredited at the college level by agencies which have either been 1) approved by the US Secretary of Education, 2) hold pre-accredited status recognized by the US Secretary of Education, or 3) are accredited by agencies recognized by the now defunct Council on Postsecondary Accreditation (COPA) and the Commission on Recognition of Postsecondary Accreditation (CORPA), or currently recognized by the Council on Higher Education Accreditation (CHEA).

I identified 12 for-profit institutions from the directory and visited each institution's website to gather background information regarding the types of degree programs they offered. I chose institutions that offered degrees in several predetermined disciplines, discussed later in this chapter, and excluded those institutions that specialized in only one field. This allowed for an examination of faculty culture using the discipline as a frame of reference. That is to say that by choosing institutions that offered academic programs in specific fields of study, similarities and differences in disciplinary cultures could be examined across the sample institutions.

Classification by Ownership

As previously touched upon in Chapter Two, for-profit colleges and universities can be classified in numerous ways. Institutions can be classified by size, i.e. measured in terms of revenue dollars generated per year or by student enrollment. The Apollo Group, the parent company of the University of Phoenix, is the largest for-profit postsecondary education provider in the country in terms of revenue generation. Another method of classifying for-profit IHEs is by the way in which they deliver instruction, i.e. distance education vs. on-ground (classroom instruction) institutions.

For-profit colleges and universities also can be classified by type of ownership, i.e. family owned IHEs, institutions that are owned by private corporations, or those owned by public corporations. The for-profit institutions represented in the study are either classified as publicly traded or privately held institutions. For the purposes of this study I refer to for-profit IHEs that are family-owned, owned by a private corporation, or a group of investors as privately held institutions.

On the surface, ownership of privately held for-profit institutions can be difficult to characterize because of the complexity associated distinguishing between different types of ownership. Approximately 55% of regionally accredited for-profit IHEs are owned by families or by private corporations (Kinser, 2004). Family-owned colleges usually are named after the president or chairman of the board, who is often the owner. However, a private corporation can own an institution that was originally established by a family, hence the difficulty in distinguishing between the two types of institutions (Kinser, 2004). Of the two privately held for-profit institutions represented in this study, one is family-owned and the other was previously a family-owned college but was purchased by a private corporation in 2002.

Publicly traded IHEs are institutions owned by stockholders and are much easier to recognize; their stocks can be bought and sold on the open market. The general public is most familiar with these types of institutions, since many of them regularly advertise on radio and television, in newspapers and magazines, and on the Internet. One of the most recognizable publicly traded for-profit education providers is the University of Phoenix; others include ITT Technical Institutes, and Career Education Corporation. Of the two publicly traded for-profit institutions represented in the study, one has campuses located throughout the US and the other is exclusively a distance-education institution.

SOLICITING INSTITUTIONAL PARTICIPANTS

As previously mentioned, the *2000 Higher Education Directory* was used to identify institutions that fell into each of the two categories—privately held and publicly traded institutions. After developing a list of potential institutional participants, I subsequently sent an introductory email letter to each institution's chief academic officer. The letter provided background information about me and the project. The institutions that responded asked me to provide them with a detailed research proposal along with the interview protocol. In the case of the two publicly traded institutions, I sent the information to each university's Institutional Review Board (IRB) officer.

It is important to mention, as an aside, that IRB departments are commonplace to traditional colleges and universities. They are designed to approve and oversee the research endeavors of their respective faculty members. For-profit colleges and universities are not research institutions; they deliver rather than create knowledge. Therefore research is not a required component of faculty work life. However, the two publicly traded institutions represented in the study maintain institutional review boards that are mainly responsible for monitoring research projects concerning the institutions themselves, i.e. research projects that involve the institution and/or its members as study participants. The implications of this type of 'protective' behavior are discussed in future chapters.

After receiving a detailed research proposal, IRB administrators from each publicly traded institution participating in the study discussed the proposal with other members of the administration and with faculty department heads. In both cases, IRB administrators also sought approval from their respective boards of directors before final approval was granted to conduct the research.

The project approval process at the two privately held institutions represented in the study also were similar to one another, but differed slightly from the process associated with the publicly traded IHEs. Academic administrators at each of the privately held institutions were primarily responsible for reviewing and approving the research proposal, although it was necessary in both cases to obtain the approval of the college president before proceeding with the research. Moreover unlike administrators at the publicly traded institutions, administrators at the privately held institutions did not consult with faculty members before final approval; specific faculty members were notified of the project only after approval was granted.

INSTITUTIONAL PARTICIPANTS

For the purposes of confidentiality, I use pseudonyms to identify each institution. Pacific-Atlantic University (PAU) is a large, multi-campus institution with numerous campuses located throughout the US. It is held by a publicly traded corporation, and offers classes both online and on ground. The faculty members that participated in this study all taught on-ground, and all taught in a specific region of the western US. Distance Learning University (DLU) is the second publicly traded institution represented in the study, and as its pseudonym states, it is a distance education exclusive university. Its central headquarters are located in the Midwestern US. DLU enrolls students from throughout the world, though over 90% of its students are domestic. Miller College (MC) is a privately held institution with seventeen campuses located throughout the Midwestern US. The Miller family previously owned the college, and although it was recently sold to and is presently owned by a private equity investment firm, it retains the family name. Miller College faculty members interviewed for this study were located at four different campuses. The fourth and final institution participating in the study is Southeastern College (SC), a privately held, single-campus institution located in the eastern US. It was originally established as a technical business school and only recently began offering four-year bachelors degree programs. SC is a privately owned institution, with the owner serving as the institution's President and CEO.

FACULTY SELECTION CRITERIA

Since my efforts to recruit faculty were contingent upon the involvement of administrators at each institution, the process proved to be very tedious and time-consuming as I maneuvered through the various levels of 'red tape.' I worked with administrators, who were essentially the chief academic officers with varying titles, in identifying potential faculty participants. Once each institution granted me permission to conduct my study, upper level administrators sent email notices to department heads informing them of my research project and asking them to provide me with a list of names and contact information of potential faculty members that might be interested in participating.

Before department heads provided me with contact information they notified faculty members of my intent to invite them to participate. In other words, faculty members were given the option to ask that I not contact them. Only after these steps had been taken, was I given contact information and allowed to solicit potential participants using email invitations. Contact with faculty members from individuals not affiliated with the institution is closely controlled and monitored by members of the administration—another behavior that is discussed later.

Faculty members were recruited in groups, by institution. Table 2 provides a breakdown of the total number of faculty who were invited from each institution, the number who participated, and the percentage of faculty participants yielded. Administrators provided an initial pool of participants' names to me. I also recruited participants by asking faculty for additional names of individuals who might be willing to participate. Miller College was the most problematic institution with regard to faculty recruitment. The administration initially provided me with a list of 16 names of potential participants. Of the initial 16 individuals, only 5 agreed to participate; the others did not respond. The remaining 3 participants were recruited with the assistance of the initial group of faculty. Conversely, faculty from Pacific-Atlantic University and Southeastern College proved to be the most amenable. Of the names initially provided to me by the administration, all but one faculty member from each institution participated in the study. Although the Southeastern College administration was hesitant to provide me with more than five names, the faculty who agreed to participate were helpful in that regard. However, before I could solicit faculty members referred to me by the initial group of participants, I needed to obtain permission from the administration. More than half of the faculty members interviewed from Southeastern College were recruited with the help of the initial group of participants.

Table 2: Number of Faculty Members Invited vs. Number Who Participated, by Institution

Institution	Number of names provided by administration	Faculty from initial group who participated	Faculty members referred by participants	Total number recruited	Total number that participated	% yielded from total pool
Distance Learning University	26	12	8	34	18	53%
Pacific-Atlantic University	9	8	13	22	15	68%
Miller College	16	5	4	20	8	40%
Southeastern College	5	4	8	13	11	85%

Employment Status

Table 3 shows the distribution of faculty participants by employment status. Note the absence of part-time faculty participants from Miller College. I initially requested the names of part-time faculty members but was told that Miller College does not employ part-time faculty on a regular basis. Their goal is to provide students with as many full-time faculty members as possible. They use part-time faculty only when a full-time member is not available to teach a course. Also worth mentioning is the low representation of part-time faculty from Southeastern College. They, too, mentioned that they make an effort to hire full-time faculty members, but unlike Miller College, they do employ a handful of part-time faculty members on a regular basis. Although they represent a small minority of the faculty at Southeastern College, part-time instructors are used regularly to teach specialized courses when full-time faculty lack expertise in the area.

Academic Fields

Participants were selected by academic program and/or by department. Although the range of academic programs offered at for-profit colleges and universities continues to expand, the number of programs a given institution offers will vary. Some institutions offer an array of academic programs that span across several different fields, while others specialize in one or two areas, i.e. business or nursing. A requisite for faculty participation is that they teach in at least one academic degree program, or are involved in teaching general education courses within an academic degree program. Faculty members that taught only in certificate programs were excluded from participating in the study.

Table 3: Distribution of Faculty Participants by Employment Status and Institution

Institution	Full-time faculty	Part-time faculty	Total
Distance Learning U.	8	10	18
Pacific-Atlantic U.	7	8	15
Miller College	8	0*	8
Southeastern College	9	2	11
Total	32	20	52

*Miller College does not use part-time faculty on a regular basis

I chose degree programs that fit into one of six academic fields. These fields represent the most common areas of study offered at for-profit colleges and universities. Of note is the absence of degree programs in liberal arts and the humanities. For-profit IHEs that offer undergraduate degree programs, and are accredited by regional accrediting bodies, offer such courses as part of the general education curriculum; it is a prerequisite for accreditation. However, it is rare to find degree programs in the liberal arts or in the humanities. Because for-profit IHEs offer training and develop skills for the workplace, their degree programs often are professionally oriented.

Faculty Participants

I asked administrators to include faculty members teaching in at least one of the following six different academic fields: Business; Education; Information Technology (IT)/Communications; Health Sciences; Social Sciences; and General Education. Table 4 shows the distribution of faculty participants by academic discipline. These areas represent the most dominant fields of study at for-profit colleges and universities. My recruitment efforts yielded a total of 52 faculty members, 21 part-time and 30 full-time employees (See Table 3).

Certain academic programs are easily recognizable. Programs in marketing, finance, and management fell into the category of Business. Other academic programs were not as easy to distinguish. For example, the Health Science category includes degree programs in nursing, and other allied health professions. In addition, programs such as computer design, information technologies, and communications are part of the Information Technology (IT)/Communications field, while degree programs in psychology, criminal justice, and legal studies make up the social science field. Of note is the General Education category. To be clear, this category represents the number of faculty participants who taught courses within their institution's general education curriculum and does not indicate the number of faculty who teach within liberal arts and/or humanities degree programs; the institutions represented in the study offered only general education courses in these areas.

As detailed in Table 1, both administrators and faculty participating in the study provided me with a total of 89 faculty contacts. I initially contacted faculty members via email, sending electronic invitations addressed to individual faculty members. I followed up with phone calls when necessary. A copy of the email invitation is included in Appendix B. In what follows, I explore qualitative interviews and discuss the data collection process. As previously mentioned, I utilized documents as a secondary data-gathering tool. I will explore the document analysis process, in general, and discuss how it specifically was used in the study. I close the chapter with a discussion of the study limitations and offer concluding remarks regarding qualitative research.

Table 4: Distribution of Faculty Participants by Academic Field and Institution

Institution	Business	Education	IT/Com.	Health Sciences	Social Sciences	General Education	Total
Distance Learning U.	3	6	1	4	4 (Psychology)	0	18
Pacific-Atlantic U.	3	2	3	2	3 (Psychology)	2	15
Miller College	2	No program	3	1	No program	2	8
South-eastern College	5	No program	2	1	2 (Legal studies)	1	11
Total	13	8	9	8	9	5	52

QUALITATIVE INTERVIEWS

Kahn and Cannell (In Marshall and Rossman, 1999) describe interviewing as a conversation with a purpose. In qualitative interviewing, the researcher relies on acute listening abilities. The interviewer listens for key words and/or phrases, particular omissions, and 'hears' the meaning of what is being said. In doing so, the researcher explores the shared meanings and beliefs that develop in the studied environment. The practice of meaning making is part of the process of qualitative research (Horvat & Antonio, 1999). Meaning making is also not free of values; at the start of a project, researchers may make judgments about the arena being studied based on their preconceived beliefs. Many in traditional academic settings, for example, do not view for-profit higher education institutions as legitimate academic institutions; they may view them as diploma mills or job training centers.

Qualitative interviewing is based on the concept of conversation as a data-gathering tool. This technique requires an individual to rely on their conversation abilities and the rules inherent in everyday conversations, such as knowing when to speak, when to listen, and when to conclude and shift to a new topic of conversation. Yet, qualitative interviewing is more complex than daily conversations and differs in a number of ways. Rubin and Rubin (1995) identify three key elements that distinguish qualitative interviewing from other types of conversations. First, the interview is a means of gathering information or data from which the researcher will analyze, create new concepts and theories, and disseminate an analysis of a particular phenomenon through presentations and publications. A second distinction is that interviews typically are held between strangers, although interviews with acquaintances can also be part of the research process. The third difference between a qualitative interview and a typical conversation is that the researcher guides the conversation topics into specific areas of importance.

Data Collection via Interviews

I held 52 in-depth interviews with faculty participants that represented four different for-profit institutions, two privately held and two publicly traded institutions. Each interview lasted approximately one hour. Faculty participants answered questions from a standard protocol developed for this study (see Appendix A) as well as other unscripted inquiries that came about throughout the course of our interviews. The interview protocol designed for the study consisted of twelve questions designed to elicit information that rendered a detailed description of the work environment. Questions prompted faculty members to reflect on situations that would provide rich, detailed data from which to understand how they create meaning. This data allowed for a thorough exploration of faculty working conditions.

It was essential to have a flexible conversation style that allowed the interviews to progress into unforeseen areas that would expand upon my understanding of faculty culture. For example, in Chapter Six I discuss the high faculty turnover rate at Miller College. Although I had not considered this as a possible topic, the open-ended interview approach gave participants the opportunity to discuss how the long hours and demanding teaching schedule made it difficult for the institution to retain faculty for more than 18 months. The discussion method utilized in this study, the semistructured interview, permitted participants the freedom to take the interview to places of importance to them. By allowing a flexible protocol and interview process numerous areas could be examined in greater detail by certain faculty members. This permitted for a broader conception of the phenomenon under examination.

In developing the research design, it was important to include methods for systematically documenting data (Marshall & Rossman, 1999). Interviews were tape-recorded with each participant's permission. In three cases, faculty declined to be tape-recorded in which case extensive notes were taken during and after the interview. I provided myself ample time to write and review interview notes, and to outline a summary of the discussion after the conclusion of each interview; I allowed for a 30–45 minute time period for a more extensive and detailed note-taking session. This permitted me to reflect on the interview itself, dissect the data and begin to develop possible themes. Additionally, it allowed me to detect patterns that began to emerge during subsequent interviews.

Audio tapes were transcribed to facilitate the data analysis phase. I examined interview notes against the transcriptions to make certain my notes were accurate. During the initial analysis of the transcripts, I found that certain faculty provided responses that were unclear or required additional details. I subsequently corresponded with various study participants by email and telephone to probe their responses and/or to make additional inquiries about new issues that had not been covered during the initial interview.

Analyzing Interview Data

The approach a researcher uses to analyze data varies depending on how she or he intends to use said data. The purpose of the study is to gain insight into the culture of faculty members, thus the interview data are interpreted through the participants' lenses. The interview approach utilized in this study is referred to as a 'cultural' interview and participants taking part in cultural interviews have ownership of the data (Mason, 1996; Rubin & Rubin, 1995). In other words, faculty members create meaning and the researcher reports the meaning through the participants' lenses. This approach obligates me as the researcher to reproduce the participants' viewpoints and ideas, yet allows for one to "make choices about what to frame" (Rubin & Rubin, 1995, p.30).

My epistemological perspective is critical in interpreting the data. In using the interview format as a data gathering tool, my ontology is based on the assumption that people's knowledge, views, experiences, and interactions construct their reality and are important in studying the researched phenomenon. Thus, my epistemology allows for data gathering through interactions and conversations with people. However, when analyzing interview data, I made certain to be aware that, although interview data regarding participants' experiences are built around these ontological and epistemological perspectives, the data cannot fully explain every facet of their thoughts and behaviors (Rubin & Rubin, 1995). In other words, it was important that my conclusions not be based on data that was not recounted or revealed during the interview.

The coding and analysis process began only after I read the interview transcripts thoroughly and became very familiar with the data. The coding of data was approached in a number of different ways. I performed a microanalysis, also referred to as "line by line" analysis, to analyze individual sentences and/or paragraphs (Strauss & Corbin, 1998). This approach allowed me to develop concepts that tied categories together. For example, as the transcripts were analyzed I performed a detailed line by line analysis and assigned codes by conceptualizing the data. The act of conceptualizing is the action of breaking down data into incidents (Strauss & Corbin, 1998). After conceptualizing the data, I created broad categories that encompassed multiple behaviors. Data were then organized and coded in a manner consistent with the issues and themes that arose during the initial analysis.

Trustworthiness

It is essential for a researcher to be able to justify why their conclusions are the most appropriate as opposed to other alternate explanations. Data gathered through in-depth interviews require the researcher to protect against interviewer misperceptions and to avoid informants that are out of the ordinary, or who may lack credibility (Tierney, 1991). This helps to ensure that data are consistent with the conclusions. A well-designed research project will help to substantiate the researchers' conclusions. One way to assure that interview data are trustworthy is to assess its credibility by reviewing multiple data sources. Constant rechecking with informants during and after an interview helped assure that I was not misreading the data. By leaving the lines of communication open between myself and the research participants, I was able to address inconsistencies that arose during subsequent interviews. This type of procedure helped ensure that the conclusions were believable and communicable to readers.

DOCUMENT ANALYSIS

Document analysis refers to a specific type of qualitative research where data are generated through a variety of sources such as books, journals, public records, government documents, and other historical records. Some documents exist before the research begins allowing the researcher to gain background knowledge before conducting interviews. Other written communication can be generated during the research process by either the researcher or the participants; these include charts, tables, and written accounts. Document analysis supplements other data generating methods, such as interviews, and is a useful tool for triangulating data. It also provides an additional dimension to the research allowing one to gain an added perspective on the researched phenomenon, i.e. faculty culture.

I utilized data obtained through documents as a secondary data source that could offer additional insight into for-profit IHEs. Documents provide a context from which to examine these institutions and supply an alternative view of for-profit colleges and universities that may not be obtained through interviews. In other words, additional insight into faculty culture can be gained by employing an alternate means of understanding the context in which faculty make meaning. I collected data from company reports that offer a basis from which to view the organization relative to its employees. I inquired of certain faculty whether they would share course syllabi; this provided information regarding educational outcomes, course design, and student expectations. I was able to obtain employee handbooks from two institutions. They provided specific information about faculty members' role in curriculum development, stipulated how and when faculty are evaluated and whether they have a voice in the decision-making process.

Data from institutional handbooks are useful to corroborate or refute previously collected data. Publications generated for marketing purposes allowed me to assess the institution's intended public image, their stated goals, and the process towards achieving them. This type of data was useful because it provided a method from which I could compare an institution's mission with the kind of work expected from faculty. Memos generated for faculty and other employees were also a useful way of understanding the relationship between the employees and the organization. I analyzed documents for literal meaning as well as through an interpretive lens.

TRIANGULATION

Data triangulation involves the use of multiple methods in evaluating research data. Mathison (1988) asserts that triangulation is a strategy that helps eliminate bias by allowing a researcher to dismiss other possible explanations; it increases the validity and accuracy of the researcher's conclusions. Documents were primarily used to support, refute, or supplement data collected from interviews. The assumption here is that bias inherent in an individual, in the investigator, and in the methods of collection is canceled out when used in conjunction with other data sources and methods (Mathison, 1988). This argument assumes that what is not 'canceled out' is the 'truth' about the phenomenon being investigated and suggests that when researchers triangulate data, the results will converge on a single perspective of the social phenomenon under study.

Triangulation can take on various methods. Patton (1987) suggests four strategies for triangulating qualitative data: (1) collecting different kinds of data from the same question; (2) utilizing multiple fieldworkers to avoid bias; (3) using multiple methods to study the research phenomenon; and (4) using different perspectives to interpret data. I will focus on the latter of the four elements, triangulating data across interviews, as it is an appropriate method for triangulating data from this study, and provides the third data source that completes the metaphoric triangle. Triangulating across interviews suggests a method for validating interview information through corroboration. In other words, I not only compare data gathered through interviews with documents and other written evidence, I consider what respondents say in comparison to the responses of other participants. In doing so, I am able to verify the integrity of an individual's responses against data from other participants. If the purpose of triangulation is "to examine a conclusion (assertion, claim, etc.) from more than one vantage point" (Schwandt, 2001, p. 257), then triangulating data across interviews provides a process to achieve that objective.

STUDY LIMITATIONS

Due to the nature of for-profit colleges and universities, as proprietary organizations, I was confronted with the first of two limitations—difficulty in locating participants. I played a limited role in identifying faculty participants. Members of each institution's administration were primarily responsible for identifying and initiating contact with potential research participants. Therefore, it was necessary to be aware of the biases that faculty participants may have regarding their employment and employer. The faculty members that were identified and who agreed to participate held strong attitudes and opinions with regard to their institutions. Accordingly, I made certain to be aware of participants' biases and one-sided responses, and worded questions in a manner that would render relevant data.

This leads to a second limitation—challenges in assessing the participant's true beliefs about the institutions that employ them. Many of the faculty members that agreed to participate in the study seemed reticent to provide genuine insight into the structures and processes that guide the daily operation of their institution. Unlike traditional colleges and universities, which are accustomed to sharing information that assist in improving their institutions, similar information is considered proprietary by for-profit education providers. Participants were aware of the functional differences between for-profit and traditional institutions, and often were reluctant to offer certain information. Some of the faculty members expressed concern about the possibility of repercussions if administrators became aware of their opinions, especially because access to faculty members was gained with the explicit consent of the institution's administration. Triangulating data across interviews and across participants became a priority in such instances. As interview data was corroborated, it was my responsibility to distinguish between different types of responses, candid vs. guarded. To help ensure that participants responded truthfully, I guaranteed their anonymity. Participants were informed on numerous occasions that their responses would remain anonymous in the final report and in any other articles, presentations, and/or reports regarding this study. Their consent to participate required that they understand that their responses, my interview notes, field notes, and audio tapes would not be heard or viewed by anyone other than myself and members of the dissertation committee, if so desired. Moreover, each participant was given the opportunity to remove him or herself from the study in the future if they felt uncomfortable participating.

CONCLUSION

Marshall and Rossman (1999) describe qualitative research as a general means from which to study social phenomena. Qualitative methodologies allow researchers to gather data that examine how individuals interpret and experience their environments. Data gathering tools such as in-depth interviews and document analysis, for example, provide insight into the unexplored environment of faculty culture at for-profit institutions, and enable the researcher to examine the social interactions of faculty members while basing the data analysis on the participant's experiences and the interpretations of those experiences.

Although there has been tremendous growth in the for-profit higher education market, only minimal amounts of empirical data exist regarding the structures, processes, and cultures that define for-profit colleges and universities. Market forces and other external factors will continue to shape for-profit IHEs, yet there are internal dynamics unique to these institutions that contribute to their culture. By studying the attitudes and perceptions of faculty members, I intend to provide an increased understanding of faculty culture at for-profit institutions, and the issues faculty members confront due to their at-will employment status and the profit-seeking nature of the institutions that employ them. These two factors are not independent of each other; they are linked to one another as well as to the institutional culture.

In the subsequent four chapters, I present case studies. Each case study is organized in a manner consistent with the methodological approach previously described in this chapter. My intent is to provide a greater understanding of how certain issues serve to define for-profit colleges and universities and how these issues contribute to the development of the faculty culture. This study offers an accurate description of faculty culture at specific institutions and provides a broader understanding of faculty culture at for-profit IHEs in general by incorporating data from faculty participants across institutions. A cultural framework provides a window from which to examine the relationship between faculty members and the for-profit institutions that employ them. This study considers how for-profit institutions situate faculty within their institutions and explores the challenges, roles, and responsibilities associated with faculty work life.

Part II:
Perspectives from Within

The priority that faculty members place on their various work responsibilities is a function of the mission of the university and the value it places on each duty. One can expect faculty roles and responsibilities to differ between for-profit and traditional colleges and universities. For-profit institutions view postsecondary education as a private commodity, which results in different missions and goals than many traditional colleges and universities. The goal of for-profit institutions is to train individuals for jobs relevant to the current market while generating a profit, whereas that of traditional IHEs is to train individuals for the workplace, develop students' critical and analytical abilities, and in many cases create new knowledge. As a result, the priorities that each type of institution sets for their faculty also will differ. Understanding these fundamental differences in institutional goals is critical when examining how faculty members at for-profit colleges and universities define their priorities, responsibilities, and institutional roles.

The next five chapters examine how faculty members situate themselves and their work in relation to the various subcultures of faculty culture to gain insight into the issues they confront. As there are fundamental differences between for-profit and traditional institutions, differences in faculty work and faculty culture should be viewed in relation to the broad missions and goals of for-profit IHEs. In Chapters Four–Seven, I offer four case studies that will focus on four different types of for-profit institutions. Each case examines a predetermined set of criteria that shape how faculty perceive their working environments. The predetermined areas are: 1) parameters of faculty work; 2) parameters of governance; and 3) parameters of employment. The parameters of faculty work provide an overview of faculty roles and responsibilities. The parameters of governance examine faculty participation in governance and decision-making activities, and the parameters of employment explore the significance of contingent status and its consequences. Each case study also will explore a unique aspect of faculty work life for each institution.

Information regarding the working conditions for faculty at each institution is specified in Table 5. Faculty members from the publicly traded institutions represented in the study, DLU and PAU, openly provided detailed information. In contrast, participants from Miller and Southeastern College were reluctant to provide details about their working conditions with the exception of their employment status. Additionally, I also

Table 5: A Comparison of Part-time and Full-time Faculty Working Conditions by Institution

Institution	Employment Status	Health Benefits	Vacation Time	Sick Leave	Retirement Plan
Distance Learning University					
Part-time	Contracted by term	No	No	No	401K
Full-time	At-will (no contract)	Yes	20 days/year	Yes	401K
Pacific-Atlantic University					
Part-time	Contracted by term	No	No	No	Stock options and a 401K after 5 years of service
Full-time	Typically a 1-year contract	Yes	Yes (# of days not specified)	Yes	Stock options after 5 years, a 401K at hire
Miller College					
Part-time	Contracted by term *	Unknown	Unknown	Unknown	Unknown
Full-time	At-will	Unknown	Unknown	Unknown	Unknown
Southeastern College					
Part-time	Contracted by term	Unknown	Unknown	Unknown	Unknown
Full-time	At-will	Unknown	4 weeks	Unknown	Unknown

*No part-time faculty were interviewed for this study

determined that SC faculty members were allotted 1 week of vacation time after each academic term, for a total of four weeks per year.

Each case study will encompass a fourth area that explores a unique aspect of the institution, which will offer additional insight into faculty work life. I begin each case study by providing background information for each institution to offer a context from which to view the institution before moving into a discussion of the four substantive areas. The presentation of the case studies begins with a discussion of the two publicly traded institutions—Distance Learning University (DLU) and Pacific-Atlantic University (PAU), followed by the two privately held institutions—Miller College (MC) and Southeastern College (SC). To offer additional insight into the issues that contribute to the development of faculty culture, I close Part II by offering a chapter that examines a number of commonalities between all four institutions represented in the study, Chapter Eight. The topics covered in this chapter span institutional boundaries and offer a broader view of faculty work at for-profit colleges and universities in general.

Chapter Four
Distance Learning University

"If tenure were important to you, you wouldn't come to work at a place that doesn't have tenure."

As its name implies, Distance Learning University (DLU) is an online exclusive institution headquartered in the Midwestern United States, holding regional accreditation from the Higher Learning Commission of the North Central Association of Colleges and Schools. DLU was established in 1969 as a distance education-based institution, offering courses via U.S. mail, i.e. correspondence courses. The university focuses on educating adult learners, and the majority of its students are working adults returning to school either to enhance or change their careers. One of the university's selling points is the flexibility and convenience it provides for "busy professionals balancing work, family, and education." Students are required to complete a residency requirement, for accreditation purposes, but the majority of instruction takes place in a web-based, asynchronous environment.

Distance Learning University is a graduate institution that offers masters and doctoral degree programs in four academic divisions; Education; Health and Human Services; Management; and Psychology. They recently began offering a bachelors degree in the Management area. The institution's mission is two-fold and is clearly expressed in terms of what it intends to provide to its students, i.e. "to provide alternative graduate-level, dispersed-residency distance education . . ." and "to prepare and inspire scholar-practitioners to be leaders in making positive social change in their areas of influence." DLU's mission, like those of many for-profit IHEs, is explicit and transparent. Students are made aware of the institution's purpose by the mission statement located on their website and can make an informed decision before deciding to enroll.

The nature of the university, as a distance education institution, makes a study of faculty culture unique. Over 90% of the faculty members work for DLU on a part-time basis and are located throughout the country. Full-time faculty are the only faculty members required to work at the central office. Table 6 provides additional background information on the participants. However, there are other important characteristics of DLU participants that are not reflected in Table 6—more specifically their educational, personal, and professional backgrounds. Faculty members from DLU typically are individuals who hold doctoral degrees and have extensive backgrounds in higher education either as researchers or administrators. Out of the 18 faculty members that were interviewed, 17 had doctoral degrees including a Juris Doctorate, and 10 currently are either professors and/or executive level administrators in education. As well, one-third of the participants had retired from education professions; 3 were retired professors, 2 were retired administrators, and 1 was a former high ranking official with the U.S. Department of Education. The backgrounds and experiences of faculty members from DLU provide a context from which to explore how these participants defined their work life and ultimately DLU's faculty culture, and are an important factor to consider as one examines the data.

Table 6: Distribution of Faculty Participants from *Distance Learning University* by Discipline, Status, and Terms of Service

Discipline	Full-time	Part-time	Number of Years at Institution		
			0–2 years	*3–5 years*	*Over 5 years*
Business	2	1	1	2	0
Education	3	3	3	2	1
IT/Comm.	0	1	0	1	0
Health Sciences	2	2	2	1	1
Social Sciences	1	3	0	2	2
General Education	0	0	0	0	0
Totals	8	10	6	8	4

PARAMETERS OF FACULTY WORK

Faculty members at Distance Learning University have responsibilities that vary depending on whether they are part-time or full-time employees. Full-time faculty members comprise a small minority of the faculty body, whereas part-time faculty members comprise more than 90% of the faculty at DLU. Part-time faculty members are hired both to teach and mentor students. Service to the university, in the form of committees, is not a responsibility of part-time faculty members although they are given the opportunity to participate in committee work. Research also is not a required component of faculty work, as with most for-profit IHEs, but there are a small number of faculty members who engaged in research on behalf of DLU. The institution may provide financial assistance for a number of research endeavors, if they include a distance-education component from which the institution will benefit. Part-time faculty members at DLU have various responsibilities but they typically fit into one of the two major faculty roles—that of a Faculty Mentor and that of an Online Instructor. The positions are not exclusive of one another; an individual can be hired to serve both as a faculty mentor and an instructor. Yet, they are distinct in the types of interactions that are required.

Full-time Faculty

Although they are referred to as professors, many of the responsibilities of full-time faculty are administrative in nature. Their responsibilities differ greatly than those of full-time faculty at traditional IHEs. Three components—teaching, research, and service—tend to encompass the typical work roles of full-time, tenure-track faculty members at traditional colleges. Full-time, off-track faculty at traditional IHEs usually have heavier teaching loads than their tenure-track counterparts and also may be required to complete a modicum of service to the university. The role of full-time faculty members at DLU encompasses a variety of responsibilities. Although they are referred to as professors, full-time faculty spend the majority of their time in administrative rather than in teaching roles.

When viewed from the perspective of traditional academia, the responsibilities of full-time faculty at DLU parallel that of a department head or dean. One of the major responsibilities of full-time faculty is to staff their departments, which means they are charged with recruiting and hiring part-time faculty members. "My title is professor but I actually administer the [program] in my department. I maintain development of all the schedules. I hire the faculty, I schedule the faculty, I monitor the faculty, and I take care of all the curriculum development in terms of academic review. I teach occasionally and I also mentor doctoral students. So, my job is very busy."

A full-time faculty member in Management echoed the previous remarks. "I am responsible for identifying part-time faculty candidates, hiring them, and assigning them to both develop and teach courses." In addition to these responsibilities, full-time faculty develop courses for their program however, they are predominantly responsible for maintaining the daily operation of their programs.

> I have to say that it is probably a lot more administrative work than I would have imagined and maybe, like I said, I don't have a background in a traditional academic setting, but it is still more administrative than I would have imagined. On a day-to-day basis, most of what I am doing is staffing, scheduling, and taking care of the administrative things that we need to keep things going with the part-timers.

Full-time faculty responsibilities at traditional colleges and universities often include course design and curriculum development. These duties are not usually part of the full-time faculty workload due to the significant administrative responsibilities associated with full-time faculty work at DLU. Full-time faculty members have the opportunity to design courses, but this is a secondary responsibility that is set aside when primary administrative responsibilities must be met. "I'm not involved in developing new courses, but I work with faculty to develop them. In fact, I had proposed to develop a Knowledge and Learning Management course and my supervisor thought maybe I shouldn't because I had too much to do. So we hired someone to develop the course, but I do the academic reviews."

Part-time Faculty

Similar to the other institutions represented in the study, part-time faculty members at Distance Learning University are hired to teach. The part-time faculty role involves more than teaching; there are other components such as being sensitive to the student-centered culture. Part-time faculty play one of two teaching roles. They are hired to teach online courses, but can also be hired as Faculty mentors. Of the institutions that participated in the study, the faculty mentor role was unique to DLU. This can be attributed to the graduate education component of the institution. There is a need to provide a certain degree of faculty to student contact outside of the classroom environment because the majority of DLU's students are pursuing graduate degrees.

Faculty Mentors

Doctoral programs at DLU are structured differently than typical doctoral programs. Students are required to write a dissertation. However, depending on the specific program of study, doctoral programs are structured in one of three ways: 1) students take courses and write a dissertation; 2) in lieu of taking courses, students write a series of papers that encompass a specific set of knowledge-based areas from their chosen field, and write a dissertation; or 3) they do a combination of courses, and a set of papers along with a dissertation. The modified structure of doctoral programs necessitates the need for a distinct faculty role, the faculty mentor.

Faculty mentors are responsible for working with students on an individual basis. Their role is very similar to that of a dissertation advisor except that faculty mentors work with students as they write their knowledge-based papers (KBP) in addition to their dissertations. In many ways, the role of the faculty mentor is to tutor students throughout their program. A faculty member described his role as that of a guide and spoke about his responsibilities as a faculty mentor.

> As a mentor, I am essentially someone that helps to guide students as they're developing their needs. I help them in their research and in their research methodology. I'm often times reviewing drafts of their thesis in the process, if they're writing their dissertations. But I'm also someone that helps them, you know, if they have questions about the university and they need someone that has to explain to them about the processes. So, it's a very wide-ranging role.

Students receive a great deal of personal attention from their faculty mentors. On numerous occasions faculty participants highlighted the amount of time they—as faculty mentors—spent with students. "There is probably more interaction with students right here than you ever get in a classroom with a professor." Another participant stated "I spend so much more time working with students online because everything they write is for posterity." The role of a faculty mentor is time-consuming and may encompass more than the typical responsibilities of a thesis advisor at a traditional institution. A full-time faculty member who is responsible for hiring faculty mentors for her department explained that "I want to make sure that they have the time they need to spend with the students."

Online Instructors

On the surface, the role of faculty members who teach online courses differs from the role of the faculty mentor. Instructors work in the 'classroom,' while mentors work with students individually. Upon closer examination the teaching philosophy at DLU yields somewhat similar roles for faculty mentors and online instructors. Both require the faculty member to guide students rather than to lead students. This is an underlying principle of the institution, given that most of the students are adults with many years of work experience. One part-time faculty explained:

> The Internet side of teaching requires that you be a 'guide on the side' rather than a 'sage on the stage.' You can't lecture, it is not lecture-based, it is really more sort of guiding discussions by posing questions for discussions and letting the students do a lot of their own pondering and reflecting from week to week. You jump on the discussion boards and try to guide the discussion in good ways and comment along the way.

The responsibility of an instructor is such that the student and the faculty member work alongside one another as colleagues. The nature of this relationship also requires that students play a significant role in the learning process. In other words, students at DLU are not simply reading their e-textbooks and turning in assignments; they are active participants in the learning process. One faculty member who echoed the thoughts of other participants commented that students "are very focused and very goal oriented, and are very active learners."

Student-centered Faculty

A central responsibility of faculty members, no matter whether they are part-time of full-time, is to focus on the needs of the student. One full-time faculty member remarked "At DLU, a focus is on being student-centered and that's a very high priority. That's not to say that other institutions are too, but it is highlighted at DLU." When asked to define 'student-centered' she explained that faculty are "really looking at whatever students needs are and you're looking at how you can provide a quality education that's going to meet their needs for education." Other faculty members asserted "At DLU, students come first." And "What makes DLU unique is that fact that it is very much student-centered. I'm not sure if this is true of other places as much as it is with DLU."

The student-centered approach brings with it new challenges. Many of the faculty members spoke about the need to be cognizant of students' time.

> I think that the students are all working and have very busy lives. I think in [the] Orientation [course], because it's their first course, they

are taking it along with another course, and I don't think that a lot of students really have understood what it means to be in a doctoral program. I think that that's probably a challenge, you know, to really help the student be successful and to understand the time commitment.

Being student-centered also requires that the faculty understand that their role is not only to teach; they have a responsibility to make certain students learn. The student-centric culture faculty are required to create and maintain was best captured by the thoughts of a full-time faculty member from the education department.

> If you take the traditional university as research, service, and teaching, I would say that at DLU we are reversed. The primary purpose at DLU is learning, which was never part of the triad at research universities. Ten years ago [people] never talked about learning. It was always number one-research, number two-probably teaching, and number three was service. At DLU, student learning is number one. Some [part-time] faculty have, I think, a modicum role in service and some might have a modest role in research, but it is almost probably 95% teaching and learning.

A faculty member's ability to create an environment that promotes open communication between students and the instructor is of utmost importance to the institution. The faculty role requires instructors to meet the needs of the student in other ways. More specifically, faculty also must take into consideration the needs of the student outside of the classroom. One full-time faculty member mentioned that faculty should ask "what are we going to do to help with their other needs, whether it's finding information or learning more about technology and what [electronic] room to go to. You know, the service side of things, how to solve their problems." Although one can argue that the student-centered approach is, in essence, responding to the needs of the student, others may view this approach as acquiescing to meet the customer's needs. The student-centric model creates a tension that highlights the belief of students as customers. Another example of the tension between responding to the needs of students vs. the needs of the 'customer' was captured by the following scenario between a full-time faculty member and a part-timer whom she supervised. "Recently, I had someone who included four textbooks [in his course], and I said 'No, we don't want to do that to our students, do you really need all those textbooks'? And, of course, he came back with one textbook and one little handbook. I look at that because we do have to be considerate of [student's] money."

Culturally Cognizant Faculty

A faculty member who does not understand the culture of the online environment at DLU will not do well. For example, a full-time faculty member in the management department who is responsible for hiring and monitoring faculty within the department spoke about how occasionally there have been part-time faculty members who did not understand their role, the proper way in which to interact with students, and the nature of the faculty-student relationship.

> Our culture is a very respectful culture and our assumption is that our [faculty] are well trained and know what they're doing. And with only two exceptions that has proven to be true for me personally, from the faculty that I work with. I have had to stop scheduling two faculty members because they just didn't do well with the culture. They were good people, we just all agreed that we wouldn't schedule them again. It just wasn't working. They were not able to form a link with the students when the students [needed to] feel free to communicate. And it was like a very hard-nosed approach.

As with most colleges and universities, open communication between faculty members and their students is important because it enhances the learning environment. The DLU culture highly encourages, if not requires, faculty to create good rapport with their students. When asked what the institution looks for in a perspective faculty member, a number of participants responded that they "look for faculty who can create good student relationships." A full-time faculty member referred to this skill as "student relationship management." A participant provided the following example:

> A technique you use is to pick out something that the student has said and you relate to it. That is something that I do personally, it can be as simple as 'I noticed something similar in your background that is similar to mine,' or 'I noticed that you are from Connecticut, so am I.' Just things like that kind of break the ice and it really helps the students understand that there is a real person behind there.

Given the nature of DLU as an online university, the method of delivery is unique not only because it is via the Internet but also because teaching and learning go on in an asynchronous environment. In other words, faculty and students do not need to be logged into the 'classroom' at the same time, which in turn creates an essential responsibility for faculty members. To maintain open lines of communication as well as good rapport with students, faculty must follow specific guidelines. For example one full-time faculty explained, "Faculty must respond to students' questions within 24 hours, and that includes the discussion boards, because many times students are working on their assignments and they might ask a question within their posting. That is why it is so important for faculty to be in there regularly, so that they can see if students are asking questions." Although there is a lack of what was referred to as "face-to-face interaction" between faculty and students—an issue I will discuss later—the culture of the institution requires that faculty members be readily available to students.

Parameters of Governance

Faculty participation in governance and decision-making is common at traditional IHEs. Participation in a shared system of governance is not only a right of the faculty at tradition IHEs, but also a responsibility. The governance structure at DLU is such that faculty members play a limited role in governing the institution. Given that DLU resides in the both the corporate and academic arenas, one would expect it to have a governance structure that deviates from traditional colleges and universities. In other words, because DLU serves the needs of both the students and the investors a system of shared governance is viewed by many in the 'corporate' arena as an inferior decision-making structure. Decisions that include faculty input are related only to courses and the curriculum, and both part-time and full-time faculty can contribute to the process.

Sharing the Corporate View

While faculty members have some decision-making authority, it is limited in scope. Academic administrators have the authority to make certain decisions. Yet, the final arbiters of most decisions regarding the institution— such as offering new programs, maximum class size, and the overall strategic direction of DLU—are corporate not academic executives. Faculty members expressed a certain degree of confidence in their corporate managers, presuming they made decisions in the best interest of the university. The organization reassures its faculty via a series of presentations that explain how senior executives make their decisions. A number of faculty members spoke about these presentations:

> We had a presentation by one of the corporate officers at a meeting in January, and she said 'I am going to give you a presentation that we just gave to an investor group, so this really isn't intended for you but I would like to give you a window into what we have to do on that end

and I know I am speaking to faculty and I respect you and so forth but just allow me to show you what we have to do in the business end to make sure that DLU is a viable institution financially.' And so she went about it and I thought it was pretty fascinating. We all did, and it was kind of like 'thank you for letting us know what your challenges are and how we as faculty play a role. . . . '

Another faculty member described the presentations as a means by which the company informs its faculty about how funds are distributed. In other words, this participant interpreted the presentation as a justification for the manner in which budgets were allocated.

We had a meeting somewhere and we were given the big corporate picture and that sort of thing. And so there's an emphasis on 'the stockholders expect this,' or whatever, 'for us to show a profit.' And they want investors to see that the company is doing well. That's quite a foreign thing for most people in academia, and so what comes from this is, probably the greatest thing, is the budgetary decisions. So there's so much money allocated, and it's based on past performance and how much money is available and how much money they want to spend on new ventures . . .

Corporate executives share their view of the institution with the faculty to help them understand the context of the decision-making process. The presentations build "a picture of the interconnectedness of it all" so that the faculty can begin to understand why certain decisions are made. Sharing the corporate perspective may alleviate some concerns and can instill a certain degree of confidence in the institution among faculty members, but there are still those who are uneasy with the profit-seeking motives of the institution and the hierarchical approach to decision-making.

Corporate-based Decisions

On many occasions participants expressed that, although faculty do have a voice, decisions about the organization often "take a top-down approach [because] that's the way corporations are." Still, participants were reluctant to trust the organization completely. Most faculty members have backgrounds in traditional higher education and, although they have taught at DLU for a number of years, they found it difficult to trust that the institution was always doing what is in the best interest of its students rather than its investors. A part-time faculty participant commented:

You have to have a kind of skepticism in your mind when you understand that when the bottom line comes down to it, a decision has got to
be made relative to how much profit is being made and what is happening to the stock. Those are the bottom line decisions because that is the
basis of for-profit education. That is it. There always will be that bottom line that if your stock is losing value you have to do something
about it. If your profits go down to an unacceptable level you are going
to do something about it and that is still a little bit different than the
kind of bottom line discussions that happen, I think, in [traditional]
private and pubic institutions.

For many faculty members corporate based decisions are, in essence,
financial decisions. Several participants explained that corporate managers
attended faculty meetings regularly to update the faculty on developments
regarding the institution. Before faculty members discuss specific topics on
the agenda senior executives, "come in to give us what they call the pipeline
[report]. That's when they give us the numbers so we know what it's looking like for students who will start the next term. Then we talk about attrition and marketing." Many discussions among faculty members take place
within the context of revenue generation, rather than within an academic
context.

What you have with DLU which you don't have with the traditional
university is the whole infrastructure of marketing and those sorts of
things that other universities don't . . . There's a whole research team to
figure out what is the best market. There's a lot of infrastructure just to
meet the needs of a for-profit organization . . . there's an infrastructure
that is really setting the stage within what the university can do. The
university couldn't say 'we want to start this new program' and go
ahead and do it. There's a whole process.

When the institution considered pursuing program accreditation,
from the American Psychological Association, for its Psychology department a participant explained that faculty played only an advisory role in
that decision. Ultimately the final decision was based on financial motives,
with the faculty having little authority.

Even though the faculty took a role in that. DLU and [it's parent com-
pany] decided that it would not be profitable. It could result in such a
reduction of student numbers that tuition would have to increase astro-
nomically, and it would be eliminating a lot of people who would be

DLU clientele and would no longer be eligible. So the bottom line is, even though faculty had made this decision, it was actually an advisory thing. If DLU administrators were to have said, 'We want to do this,' it would have happened regardless of the faculty.

Even more surprising, when asked whether the administration would have reconsidered their decision had the faculty strongly objected, the faculty member remarked, "If the faculty would have said 'Well, we want to do it. It is important.' It still would not have happened." A part-time faculty put it best; "Everything is a business decision."

Tension Between Corporate vs. Academic Units

Faculty members spoke about the tension between the academic and corporate branches of the organization. "Faculty really have issues with corporate influencing or trying to influence the academic side of the business." A major issue of contention pertains to the growth of the institution. As enrollments in the institution increase, the corporate office has responded by increasing the maximum number of students allowed per class. One faculty member explained, "The push from corporate is to conduct [a class] with twenty-five students whereas in the past we definitely would have split the class." She asserted, "I believe it has changed to meet the corporate goals. [To meet] the budget goals, and revenues and profits, we are finding that we need to increase the caps of our classes." Yet, faculty members also explained that "quality is very, very important and most faculty say they won't sacrifice quality for numbers." DLU's parent corporation views the opportunity for growth as enormous. This is not to say that DLU executives will sacrifice quality for profit. Rather, these circumstances provide insight into how one side of the organization—the corporate side—is the final arbiter of many decisions regarding the institutions.

A part-time faculty member in Management described the tension between the corporate and academic sides as healthy, and as part of the institution's "growing pains." Yet, he was clear in his understanding that the university's goals are synonymous with corporate goals.

DLU is clearly a for-profit company, and [a] publicly traded company. Their primary motivation is growth and every company is responsible for showing a return to their stockholders. So, DLU wants to grow and the academic side wants to grow. Yet, to what degree [the academic side] wants to grow, there may be some friction. But they are both in agreement that we need to grow. It's healthy for the business.

Decisions about Curriculum

Faculty members at traditional institutions often times develop and teach their own courses, which do not have to meet with the approval of others. At DLU, decisions about courses do not rest with a single individual. Once a course is developed it must meet the approval of the faculty chair and proceed through a systematic review process before it can be taught. Once the course has been developed, it is submitted to the chair of the department. At that point,

> I look to see if the design is instructionally sound . . . and that it is user friendly. I look at the overall format of the syllabus before it goes anywhere, and then once I approve [the syllabus] it goes to the curriculum and design (CID) group and they look at it. Then we give the course to a shell developer, when the syllabus has been approved they lay it into the course shell. Then CID looks at the course shell, and then finally I look at the course shell before it is taught.

A full-time faculty member explained that after a course goes through an extensive review process, decisions about whether to offer the new course or a new academic program also are based on their financial viability. Faculty authority in the curriculum stretches only so far before curricular decisions become business decisions. "And that's the other thing, to get a program approved, there are many different people looking at it. And in the end, it's truly a business decision. What is the likelihood of this degree being profitable? That's what it comes down to. How much are we really going to invest to get to the point of profit building?"

Full-time faculty members are not required to be involved in the development of curriculum, but they have some decision-making authority over the courses in their department. The decisions they make regarding the curriculum deal with evaluating rather than developing courses. A full-time faculty in Management explained, "We have part-time faculty we hire to develop the courses. I do all of the course reviews from an academic standpoint when [the faculty member] finishes the development of the course." Once a course has been developed it is evaluated by other faculty members. A full-time faculty member described her role in approving new courses for her department. "We have to look at each course, you know, [and ask] 'Where are we going to provide content and learning activities and assignments that will meet the overall outcomes of the program objectives'? In some instances, decisions about the curriculum may have previously been made by others. For example, a faculty member explained how he was responsible for creating courses for a new degree program, but the course outlines (master syllabi) from which the courses were to be developed had already been written by someone else. "When I joined DLU about a year ago many of the courses had not been developed yet because the program was so new. Early on, my responsibilities were for the development of the program because the curriculum was set. We had all the master syllabi for the courses, but not all of the courses were developed."

PARAMETERS OF EMPLOYMENT

Before discussing the effects of contingent status on faculty members at DLU, it is important to remind the reader that the majority of faculty members from DLU who participated in this study had professional backgrounds in traditional higher education. As previously mentioned, 16 of 18 participants previously were or currently are employed in the traditional education arena. "At DLU, we have people who are teaching at another university, more people like myself." I asked several participants if DLU makes an effort to hire individuals with administrative and/or faculty experience at traditional IHEs and many responded in similar fashion. "Over the last two or three years, DLU has been hiring more academic type of people. Fewer people have been hired who are of the strict clinical practice . . . because at the doctoral level you have the research requirement. So, DLU is sort of strengthening the faculty with respect to their background." As a consequence of offering masters and doctorial degree programs, DLU seeks faculty with backgrounds in research and publishing, i.e. current and former faculty members.

Accomplished and Aware

The personal and professional backgrounds of the faculty members at DLU are important in exploring the effects of contingent status on faculty work. Thirteen of the participants had achieved tenure or were seeking tenure at another university, and four were central administrators in either the K-12 public education arena or at traditional higher education institutions. Moreover, one-third of the participants were retired educators who chose to teach at DLU to keep connected with the field. Consequently, their contingent status did not pose a significant problem. "A lot of faculty are working elsewhere, and they have worked elsewhere and they've been through that tenure thing, and maybe it's not as important to them at this point in their career." In other words, faculty who make the decision to teach for DLU do so knowing that the institution does not offer tenure and that they will be hired on a contingent status; tenure or lack thereof was of little consequence.

I've never heard that [tenure] is an issue because the majority of the faculty are part-time and there are not that many full-time faculty. [DLU] has policies and guidelines, you know, about termination and all that. But there's no tenure like at a traditional university, and I've never heard anyone say anything about it, as far as it being an issue. I don't think tenure is an issue. If tenure were important to you, you wouldn't come to work at a place that doesn't have tenure.

A retired faculty member tenured at a traditional university and who now teaches full-time for the DLU explained, "My scholarly days are pretty much over. I am not going to be writing any more grants, I assure you." In speaking about other faculty who teach at DLU, he remarked that many are not unlike himself, "They have already achieved."

Other faculty members were interested in working at DLU part-time because it provided them the opportunity to work with a different type of student; students who have extensive professional backgrounds and whose interests lie in being practitioners rather than educators.

Another feature that attracted me to DLU was the fact that their student body, as far as doctoral and masters students, are very different clientele than students at [my university]. They are all for the most part mid-career people coming with a lot of practical experience in whatever venue. I have worked with people at DLU who were corporate CEOs or who have been working in clinical practice. . . .

Faculty chose to work for DLU for a number of reasons. Whether or not they are contingent employees is an afterthought. Tenure is not important to them for a variety of reasons. Other elements of the job are much more significant to faculty. The only issue that faculty mentioned as somewhat problematic, which is peripherally related to contingent status, is the lack of faculty autonomy.

Efficiency vs. Autonomy

While autonomy and academic freedom are closely linked to one another in the realm of traditional academe, the corporate culture of the institution does place restrictions on the amount of freedom faculty have. The topic of academic freedom will be discussed in greater detail later in subsequent chapters. The following section focuses on the issue of faculty autonomy as it relates to the culture of the institution. The need to be efficient creates a dynamic that restricts autonomy.

The corporate branch of the organization has little input into decisions regarding course content. However, it is important to keep in mind that in the business realm, quality is achieved through standardization. The way in which quality is maintained at the academic department level is by creating a 'Lead Faculty' position. Lead faculty is not a title. Rather, it is a role that requires an appointed faculty member to coordinate the activities of the entire faculty who teach a specific course or set of courses. In essence, the lead faculty role diminishes faculty autonomy by restricting the choices individual faculty members can make.

> The lead faculty role includes getting the course ready every term so that it can be copied for other instructors, and also maintaining the textbook information, particularly new editions or changes in textbooks. So, they are the point person, if you will, for that particular course . . . [The] lead faculty decides on the textbook, sets up all the assignments, the syllabus. And everyone who instructs must follow that.

The lead faculty role was not created to diminish academic freedom, although that may be the result. The culture of the institution mandates there be some degree of course standardization as a means to efficiency. In much the same way that a department head coordinates the activities of the department, the lead faculty role goes one step further by coordinating the activities of faculty members. A lead faculty member offered his perspective. "We have a very stringent schedule and a step-by-step of what we need to do to make sure all of our courses are ready for the students two days before the term starts. If you think about it, we have turned something that perhaps was every instructor's right to set up the way they want and how they want, to something that is really somewhat of a machine." Another faculty participant explained his view on how the need for efficiency affects faculty autonomy. "I think there have been some restrictions on [autonomy] by virtue of course definitions that appear in the catalogue and required textbooks that are being used . . . I think that is because of privatization, standardization, [and] the online delivery format."

Standardization

The loss of faculty autonomy in favor of standardization and efficiency has a direct affect on students. A number of faculty members mentioned that their lack of ability to choose their own texts and develop the courses they teach diminishes the student experience. The need to maintain standardization and follow a prescribed course outline can have detrimental affects on the education that graduate students receive. A number of participants questioned this approach.

> If you are [standardizing] at the undergraduate level maybe that works. But if you're talking about doctoral level, you need to have people who are not just reading the same old textbook and memorizing for a test. You need people who are critically examining the literature, developing their critical thinking and writing skills, people who are going well beyond any required textbooks in terms of what they are reading and what they are researching . . . I have raised this issue, that we may not be doing masters and doctoral students a service if we are putting so much emphasis on the textbooks . . . and not going beyond this pre-scribed curriculum in the course—the objectives that are defined and associated with this course description and so forth.

A number of faculty accepted standardization as a component of the institution's culture. "They want to keep it pretty consistent from class to class . . . I don't have a problem with that. [DLU] has certain guidelines, certain information. So, I go along with it." Nevertheless, participants seemed apprehensive over the need for standardization but were aware of its importance to the institution. "Everybody has a concern about [standardization], but at the same time there is a need for the standardization that people are feeling." A faculty member from psychology commented that although the corporate division of the organization believes in standardization to increase quality, it may not be the best approach to graduate education.

> Because of the graduate focus, I think there has always been the sense that faculty should be allowed maximum freedom in terms of how they structure their courses . . . As DLU grows there is a kind of thinking seeping in, in terms of 'Can we start to reduce some of the variability across our courses'? with the premise being that if you do that you increase, potentially, quality.

While standardization of courses and curriculum was a major concern for most participants, there was another issue that was consistently mentioned by faculty participants. The issue directly relates to DLU's institutional type, more specifically its method of delivery. As its name states, Distance Learning University is a distance education institution. Contact between students and faculty occurs electronically, rather than face-to-face.

The inherent nature of the institution leads to issues that are unique to DLU.

DISTANCE AFFECTS COMMUNICATION

The lack of face-to-face interaction across and between various groups including students, faculty, staff, and administrators created circumstances that were unique to DLU. Communication between faculty members was most problematic. The loss of interpersonal interaction between faculty members and administrators and between faculty and students also had its consequences. I focus on three areas that were consistently mentioned by faculty participants as problematic issues related to communication and distance.

Communication Amongst Faculty

Unlike on-ground colleges and universities, faculty members at DLU are located throughout the country and interact mostly in a virtual environment. There are opportunities for faculty to come together; DLU hosts a number of regional meetings that faculty are invited to attend. In addition, faculty members can attend summer student residencies; programs of study often require a residency for students. Not all faculty members attend student residencies. Faculty members attend by invitation only, making it difficult for them to become familiar with one another outside of the virtual environment. "I think faculty members that meet at residencies know each other better, and I don't do residencies so I'm sort of missing out on that . . . There is sort of a small percentage of DLU faculty that participate in that, from my understanding."

As a result, faculty members communicate primarily via email and a listserv created by institution. The 'virtual communication' between faculty members has its drawbacks. Many faculty members do not use the listserv. After inquiring whether the listserv was underutilized a part-time faculty member in Public Policy responded, "Absolutely." He continued, "The listserv is a way to promote conversation among the faculty, but I always think to a certain degree that the listserv will never really duplicate having a strong relationship with other faculty."

The lack of communication between faculty members was described on the one hand as a minor issue, and on the other, as problematic for both faculty and students. A part-time faculty from psychology mentioned that inadequate communication between faculty members resulted in the lack of a faculty community. "I wish there were more [communication]. We do kind of get together at the regional meetings and seminars in the summer, for those of us that go to summer sessions. I think it's not so much with the student work that I miss; it's the collegiality that I miss, just not being part of a faculty that knows each other." He also explained that the university has attempted to mitigate the lack of contact between faculty by using an online discussion board called the Academic Faculty. However, there are residual problems stemming from asynchronous communication between faculty members—poor faculty morale. "We have this thing online called the academic faculty. We are able to carry on conversations asynchronously. When you have been there for a while you get to know people . . . I do think [the online environment] makes it much more difficult to keep morale up, that is a problem."

Another part-time faculty member pointed out that the lack of face-to-face communication has negative consequences on the students. Minor dilemmas become major hassles when faculty members are unable to communicate informally with one another.

> I think one of the frustrating things for me is the kind of 'water cooler' conversations that you would have around 'What are you doing with students who are having writing problems in this class? How far are you willing to go'? and 'What is acceptable and what is not acceptable from your viewpoint at this stage'?—these kinds of conversations. You can do that online but somehow it isn't the same thing. You have to disclose a lot more online than you do at a water cooler.

Faculty members are left on their own to determine whether a student is measuring up. Many have difficulty determining how well their students are doing, and whether they measure up to the learning curve of the university as a whole. "It turns out that standards, which is what I was talking about in the last situation, you just have to make your own mind [as to] where you are going to draw the line." Another faculty member asked, "What level of writing should you insist upon? The question comes down to the kind of quality of writing . . . what standards should apply"?

Communication Between Faculty and Students

The majority of communication between faculty and students occurs online. Students and faculty communicate using discussion boards that are set up for each course. Yet, it is not uncommon for faculty and students to communicate by telephone. "The work that I do takes me outside of the discussion board environment. I will contact students via email or sometimes even telephone calls to people, depending on issues that come up.

Even though we are not seeing each other face-to-face, we are still communicating with one another on a one-to-one basis . . . I am there, virtually."

The lack of face-to-face communication poses particular challenges for faculty. One faculty member remarked about the difficulty he faced in communicating with students over the Internet, and the skills one must possess to be able to teach in an online environment.

> I think you have to have a very good deft touch when it comes to writing and corresponding with students in the discussion boards. It is the challenge of expressing yourself well in an e-mail and really trying to capture the nuances of what you are trying to get across. It is a challenge for the students when they are trying to get a point across and certainly a challenge for faculty to comment in a way that isn't going to be taken the wrong way or that I don't come across as mean, harsh, or unclear in what I am saying.

Faculty members who work with doctoral students in an online environment are aware of the challenges they will encounter due to the lack of face-to-face interaction with students. Faculty must be flexible enough to work through this process to overcome the challenges of an online environment. One faculty member considered departing DLU because of the difficulties of teaching online. He remarked, "There was a point when I thought that I wasn't going to [continue], but I stuck with it and, right now, I have no problems with it. The one thing that is frustrating is working with some of the students in the dissertation process. I guess that's just part of it, part of this university." Another faculty member spoke about how it is more difficult to monitor whether students are able to comprehend the course materials without the face-to-face interaction. This particular challenge was mentioned on numerous occasions.

> One of the biggest challenges is that you don't have that face-to-face contact with students . . . and I think of not having that face-to-face contact as inefficient. When students are not initially responding to you, when you have them in the classroom you can say 'I need to talk to you.' But if you tell them online 'Do you really need to talk? Just tell me a time.' . . . They can just ignore you.

Communication Between Administrators and Faculty

DLU continues to grow in terms of its expanding student population and faculty body. The rapid growth of the institution has caused problems with respect to unclear communication channels between the administration and the faculty. The preferred method of communication by the administration is email. Many faculty members felt the institution was unable to keep them abreast of changes in policy. Some faculty members questioned whether email was the ideal method for communicating detailed information regarding policy.

> There's been a change in the process lately, and it's been [frustrating] to get all the information. We had meetings, and we have had a change in process and we made sure everybody knew what was going on, but we're just not getting the total picture, partly because we are at a distance . . . I just think through emails alone doesn't—I mean it can—but there's just going to be sometimes something missing or something that comes out not understandable, or you misunderstand.

After asking whether the administration, in an effort to more clearly communicate with the faculty, attempts to communicate policy changes using other means that do not include the Internet, one participant replied, "Well, it's basically through email. Sometimes phone calls, but rarely has that happened. Sometimes through the mail, but rarely has that happened. So, it's basically through email."

Faculty members consistently mentioned that one of the challenges they face as distance educators is maneuvering through the institution in an effort to learn about its processes and policies. The following quote was offered by a part-time faculty member; she partially attributed the breakdown in communication to her part-time status.

> I think the lack of clarity about how to do things is certainly one of [the challenges] and I think it is one of the problems of having a part-time role. I would suspect that some of this is true if you are sitting on a campus, but there is not a good connection between what you really need to know to get things done and the communication of how to do things. It isn't very good.

Other faculty members explained that because they are not kept abreast of changes, simple tasks such as turning in student grades and maintaining electronic course materials are not only frustrating, but also can be time consuming.

> You have to submit your evaluation for a student's knowledge-based report to an electronic database and it really works well but no one

ever tells you that you have to do that. So, you sort of have to figure it out on your own and that is frustrating, and it uses time that is better spent doing other things. One of the things I like about DLU is that it has expanded fairly rapidly in the recent past, [but] keeping material up to date has been a problem. Like the faculty handbook, it's totally out of date. Some of the curriculum hasn't been updated on the website.

These ordeals along with other challenges faculty face when teaching in an online environment can be demanding and frustrating. "Working with students, and trying to figure out for yourself what is going on isn't always easy . . . If you don't know how to do something, that is really a waste of time."

CONCLUSION

Distance Learning University is an innovative institution with highly qualified faculty. Its focus on masters and doctoral level training makes it unique in the for-profit higher education arena. The institution is not afraid to use innovative teaching methods that fit the needs of their students, as exemplified in the KBA (knowledge-based areas) method of instruction. Overall, faculty members at DLU are satisfied with their work and with the institution. Although most of the participants had extensive experience as educators, they chose to teach at DLU for a variety of reasons, which include working with a different student clientele, and keeping connected with their discipline. The institution's profit-seeking motive creates issues that were distinctive to for-profit education. There exists a tension between the goals of the corporate division and those of the academic division. In addition, faculty members must contend with the challenges posed by the online environment, including problematic communication amongst the faculty and between faculty members, students and administrators.

Chapter Five
Pacific-Atlantic University

"In order to teach at PAU you have to be working in the area you are going to teach. For example, if you want to teach accounting you had better be an accountant."

Pacific-Atlantic University (PAU) is a large, multi-campus institution, with campuses located throughout the country. A major difference between Distance Learning University and Pacific-Atlantic University relates to the professional backgrounds of their respective faculty bodies. While 17 of the 18 DLU participants were current or former educators with extensive professional backgrounds and training (doctoral degrees), only 5 of 15 faculty members held a doctorate; the remaining held masters degrees. Part- and full-time faculty participants from PAU currently were or had been employed in the fields in which they taught. The difference in educational backgrounds between faculty members from DLU and PAU can be attributed to the academic focus of each institution. DLU primarily focuses on graduate education with a research component, thus requiring faculty to hold advanced degrees, whereas PAU focuses on applied training at the baccalaureate and masters levels. Table 7 provides a breakdown of faculty participants by discipline and employment status.

Student enrollments at PAU continue to grow as the institution offers courses both online and on-ground (in the classroom). Nationwide, over 95% of the faculty body are part-time employees with full-time faculty comprising only a small minority of the instructional staff. All the faculty members from Pacific-Atlantic University that participated in this study taught in the same geographic region of the United States, under the same regional director of education. PAU is owned and operated by a publicly-traded corporation, and holds regional accreditation from the Higher

Learning Commission of the North Central Association. In addition to regional accreditation, the institution's health-related programs hold national accreditation.

The institution's mission is focused on assisting adult learners to "develop the knowledge and skills that will enable them to achieve their professional goals . . ." through active learning and collaboration. The institution's learning and teaching model is grounded in adult learning theory, provides relevant and applicable skills, and is based on the adult as an active learner. This philosophy guides the development of courses and academic programs, and responsibilities of the instructional staff. Pacific-Atlantic University is forward about its for-profit status as acknowledged in their statement of purposes. Two of the institution's purposes are: "To be organized as a for-profit institution in order to foster a spirit of innovation . . ." and "To generate financial resources necessary to support the University's mission."

Whereas Distance Learning University concentrates on graduate training, Pacific-Atlantic offers academic programs at the undergraduate and graduate level in five broad areas: 1) business and management; 2) nursing and health care; 3) counseling and human services; 4) education; and 5) information technology. Students attend PAU on a part-time basis, and are required to be employed at least part-time in a field related to their

Table 7: Distribution of Faculty Participants from *Pacific-Atlantic University* by Discipline, Status, and Terms of Service

Discipline	Full-time	Part-time	Number of Years at Institution		
			0–2 years	*3–5 years*	*Over 5 years*
Business	2	1	0	1	2
Education	1	1	0	1	1
IT/Comm.	1	2	1	0	2
Health Sciences	1	1	0	0	2
Social Sciences	1	2	0	2	1
General Education	1	1	0	1	1
Totals	7	8	1	5	9

program of study. Since the majority of the faculty are employed by PAU on a part-time basis, faculty members typically are employed full-time in a field related to the courses they teach. Their part-time status also impacts the nature of their roles within the institution. Full-time faculty participants were employed in fields outside education, but within their teaching discipline, before being employed by the university. The university refers to their teaching faculty as "professional practitioners" in marketing materials, a label that personifies their role within the institution and the goals of the university, i.e. to provide relevant and applicable knowledge to students.

PARAMETERS OF FACULTY WORK

Not unlike part-timers form DLU, PAU's part-time faculty members' responsibilities lay primarily within the classroom. Full-time faculty members play administrative roles, with teaching as a secondary responsibility. The roles of part-time and full-time faculty are very distinct as evidenced in their titles. Part-time faculty members are practitioner-faculty whereas full-time faculty members are core faculty or simply are referred to as faculty. In what follows, I explore each faculty type by focusing on their respective responsibilities and the roles they are expected to fulfill. I follow with a discussion of faculty participation in governance activities by examining the 'exclusive' participation approach. I examine how faculty members perceive of their at-will status before concluding with a discussion about participant's perceptions of the non-hierarchical faculty structure.

Part-time Faculty

As their titles indicate, part-time faculty members—or practitioner-faculty—are individuals who are currently practicing in their respective fields of expertise. Part-time faculty members are hired to teach on a 'per course' basis; the terms of their contract are for the duration of the course. In essence, part-time faculty are independent contractors who rely on their full-time profession for the majority of their income and benefits. They teach part-time to earn additional income and to fulfill their personal aspirations as educators.

Participants responsible for hiring part-time faculty stressed the importance of hiring individuals familiar with the work environment. "We want practitioner-faculty that bring to the classroom real world experience. We look for people that [work] for a living, not the unemployed trying to make their rent." Another faculty member explained, "In order to teach at PAU you have to be working in the area you are going to teach. For example, if you want to teach accounting you had better be an accountant. That is one of the things we push pretty heavily at Pacific-Atlantic University. You'd better be working in the areas you are going to teach." Practitioner-faculty members teach the majority of the curriculum, and must meet certain requirements before they are able to teach.

Faculty Requirements

PAU goes to great lengths to screen prospective practitioner-faculty. The process begins with an initial screening by a faculty recruiter who confirms that a potential faculty member meets the minimum requirements, i.e. the proper degree and relevant work experience. Applicants also are carefully screened for their writing abilities. "Before you even come in you need to do an essay. The topic is not important. It's to see whether you can write and whether your English is fine, and so 'how do you use grammar appropriately'? That kind of thing." After an applicant is initially screened they undergo an assessment in which senior faculty interview the potential faculty member and evaluate the applicant's 10–15 minute presentation. A leaderless group activity is used to help select the final candidates.

> The last part is called the leaderless group. This is where you are with eight or nine other applicants for the position and you are given an assignment to do that you develop as a group. The process is monitored by two faculty members who look to see whether you are overbearing, whether you don't want anyone else to have a word, whether you get mad because they don't agree with you, or whether you never say a word and just sit there like a plant.

Many described the leaderless group activity as the most critical step in identifying potential faculty members. Senior faculty members that monitor the leaderless group activity consider, among other things, whether potential faculty "use inappropriate language, or inappropriate body gestures." If so, then "you're not someone that we want to teach, and we deny you a position." After applicants meet with the approval of the observation team, they are required to successfully complete a training course to become practitioner-faculty members.

Prior teaching experience is not a requirement to be considered for a faculty position. In the words of one participant "we can teach them how to teach." In fact, the university offers faculty workshops where PAU faculty are provided with the skills needed to educate students because many of the faculty-practitioners do not have classroom experience. A faculty member in education who teaches the faculty workshop explained,

I have IT people in there with clinical psychology people. There are even nurses and anyone who is not in education. [They] can see what I'm presenting and it is just so obvious [to me] and people are blown away. And I'm going 'What'? [and] I realize that they don't have a clue how to educate . . . When my bosses asked me to teach this they said, 'Of course it's second nature to you, but you're going to find that people don't have a clue how to teach.' They might be experts in their field, they might be a great nurse, but they have no clue how to communicate that information.

While a number of newly hired faculty members at traditional IHEs may have a modicum of formal classroom teaching experience; they have been socialized into a university teaching environment as doctoral students. Yet, the majority of faculty members at PAU are socialized into a teaching environment that is designed specifically for that institution, one that favors the use of field experience as opposed to teaching experience in the classroom. This is not to say that one approach is more valid than the other. Rather, my intent is to provide a basis from which one can begin to consider why faculty members at PAU view the classroom teaching environment differently than professors at traditional IHEs.

Facilitation vs. Lecture

The approach practitioner-faculty adopt in teaching their classes is referred to as facilitation. Recall that a similar approach to working with students also was part of the 'instructional culture' at DLU. While in the classroom, PAU faculty members refer to themselves as facilitators not instructors. Practitioner-faculty "have to be facilitative in their approach." It is an integral part of the learning experience at PAU. "One of the things we use at Pacific-Atlantic University is facilitation rather than lecture." Participants defined facilitation as "getting the class involved in the discussions and everything else." A faculty member in information science and technology further explained,

If I have got a guy that is in the class and is experienced in the area we are in, I have had them do as much as half of a night of discussions about 'Well, this is how I do it and this is what I do.' Basically it is, for a lack of a better term, a demonstration between myself and the students that have experience in the area talking about different ways of approaching how they do it, how they approach it, and how it gets done.

Faculty members de-emphasize the lecture format in favor of facilitation as a way to incorporate the professional experience and knowledge that PAU students bring into the classroom. A part-time faculty member commented, "These are adult learners who are already employed and they come already with a rich background, and our role at PAU is to be able to extract the elements of that background that the students already have and have them think at a higher level, a more critical level . . ."

Practitioner-faculty members are expected to offer students their personal insights of the field with the assumption that students are likely to appreciate that knowledge because it has been gained from experience in the workplace rather than from a textbook in the classroom. The assumption is that students will utilize a faculty member's knowledge along with the classroom information and apply it in their own working environments.

> The big thing is [that] our faculty are working in the fields and are experienced in the area. For example, if I have a student sitting in a telecommunications class and he says 'Well, how would we set this up and how would we do that'? And the instructor can say 'Well, in my experience I have done this and when I did this for Pac Bell I netted thirteen million dollars profit.' The students tend to listen rather than hear someone say 'I have a Ph.D. and I have been teaching for 32 years.' The fact that faculty members can say 'Hey, I've done this and it works very well. I have done this type of thing and it works this way' . . . To me it brings reality to the textbook and I think that is one of our bigger, stronger selling points.

Full-time Faculty

All of the full-time faculty from PAU (7) interviewed for this study began their careers at PAU as part-time practitioner-faculty. Full-time participants had worked for the institution in a faculty capacity for at least 6 years. In speaking with full-time faculty participants, the consensus was that PAU commonly recruits for full-time positions from their practitioner-faculty "because they tend to understand the culture of the university."

A number of participants explained that full-time faculty do not exist, implying that there are no full-time faculty members that spend the majority of their time teaching. "There really are no full-time faculty. There are full-time employees that also teach, but there are no full-time faculty." Full-time faculty are essentially administrators, but are required to teach a minimum of four courses per year. Courses are either 5 or 6 weeks in length depending on whether they are undergraduate or graduate courses. The remainder of their time is spent on administrative duties. In effect, full-time faculty members are required to teach 20–24 weeks per calendar year. "I will do maybe six [courses] a year which in a traditional sense still sounds like a lot, but when you think about it we are only talking five weeks [per course]. That means I am only teaching 30 weeks out of 52. . . ."

Full-time Faculty Roles

At PAU, full-time faculty members are designated as Campus College Chairs (CCC), a position that can be likened to that of a department head at a traditional college or university. However, there are other full-time administrators that are considered faculty. A participant explains, "All the college chairs here are full-time faculty, [but] we have several others that are considered [full-time] faculty. The scheduler, the faculty services coordinator, the person who does all the contracting and signing of the contracts for the faculty to get paid and that kind of stuff are full-time faculty." The CCCs have a variety of administrative responsibilities which include hiring and training practitioner-faculty, evaluating faculty members in their college, and maintaining the curriculum, to name a few. In addition, all full-time faculty participants repeatedly spoke about their chief responsibility—maintaining quality.

Maintaining Quality or 'Towing the Company Line'

Campus college chairs consistently remarked that their primary responsibility was to maintain quality. The term 'quality' was constantly used both by part- and full-time faculty members; the word is ingrained into the PAU culture. Moreover, the repeated use of the phrase "ensuring quality in the classroom" by full-time faculty may have implications regarding the merit of the data. Campus college chairs explained that quality in the classroom is achieved through excellent faculty hires and meticulous curriculum oversight. "My predominant role here is to make sure we have quality faculty and quality curriculum in this program. I need good faculty and I need good curriculum and a large majority of my time is spent on those two issues." Another full-time faculty member remarks, "I would say that my role is to ensure quality in the classroom, and I'm going to do that with quality faculty and quality curriculum." Another CCC explains, "My job is quality in the classroom and quality curriculum." And still another remarks, "My main responsibility as college chair is to bring quality to the classroom and I do that mainly through faculty recruiting, faculty training . . . My philosophy is I am really there to coach and guide the faculty so that they can bring quality to the classroom."

My reasons for offering what are essentially the same quotes are twofold: 1) they show a commitment to quality by PAU faculty, and 2) they also show that full-time faculty may be employing a 'company line' when speaking to individuals outside of the institution. While I do not intend to imply that the latter affects a commitment to the former, the fact that the responses are identical may illustrate the reluctance of PAU participants to be candid and the difficulties for a researcher attempting to understand the culture of an institution and its faculty. In other words, a study of faculty culture necessitates an understanding of an institution's culture. Accordingly an accurate representation of the institution's culture aids in the development of an accurate depiction of faculty culture. However, if guarded responses and the 'company line' obstruct an accurate portrayal of an institution's culture, an exploration of its faculty culture is hindered. As a result, data from PAU faculty members—especially full-time faculty members—should be considered with caution. I will delve deeper into the 'culture of protection' at for-profit IHEs later.

PARAMETERS OF GOVERNANCE

Governance at PAU can be described as top-down in nature. While faculty members are given the opportunity to provide input, decision-making authority essentially rests with administrators at central headquarters. Moreover, faculty members have input only into specific academic decisions, i.e. course development and program design. A practitioner-faulty remarked, "It's pretty easy on my level, I do not have any voice on the business side of things, and it's just that simple. I am aware that it exists." A number of participants described governance activities as decentralized at the campus level. "The campuses are generally managed, you know, we don't have the central management. We have a decentralized management; [our campus] has a VP-Director." The decentralized authority at the campus level is meant to allow individual campuses to manage their growth and choose the programs they would like to offer. The central administration does not grant individual campuses the authority to create new degree programs or develop new curriculum without their approval. Such decisions affect the institution on a national level and are made at the central office. An example of an academic decision that did not involve faculty was the institution's decision to make all course readings and textbooks for students and faculty available only online; it is referred to as Resource. "I am sure if my faculty had a vote, they would not have us going to resource because faculty, for the most part, like books. There are some decisions that are simply corporate decisions, and faculty won't have even a vote in that."

At the national level, participants described governance as "very corporate," implying that the organization uses a hierarchical approach to decision-making. A practitioner-faculty shared his view of the governance structure at the central administration level in relation to individual colleges and degree programs. When speaking about "each college," the participant is referring to the college at the national rather than campus level, i.e. College of Nursing, College of Education.

> The central administration is focused around a pretty standard governance [structure]. We have programs, we have a number of teams, each college has a [national] dean, and then there is a small administrative staff that surrounds that dean. The dean's [job] is to enhance a number of degree programs. Within the degree programs there are clusters of courses that support the degree program.

Faculty participants were clear about the flow of information that characterizes the decision-making structure. The flow of information is such that a faculty member's concerns or suggestions flow up the communication chain through predetermined channels and an established decision-making structure and directives flow downward from the central administration to the faculty. Faculty must abide by the policies and decisions set forth by the deans in central administration, whether or not they concur. "From a corporate standpoint, we have a couple of associate deans who I think don't do a very good job being associate deans, either in terms of being leaders or knowing their programs very well. That gets frustrating."

Curricular Decisions

The majority of the courses and the curriculum are designed by faculty at central headquarters with input and the assistance of program advisory groups. Courses also are regularly evaluated and revised by faculty. The courses are referred to as modules, a part-time faculty member explained, "Modules are designed at central administration and updated by input from [faculty] . . . The curriculum comes from the practitioner-faculty, so they develop the modules, they develop all of that stuff. . . ." Another part-time faculty member added,

> They have these intensive sessions at [headquarters], and they call faculty in, it's usually three or four faculty members, and you review the current curriculum, and review all the complaints, and look at what the problems are . . . All the curriculum gets reviewed on a schedule. So every 'so many years' the curriculum gets reviewed even if everybody says it's wonderful.

Distance Learning University and PAU share similar approaches with regard to decisions about the curriculum. While PAU faculty members are responsible for developing courses and designing the curriculum, they do not have the authority to offer the courses and programs to students without the approval of central administration. "Deciding what courses to offer is strictly a business decision, but the development of the program itself is an academic decision or is a series of academic decisions." A full-time faculty member emphasized that all faculty members can have a voice in curricular decisions if they are cognizant of the institution's decision-making structure. "Faculty members have, if they utilize the system appropriately, a voice on a continual basis to the curricular teams made up of those faculty members. There is a person that coordinates that so that adjustments in the curriculum, issues that are raised, can be considered by the faculty team." Yet, unlike faculty members from Distance Learning University, the practitioner-faculty from PAU expressed satisfaction with the structured curriculum.

> We are told, you know, 'This is a guideline, there are objectives you have to meet,' but if you've taught the course before and you've found some things that you would like to tweak. Go for it. Go ahead and make the tweak . . . One of the things I like about PAU is that you're not creating something from nothing. It is standardized, 'Here's what you're going to do now and how you get there.' . . . It would be a mess if everyone just taught whatever they wanted.

Campus college chairs have direct access to the national deans of their college. As a result, CCCs have the opportunity to make curricular suggestions that will be heard by individuals with decision-making authority at central administration. On numerous occasions, full-time faculty participants spoke about their access to central administrators implying that all faculty members were extended this opportunity.

> I like the idea that Pacific-Atlantic University is not stuck in a box. That when faculty come to them and say, 'I got an idea' they say, 'Cool, let's hear it.' Not 'We've never done that before, we can't have that.' It's like, wow, I can go right to my national dean and say 'I've got this crazy idea.' And she'd say 'Let's hear it.' So there's an open line of communication . . .

Most faculty members do not have access to central administrators with decision-making authority. Faculty input is limited to the curricular realm at the campus level and suggestions regarding the curriculum may or may not be considered at the national level. Suggestions by part-time faculty travel through several filters before they reach central administrators in charge of academic programs at the national level. To be clear, unless faculty members are invited to participate in the course development process by the central administration, they do not have direct impact on a course or an academic program.

Moreover, the ability for faculty to make changes to the courses they teach is constrained. For example, if faculty members were to deviate from the course objectives they must justify to students the reasons they will deviate from the prescribed material. A practitioner-faculty in education provided the following example.

> I do feel an allegiance to teach the curriculum here because it's there, and that's my job, and so I would present that to students. But I would also do a little thing I would say 'OK. Now I have taught you their curriculum. But let me share with you my personal experience.' And I would say to them. 'This is not necessarily what PAU is saying I should teach you, but I think that as an educator in the field, you will benefit from knowing my experience.'

The response was similar to that of other faculty members, in that participants felt compelled to teach the curriculum even if they did not agree with it.

Exclusive Participation

Given the size of Pacific-Atlantic University, the number of faculty the institution employs, and the nature of their employment as part-time faculty, one would not expect all or even most practitioner-faculty to be able or interested in participating in governance activities. Additionally, it would be very difficult to organize a system in which all faculty members could have the opportunity to participate in the governance process. Consequently, faculty participation in governance—meaning curriculum development—is limited. Faculty members are chosen to take part in 'governing' the institution based on merit.

> I began to move through the 'governance chairs' so to speak [because] I demonstrated quality in the classroom. My [student] surveys at the end of each course were close to 5.0, which is the top number. I did very well in class so I began the governance role and that is sort of how I became aware of the system that was evolving and how they became aware of me.

Expressing an interest to take part in governance activities such as course development does not guarantee that one can participate. A CCC explained that when he becomes aware that a course will be rewritten, he makes an effort to include his faculty, yet the final arbiter is someone other than himself.

> If I hear about a course, I will try to think who [in my faculty] teaches that course, who does a really good job in it and I will immediately try to see that the dean or the associate dean knows there's somebody who can be really good at helping with that course and I will try to get them asked to be involved. [Faculty] could not just say 'I would like to be involved.' They would have to be asked, but I try to advocate on their behalf.

Although all practitioner-faculty have the ability to provide feedback regarding the specific courses they teach, many of them are not given the opportunity to write or update courses. On several occasions, participants explained that faculty members who are asked to participate in the curriculum development process must be active participants in the PAU community as well as experts in their field.

> I will receive a phone call from the associate dean [at central headquarters] who says, 'We are teaming this particular course, who do you think from your campus can make a valuable contribution'? So, I'll prepare a short list of those that I think know the course. They're experts in that particular field and they are regularly participating in faculty life and make valuable faculty contributions.

The culture of the institution includes faculty in the governance process as a reward for good work and involvement in the university community. The institution permits faculty to participate in designing curriculum only after they meet certain criteria and show a commitment to the institution. In contrast, faculty members who design courses for Distance Learning University are chosen strictly on the basis of their expertise. In some cases, DLU will hire faculty from outside the institution to develop courses or participate in the design of new academic programs. Nevertheless, faculty participation in governance activities—curriculum development—is exclusive rather than inclusive at both institutions. All tenure-track faculty members at traditional IHEs are offered the opportunity to govern their institution. One may argue that faculty participation in shared governance is an implicit responsibility of the professoriate, i.e. a civic duty of the academy. Tenure provides for and protects this responsibility. However, tenure is not part of the culture at for-profit IHEs and contingent faculty employment is the norm; faculty participation in governance is controlled.

PARAMETERS OF EMPLOYMENT

PAU faculty members are employed in positions within the field they teach. Practitioner-faculty are contracted to teach courses at their convenience, as they become available; each course is a separate contract. A practitioner-faculty member explains. "I view myself as sort of an independent contractor. I teach when there is a course available to me and it works on my schedule, I am not bound to do any specific number of courses." Faculty members are free to choose the courses they would like to teach. Senior faculty members, such as area chairs and lead faculty, usually are given first priority to select courses before the remainder of the practitioner-faculty can choose. As an added convenience the entire process, from course selection to the contractual agreement, takes place online. Yet because they are contracted employees, faculty members can be replaced if either students or senior faculty are not satisfied with their classroom performance. The university can choose not to assign them courses or can dismiss them from their posts altogether.

In speaking with participants from PAU, two related issues frequently were expressed as top priorities for faculty—quality and consistency in the classroom. They are fundamental elements faculty are obligated to maintain in the classroom. The foundation for quality rests in the curriculum, whereas consistency is maintained via faculty members' adherence to the standardized curriculum. Additionally, both quality and consistency are sustained through constant evaluation of both students and faculty members. Academic Quality Management Systems or AQMS evaluates course "rigor" whereas the Adult Learning Objectives Assessment or ALOA evaluates student learning. Each of these elements—the quality of faculty and students and consistency of the curriculum—has implications on faculty work.

Consistency via Standardization

Pacific-Atlantic University maintains consistency by offering a standardized curriculum. As was the case with Distance Learning University, standardizing the curriculum is not meant to convey to faculty the notion that their expertise and input is irrelevant. To a great extent, standardization is a result of the corporate philosophy that asserts that quality is produced and maintained through consistency. Every academic program consists of a set of specific courses containing learning objectives that remain identical regardless of where the classes are taught or who is doing the teaching. "If a student takes a course here or on the east coast, the objectives remain the same." The standardized curriculum or more specifically, the established learning objectives are intended to maintain quality by assuring that students at all PAU campuses have achieved specific learning outcomes, both for academic programs and individual courses. Furthermore, terms used by participants that relate to teaching such as "competencies," "domains," and "deliverables" are not used to describe teaching in a traditional higher education environment and are more commonly utilized in the business realm. "We make certain that our core competencies meet specific domains. Pacific-Atlantic University has identified specific domains and then specific deliverables within those domains. That provides documentary evidence to the fact that our students have in fact demonstrated a proficiency in a specific area."

The consequences to faculty, with regard to curriculum standardization, are evident. Faculty members teach from a prescribed course outline that specifies what must be taught on what day, and to a certain extent, how it should be taught. Faculty are required to "teach to the objectives" or risk poor evaluations. Nevertheless, it is reasonable to assert that faculty members are aware of such constraints before entering a classroom.

When potential faculty members are initially screened, they are cognizant of the fact that they will be required to follow the university's approach to education. Faculty recruitment material reads, "Faculty must show a willingness to utilize Pacific-Atlantic University's teaching and learning model." Still, most participants felt that the PAU educational model provides them with sufficient latitude to deliver course content without limitations, and also spoke about the importance of keeping to the prescribed course goals. One participant commented, "The objectives must be met by the instructor. They have the freedom to meet those objectives any way they see fit." However another participant's remarks were more pointed.

> Pacific-Atlantic University is pretty intense on meeting course objectives and covering all of the topics, and making sure that the student is in good shape . . . So, the idea that I could go and, at a conventional university, write a broad ranging syllabus and present things pretty much in the sequence I wanted, we don't do that here. I'm going to present this sequence that is recommended by the university to ensure that each workshop covers the objectives that have to be done and if I'm really skilled I can bring in augmented materials.

Under such circumstances 'freedom in the classroom' applies only to the method of delivery and offers faculty members little latitude in modifying content and objectives, an issue that is discussed in a subsequent chapter.

When participants were queried more closely, many gave specific examples as to the type of constraints faculty members face. "For each workshop there are objectives that you have to make and for each workshop there are reading assignments. You cannot change the reading assignments and you cannot change the objectives." Another participant mentioned, "Faculty notes come built within the curriculum . . . I can take them or I can leave them, those faculty notes, but usually they're really good." A full-time faculty member provided an example of a learning objective for a philosophy course and the specific points that must be covered under the learning objective. Of note is the specificity of the content that must be delivered to students.

> One of the learning objectives for week one is to describe critical think-
> ing and purpose and process. 'Identify the process, relate the stages of
> cognitive development and the stages of logical and critical thinking,
> explain the relationship of logic and critical thinking, and define think-
> ing in general.' All those ideas are under the objective of 'purpose and
> process of critical thinking.' Those points need to be covered.

The learning objectives and the specific points contained within are, for lack of a better term, non-negotiable. That is to say, faculty members are contractually obligated to deliver the course content; how they deliver it is their prerogative.

A major difference with regard to method of delivery between PAU and DLU relates to the training faculty members receive by the institution. Since most PAU faculty members do not have extensive teaching backgrounds, PAU requires that they successfully complete a training course, which demonstrates PAU teaching methods to the participants, i.e. adult learning theory. The training that faculty members from DLU receive is much less focused on the teaching process, and much more focused on providing faculty members with the skills needed to utilize the technology. In other words, PAU faculty members learn how to teach whereas DLU faculty learn how to teach online.

Until now, I have spoken specifically about the classroom requirements for faculty members. Their classroom performance is the primary means by which faculty are evaluated and rewarded. If faculty members perform well in the classroom, they are able to remain on the instructional staff and if they consistently perform well they are invited to participate in governance roles. Likewise, when faculty members display poor classroom skills, they are removed from the classroom and possibly from the institution. Since faculty performance is central to the function of the PAU, evaluating faculty becomes essential; it helps to ensure quality and consistency in the classroom.

Quality via Evaluation

Pacific-Atlantic University has a formal faculty evaluation process in place for part-time faculty. Practitioner-faculty members are evaluated by their peers at least once a year and by their students at the end of each course. The peer evaluation process for faculty is referred to as QAV, or quality assurance visit, and the students evaluate faculty using SEOCS or student end of course surveys. "QAVs are a fundamental part of the faculty culture at PAU. We do quality assurance visits at least once a year and in most instances, those will be a little closer together. So we're looking at somewhere between every 10 months to 12 months, and every faculty. And it's basically a peer review system."

Pacific-Atlantic University uses peer review as a quality control tool to ensure a high quality faculty body. Moreover, QAVs are used to assess whether a faculty member is following the university's learning and teaching model.

> There is lots of quality control, and each year, every faculty member has a QAV, a quality assurance visit. And at that point, a senior faculty member can enter your class and fills out a very detailed form on clear teaching technique, or your handouts or your feedback to the students and whether or not you followed your syllabus and whether or not you covered the course content for the night.

Faculty members whose evaluations are not satisfactory either are placed on probationary status or are removed from the classroom. "If there are major difficulties then normally that faculty member is pulled off the line and is probably going to be placed in an 'observe' status . . ."

SEOCS or student end of course surveys also monitor faculty performance and student satisfaction. The university values student feedback; it is continually utilized to assess a faculty member's classroom abilities. "We use basically two different [faculty] evaluation systems. One is what we call SEOCS, which is a student evaluation. We look at what our students are saying about the facilitator." Faculty members that display problems in the classroom are offered the opportunity to improve their teaching skills. "If we have indications in student evaluations that we have a specific problem, we may either run a quality assurance visit to take a look at the facilitator in the classroom, or we might go in and do some mentoring and try to correct some minor difficulties."

A full-time faculty member comments on the use of student evaluations as a tool to assess a faculty member's merit. Stark criticism from student evaluations provides the basis for an additional quality assurance visit, and can result in the loss of one's job. "If we get instructors that continually get negative feedback from students, then that's another quality assurance issue that we can use to determine that Pacific-Atlantic University is not for you."

PAU is responsive to students' concerns and values their opinions. The institution allows students to have a voice in their education, and their voice is as powerful or more powerful than that of part-time faculty. Few traditional institutions furnish students with as much influence in matters regarding quality of instruction. However, providing students with such a powerful voice has its drawbacks for faculty. If a student lodges a complaint against a faculty member it is taken seriously by the administration, as should be the case. However, the influence students have provides strength to their assertions, and places the onus on the faculty member to justify their conduct rather than on the student to prove their case. The following scenario offered by a full-time faculty member regarding a student who was displeased with their course grade illustrates the point.

> If the students have a complaint, a grievance that in any way ties to a faculty member, it comes to me and I have to look at, ok, what is their grievance? I have to go through and figure out specific issues that cause it; 'This guy doesn't know how to grade, he is giving grades away or he is not being fair on grades.' I have to go and look at 'What did he do, what wasn't fair'? . . . I review what the faculty member did . . .

Whether or not such situations are resolved in the faculty member's favor is not the point. Instead, it is important to consider that the contingent status of faculty members makes them vulnerable to such complaints and places faculty in a position in which they are required to substantiate their conduct rather than placing the burden on the student.

FACULTY HIERARCHY

One of the most interesting features about Pacific-Atlantic University relates neither to the institutions policies and practices nor issues of faculty discontent. In an effort to differentiate themselves from traditional colleges and universities faculty participants consistently remarked about the lack of a faculty hierarchy. Full-time faculty, for the most part, are designated as Campus College Chairs, i.e. department heads. They have an authoritative relationship with practitioner-faculty in their college, as CCCs are responsible for hiring and dismissing part-time faculty. Yet, on numerous occasions participants spoke about the flat hierarchical structure within the faculty ranks as a unique aspect of the institution; one that separates them from traditional colleges and universities. A full-time faculty shared his perspective.

> Universities are traditionally very status conscious. Titles and all those things are very important. It's part of the social structure of universities . . . Part-time faculty are the heart and soul of what it is we do as a university. They are as much a part of this university as full-time faculty at the university. And that's what separates us from what other places are doing.

A part-time faculty member offers his viewpoint, "People have to understand the culture issue, the fact that we have no real hierarchy. I mentioned that while I am area chair, coordinating is not a command function. There is no real hierarchy. . . ."

It was perplexing how participants continually commented on the absence of a faculty hierarchy, given that the institution clearly differentiates within the practitioner-faculty ranks.

> I'm in the B faculty. You start at A and after you teach for one year successfully, or I think 5 or 6 courses, and after you've taken three of their faculty training sessions, then they move you to B faculty where you make a little bit more money. You can also move into C faculty, and I think that's after about 5 years of being there. There is also a designation called Lead faculty. I don't understand all the levels because, you know, this is not my main career.

A full-time Campus College Chair elaborated on the lead faculty title, asserting that the position is not one of authority. Rather, it is a designation reserved for experienced practitioner-faculty who display potential for leadership within the institution.

> Lead faculty are people who have been around for a while, [who] understand the culture, are active in campus activities. I mean they show up at campus meetings, etcetera. We give them the title to kind of

recognize their leadership capacity . . . I function as the head area chair and every college has someone who is called head area chair. It is not a command relationship, it is simply a recognition that a person is doing something other than and in addition to what others are doing.

Implicit in their justification of a flat hierarchical structure is the assumption that a hierarchy indicates that individuals located higher up in the organizational pyramid have authority over those below them; this is an assumption many would agree with. However, faculty members who are in the 'governance' structure—lead faculty and area chairs—often are placed in a position of authority when they are asked to evaluate other faculty members as well as mentor new faculty hires. A practitioner-faculty who is designated as an area chair explained,

We do a thing called quality assurance visits. It is a collegial visit and annually every one of us has another faculty member come in and sit in our classroom for a couple of hours and provide us [with] some feedback on things that are working well and things you can do better . . . Most often it turns out to be the areas chairs [who visit] or we have this other term called lead faculty.

The faculty hierarchy also is evident within the context of governance. Faculty members who achieve a particular rank become part of the governance structure, meaning they have a greater role in developing the curriculum in addition to other duties outside of teaching.

The governance team—the area chairs are very involved in decision-making. I really trust their input because they have become experts in their content area so when a question comes up about something in their content area I really work very closely with them and I trust their input on what might be most effective in those issues. The lead faculty are somewhat involved in terms of committees.

In addition, other participants spoke about the faculty governance structure at the campus level as consisting of various titles or designations for practitioner-faculty.

We have several levels of governance. Lead faculty are those faculty who have been with the university at least two years and have a certain score or better on their end of course surveys which shows that they are doing a good job in the classroom. The next level up from that are the

area chairs. The area chairs are people who are part of the lead faculty
who have just really demonstrated excellence in their commitment and
teaching abilities . . . Within that group I have what is called a head
area chair who is stipend, she is not full-time . . . she is more of my
right hand man . . . if people can't reach me for something they get in
touch with her.

Although participants perceive of and assert that the university does
not differentiate between faculty members, one can argue that a clear hierarchy exists with the faculty body. There are two key factors that faculty
participants neglect to consider; 1) individuals who either evaluate or mentor other faculty members are in a position of authority because they have
the ability to affect one's employment status and; 2) although participants
may believe no hierarchy exists within the faculty ranks because the institution allows all faculty to have a voice in the curriculum development
process, the extent of faculty members' input can vary, and their ability to
participate in governance activities is dependent upon their standing within
the faculty ranks.

Moreover, the institution is a profit-seeking organization with the
majority of the decision-making authority residing at the highest levels of
the corporation—at central headquarters—which reinforces the hierarchical governance structure. This is not to say that practitioner-faculty are not
held in high esteem. In fact the university makes efforts to include practi-
tioner faculty in numerous activities such as course content meetings. The
flat hierarchical structure faculty members perceive is the result of an overt
gesture by the institution to treat all practitioner-faculty the same in terms
of their decision-making authority, which is not necessarily the case. Yet,
one can argue that the decision-making authority for most practitioner-faculty is somewhat comparable because of the profit-seeking nature of the
institution. In other words, the major decisions regarding the organization
are made by individuals on the "business side" at central headquarters
rather than by practitioner-faculty at the campus level. Consequently, decision-making authority at the faculty level is limited in scope. The lack of
clarity among faculty participants with regard to this issue is evident. Yet, it
can be argued that their misconceptions, while unintended, may be justifi-
able.

CONCLUSION

Pacific-Atlantic University defines itself through the concept of providing a
practical education to its students. Part-time faculty, who make up over

95% of the instructional staff, are referred to as "practitioner-faculty." While faculty members from Distance Learning University had extensive professional backgrounds in education and held advanced degrees, both part-time and full-time faculty from PAU had extensive professional backgrounds in the fields in which they taught. All of PAU's faculty members held graduate degrees, but the degrees they held were not as significant as their professional field experience. Given that the university trains all its faculty members to teach using the PAU model regardless of whether they have taught in the past, teaching experience is appreciated but is not a requirement for employment. Once in the classroom, faculty members become "facilitators" rather than lecturers. Like DLU faculty, PAU participants expressed their job responsibilities in terms of assisting students during their learning process. In addition, faculty members must provide relevant insight based on their professional experiences. The predetermined learning outcomes preclude faculty from modifying course goals without approval from the administration. Nevertheless, participants expressed satisfaction with the standardized curriculum asserting that the institution offers a quality education delivered by quality faculty.

Chapter Six
Miller College

"One thing you have to remember about Miller is that we are a career school."

Miller College was founded in 1969 by the Miller family, but is currently owned and operated by a private investment firm. To date, the college is comprised of seventeen individual campuses located in seven states throughout the Midwest, serves about 8,000 students per year, and holds national accreditation from the Accrediting Commission of Career Schools and Colleges of Technology (ACCSCT). Although seventeen campuses may give the impression that Miller is a sizeable institution, the total student enrollment averages about 470 students per campus. Campuses were described as "modest" with "no frills." They usually consist of one or two office buildings located in a metropolitan area of the city. Unlike the previous two institutions, Miller does not offer graduate degree programs, and only recently began offering a bachelors degree program. Most of Miller's academic programs lead to certificates or associate degrees. The bachelor's degree in Computer Engineering & Network Technology, introduced earlier this year, is the first Bachelor of Science degree the institution has offered. Academic programs fall under one of three major categories: 1) Information Technology and Business Operations; 2) Trades; and 3) Health Care. Each category offers both certificates and degrees. It is important to remind the reader that only faculty who teach in degree programs were interviewed for this study.

Miller's goal is to provide "hands-on access to IT and other cutting-edge technologies in a collaborative classroom environment." Like many for-profit organizations, Miller attracts its customers by providing them with incentives. Miller's selling point, similar to Distance Learning University and Pacific-Atlantic University, is that it offers students an education that differs from traditional IHEs—one that is equated to professional training that improves an individual's earning potential. A marketing statement asserts that Miller College provides "training you'll use to achieve the standard of living you want"; another statement proclaims that Miller College offers, " . . . training designed to get you a job faster."

Until recently, the college was owned and operated by the Miller family with its founder James Miller, Sr. and his son, James Miller, Jr. serving as the institution's first and second presidents. The institution's polices and practices were in transition when interviews were conducted. Miller College was in the midst of re-organization as a consequence of new ownership, and the governance structure was evolving as well. Data from the interviews will be presented in the context of an organization in transition. In other words, many of the issues that the participants spoke about dealt with comparing the previous ownership with the new ownership. Some faculty spoke positively about the changes taking place, while others did not. Table 8 provides background information regarding participant's length of service and employment status, by discipline.

Students at Miller College attend classes four times a week, Monday-Thursday, either in the mornings or in the afternoons, with class sessions or "phases" beginning every ten weeks. Diplomas and certificates require

Table 8: Distribution of Faculty Participants from *Miller College* by Discipline, Status, and Terms of Service

Discipline	Full-time	Part-time	Number of Years at Institution		
			0–2 years	*3–5 years*	*Over 5 years*
Business	2	0	2	0	0
Education	No program	No program	No program	No program	No program
IT/Comm.	3	0	1	1	1
Health Sciences	1	0	0	0	1
Social Sciences	No program	No program	No program	No program	No program
General Education	2	0	0	1	1
Totals	8	0	3	2	3

anywhere from 13–60 weeks of instruction, associate degree programs require 80–90 weeks of instruction, and the bachelors degree requires 170 weeks of instruction. In what follows I offer a description of faculty responsibilities before exploring issues of governance and faculty involvement in decision-making. As with the other case studies in this chapter, I address the issue of at-will status before moving into a discussion about how campuses are fairly autonomous from the central administration. A major difference between Miller College and the two publicly traded institutions pertains to the use of part-time faculty. As indicated in Table 8, no part-time faculty members from Miller College were interviewed for this study. Miller does utilize part-time faculty members, but only on a limited basis.

PARAMETERS OF FACULTY WORK

Miller College focuses on technical training through an accelerated format. "One thing you have to remember about Miller is that we are a career school"; "Students that are here, most of them are here for the technical field purposes." Given the nature of the institution, faculty members are cognizant that the courses and training they provide must fit employers' needs. "From the business perspective, employers would like for [students] to be better prepared to communicate with others in their organization and others outside of the organization such as customers, clients, etcetera. So, that gives us the focus on how [and] as to what direction we want to go educationally."

Faculty members, the majority of which are full-time, work split schedules. They teach class five hours every morning and every evening, Mondays thru Thursdays. Faculty members are off between morning and evening sessions; most do not remain on campus in the afternoon. Technically, faculty members are off on Fridays, but most spend their time grading papers and preparing for the following week's classes. While there is "some interaction among faculty members," the split schedule hinders faculty interaction and "many faculty mostly interact with faculty that are in the same building," who are not necessarily in the same department.

Professional Experience

While many of the faculty members are full-time instructors, prior professional experience in the fields in which they teach is essential. "Something particularly important about the instructors we have here, they are all from the field themselves. They have to have that experience [so] they can talk to the students with the straight line." Similar to Pacific-Atlantic University, Miller College values professional experience over educational background, given that the mission of the institution is to train students for the workplace. "I don't know if all schools do this but Miller tends to prize professional work experience above, you know, just taking someone straight out of school." The highest degree of attainment for six of the participants was a bachelors degree; one participant completed a J.D. In addition, all participants had numerous years of professional experience in their respective fields. Participants explained that while degrees and academic backgrounds are important to the institution, individuals with a wealth of professional knowledge can teach at Miller. "We have some instructors who do not have bachelors degrees." However, faculty teaching general education courses, at minimum, must have a bachelors degree.

Since Miller awards associates and bachelors degrees, students are required to enroll in general education courses. The institution seeks faculty for the general education department "who at least [have] a masters degree and preferably has had experience in a work environment." Nevertheless, the institution views professional work experience as a favorable trait and, on occasion, faculty members with bachelors degrees are allowed to teach general education courses specific to their program.

> We have a handful of instructors that do have their own bachelors degree and teach a [general education] course particularly for that program. One of our welding instructors has a bachelors degree. He is a former teacher himself, a high school teacher. He has that as his educational background. So, he teaches the general education part of the welding program.

Facilitators

What sets Miller College apart from DLU and PAU is that, unlike full-time faculty from those institutions, teaching is the chief responsibility of full-time faculty members at Miller College. A participant explained that while faculty may have other duties, teaching is their central responsibility. "Well, teaching is the most critical, but we also do some curriculum development." At Miller, as with the previous institutions, the act of teaching is the act of facilitating.

> Well, what I see an instructor as, I see us as a facilitator. And the way I look at it, I tell students since the very first day of class I say 'We are a learning team. I do my part. I seek to convey the right information to you and give you the right tools and resources to succeed. Your part is to come everyday, come on time, read the material that I ask you to read, and put a real effort forth.' And so I see myself as a facilitator. We're basically there to provide support, to provide help, to guide the students . . . '

As previously discussed, classes meet in four and a half hour blocks. Each class session is divided into a lecture and a lab. Participants agreed that the lecture portion of the class was not as valuable as the lab, thus many devoted more time to lab than lecture. The lab refers to the practical training portion of the course and is considered a valuable part of a student's education. A faculty participant explained, "The hands-on approach, the lab approach, on a daily basis is particularly of importance. So if you're in computer technology, you have an hour of lecture, but then you may have two or three hours of lab dealing with what you learned on that particular day. That's the advantage that I would say [we have] compared to the traditional institutions.'

A faculty member discussed his classroom teaching style, which also emphasized fewer lecture hours and more lab time. He, too, described his lectures as facilitative and inclusive.

> I try to keep lecture time or discussion time as short as possible. I have a four and a half hour class every day, and at the very least I try to make that half and half. I try not to go longer than two hours of lecture and when I lecture, I don't really lecture. I talk for short periods of time and then I ask them questions . . . So, I try to form my lectures, more kind of me talking to them and asking questions, and try to keep them involved as much as possible.

Outside of their teaching duties faculty members can participate in non-academic committees such as the school spirit committee and the graduation committee. In addition, faculty members are given much more latitude in designing their own courses and working with advisory boards to develop new academic programs. Increased authority over the curriculum is a fundamental difference between faculty work at Miller College versus faculty work at PAU and DLU. Decisions regarding the curriculum allow faculty to participate in governing their respective campuses more so than faculty members from the previous two case studies.

PARAMETERS OF GOVERNANCE

As a result of new ownership, Miller's governance structure continues to evolve and policies and procedures are continually modified; some of the data presented in this case study reflects an institution is in a state of flux. Three Miller College campuses are represented in this study. When necessary, I will refer to Campus A, B, or C to maintain their anonymity. Table 9 describes the breakdown of faculty participants by campus and discipline.

Table 9: Distribution of Faculty Participants from *Miller College* by Campus Location and Discipline

Discipline	Campus A	Campus B	Campus C
Business	1	0	1
IT/Communications	1	2	0
Health Sciences	1	0	0
General Education	0	0	2
Total	3	2	3

The institution's governance structure as it currently exists is such that each campus is loosely tied to corporate headquarters. In other words, campuses are fairly autonomous and have the freedom to design their own courses and tailor their academic programs to meet the needs of their students and their local communities. The loosely-coupled governance structure has both advantages and disadvantages.

First, because each campus has the freedom to design programs as they see fit, students are prepared with the necessary skills for employment in their local communities. Second, the governance structure allows instructors to have the freedom to design their own courses. The disadvantage, however, is that policies and procedures vary from campus to campus and instructors at Campus A may experience their working environment differently than instructors at Campus B. Moreover, as the institution attempts to find its new identity, faculty members and administrators struggle to determine their respective roles and responsibilities. Their confusion is reflected in the data. Miller's loose governance structure makes a comparison of faculty culture across campuses challenging. Therefore, the following case study will attempt to explore the similarities in faculty governance across the sampled campuses to understand the institution as a whole; differences are examined more closely in the later in the text.

New Management

Each Miller College campus represented in the study is under the leadership of two campus directors. Participants indicated that Miller campuses typically have two co-directors who are administrators rather than faculty. They are charged with managing the daily operations of their respective campuses including maintaining the budget and implementing policies. According to numerous participants, Miller has replaced a number of campus co-directors as a result of the new ownership. This has caused some turmoil in the faculty ranks. "Well, one by one they got rid of our directors. The one that was probably, I don't know, [he was] a man that actually I had several brushes with. But he was a man that I respected greatly, apparently he was chased away. They just they drove him nuts. Apparently the new management just was making him crazy."

There also has been an excessive turnover of campus directors at Campus C "Well, basically like I said we've had some turnover in the administration . . . probably three or four different sets of directors." Changes in the administrative ranks have led to a growing disconnect between faculty and administrators, which affects campus governance and faculty morale at the participating campuses. One faculty member remarked,

> [Faculty morale] has completely bottomed out . . . I guess it was because we were family owned, we were like a family. Everybody pulled together, everybody enjoyed their work. It was really, I mean, we were successful. Everything was great. And you know, morale totally has gone into the ditch. It has been like a cancer that has spread to the entire campus.

The negative consequences associated with a governance structure in transition have led to a growing distrust of the administration. A faculty participant from Campus A shares his perspective.

> I think there is some distrust. Only because the directors were let go one at a time. Probably about nine months in between. And basically it seems like the first new co-director that came in, he's kind of the main one now . . . He more or less came in and learned as much as he could. And then let the other one go, once he thought he had a grip on things. That's when the second co-director was pushed out and they brought in their own guy. So, there's a little distrust there just because of that factor.

Lead Faculty and Program Heads

Similar to Pacific-Atlantic University, Miller designates certain individuals as lead faculty. They, too, coordinate the academic activities of their department and are usually the most senior faculty members. "Usually within any department there is a lead instructor. It is usually the person who's been around the longest and knows the most." Another faculty member added, "When I was teaching dental assisting I was the lead instructor, because I had been there the longest." Lead faculty, for instance, will act as the buffer between faculty members in their department and the administration, but responsibilities may differ by campus. Rather than a lead faculty member, "some schools will have a director of education that serves as a go-between the faculty and [our] school director for example." Additionally, lead faculty members are asked to be in charge of curriculum changes within their department.

> If the school wants to change [a course] and the state has certain requirements, whether you have to file an application for a new class, or if you change so much percentage and a large percent of the course content is really different . . . Usually a new course description, the new syllabus, and new lesson plans all have to be drawn up so that they are applicable to the new way it's being taught. At best, the lead instructors are those who have been here the longest and are more knowledgeable about the history of a particular class and how it's evolved to be what it is.

Miller designates certain faculty as program heads, but their responsibilities tend to differ from campus to campus. A program director at Campus B described herself as an administrator rather than a faculty member and also described her major responsibilities.

> They call me their principal, if that gives you any idea [laughs]. Like I said, I have over nine instructors and right now, I think I have about 120 students, give or take a few. My job as an administrator is to make sure that the instructors are dealing with what they're supposed to be doing. I have to take care of any absentee problems like if I have a student who is not coming or is having trouble with tardiness all the time. There are academic problems like when students are failing their classes and I have to step in and say 'Where is the problem here'? I am also in charge of training new instructors. We recently added three new instructors and I had to train them. So just day-to-day things like that I just have to take care.

A faculty member from Campus C explained that, unlike the previous example, his program head spends as much time in the classroom as other full-time faculty. "She teaches a full load, and then she does the department head thing in addition to that. So actually it's more of a headache more than anything. I guess she gets compensated, but that I really wouldn't know about. But she teaches a full load."

Program heads are considered full-time faculty. A program head at Campus B commented that in addition to his administrative responsibilities, he teaches on a regular basis but does not carry a full course load. "I spend more time administering more than I do teaching. I'm still teaching in the classroom, but I'm not a full-time teacher anymore. I am still a full-time faculty member but my teaching duties are not full-time. Our regular faculty members teach 40 hours a week and mine is less than that because I have administrative things to do."

Curricular Decisions

With the exception of teaching, curriculum development constitutes a major responsibility for faculty at Miller College. Faculty members are given latitude in designing their own courses. Faculty members are provided with a fair amount of autonomy when designing and revising courses, within accreditation guidelines. "One of the more fun things is working on curriculum because to me it's a real challenge to get curriculum that'll really meet the student's needs, that'll be something I can feel good about teaching . . . we do lots of curriculum development." Courses are approved at two levels—at the program level by each campus and at the corporate level. Program level approval refers to the process in which either a campus director or a program head approves a course. A program head described the process.

> I guess the first thing I look for is consistency in the curriculum. Our courses are presented somewhat sequentially, and they build upon each other as they would in the traditional school so I think if an instructor is going to change a textbook, I look to see what benefit that has from the current textbook and look to see the objectives that they are hoping to accomplish and the outcomes or whatever you call them. I look to make sure that they are consistent with what we're trying to accomplish in that particular class. We need to make sure it still fits in within the guidelines that the class is trying to accomplish.

In addition, program heads will include other faculty member's input prior to approving a course. A faculty member offered his perspective regarding the course development process. "Well, it's usually one instructor will actually puts the course together, usually it's the instructor who's going to teach it. Then it might be shared in a group meeting, in which you say, 'Okay, this is what I plan to do with this class.' And the instructor gets feedback on it . . ." He added, "Our program director has to approve it. She's in the meeting with the instructor when they are discussing it, obviously. But it's my understanding and maybe I'm wrong, but it's my understanding that when she says its okay then that's it."

Course approval at the corporate level is a separate matter. Miller College employs a compliance officer whose job is to make sure that all new and revised courses meet the accreditation standards set forth by ACC-SCT. New, and in some cases revised courses, need the approval of the institution's compliance officer before they can be taught. The compliance officer does not judge content, rather her job is to ensure that the course fits within the guidelines of the accrediting commission. "[Our compliance officer] is the one that helps us make sure that it's going to meet the accrediting commission's guidelines. She is not the subject matter expert necessarily, but she knows what the accrediting commission looks for."

Although faculty members have a great amount of latitude in designing courses, they have little say in other areas of governance. With only a small number of participants representing the institution, it was difficult to gauge the level of faculty satisfaction with their working environment. Nevertheless, their at-will status precluded faculty members from making significant changes to improve their working conditions.

PARAMETERS OF EMPLOYMENT

With regard to their contingent status, faculty from DLU and Miller College shared similar opinions; the issue of contingent status was not a major concern for many of them. Participants from Miller College were cognizant of their at-will status and, for the most part, were content with their jobs. They felt that administrators treated them with respect and valued their expertise. "[Miller] regards their faculty; they are verbally appreciative and verbally admit that the faculty, the teachers, are effective." Another participant stated, "I have two wonderful bosses, these ladies have just been wonderful to me. These are intelligent ladies, and they're fair." However, faculty spoke about two problematic issues with regard to their working environment—their work schedule and student evaluations.

Fixed Schedule

Several participants made reference to the long work hours. Faculty cannot set their work hours and are on a fixed schedule; they work 5 hours every morning and evening, Monday thru Thursday. The split schedule creates an extended day for faculty. A faculty member who recently began teaching at Miller offered his point of view. "We're basically teaching ten hours, four days a week. You get used to it. We are here from 7:30am to 12:30pm then we are back at 5:30pm. It's a little rough after being here 'til 10:30pm to be back the next day at 7:30am. It is a four-day week, and the three day weekend makes up for that. Once you get used to it, it is not bad." The unique work schedule hinders faculty interaction. Many faculty use the break in the day to take care of personal errands while others choose to go back to their homes.

> We work a split shift and honestly when classes end at 12:30 pm, most people cruise, and then the same way at night. We get out in the evening at 10:30 at night. So most nights by the time I leave, the build-ing is pretty much empty . . . I really don't go out around the hallway and talk [during the day], unless it's a student. If a student needs to talk then that's fine. I just don't do a lot of social conversation with faculty.

Student Evaluations

Classroom interactions between faculty and students are closely monitored by the institution. Faculty are aware that they are being evaluated on their classroom abilities and are not guaranteed employment if they do not per-form up to par. "Our teachers aren't under contract. So, somebody that has been here for 10 years has to continue to perform to remain employed. So, I think that affects how they interact in the classroom, and I think to a good extent that it affects [the classroom] positively."

Student evaluations play an important role in assessing a faculty member's performance. Students evaluate their instructors on a regular basis, at the end of each course. "Student critiques are something that is done throughout the Miller system." Two faculty members, from different campuses, felt that while student critiques are valuable they are not the most accurate or most valuable means of assessing a faculty member's classroom performance. Faculty asserted that in-room observations and cri-tiques by other faculty members provide a better assessment of a faculty member's abilities.

> Once a phase we have students fill out a critique form about the class. Now there's nothing wrong with that, I think that's valuable. It can be useful. We get some good information from those things. I'm certainly not disparaging them, but as a measurement of the teacher's effective-ness, a student critique is not a good measurement. They may fear repercussions if they write the honest truth, even though they are confi-dential and we never see them. I think there is pressure on [students]. There is the personality issue where they like somebody and, you know, I just don't think that they're a valid appraisal. You need a professional to come in and give you an honest, unvarnished, true, opinion of what you are doing.

A faculty member and program director from Campus B explained how she used the student critiques in tandem with her classroom visits to evaluate faculty in her department. She, too, placed more import on observations and used student critiques as a means to validate her assessments.

> Most student critiques, we'll call them that for lack of a better word, substantiate what you already know went on in the classroom, and you'll know what's going on in the classroom by observation. So, I try to sit in on classes and talk to students in the hall during the breaks and get an idea of what's going on in the classroom. And those critiques substantiate it. I don't think they've ever been surprised by anything in those student critiques and as far as those go. If I had one comment that said something about a teacher, you can take that with a grain of salt. If two people are saying the same thing, then that's starting to be trend. If three or four students in the class are saying the same thing, then maybe you have an issue.

While the consensus among participants was that in-class observations provide the best means for assessing faculty members' teaching abilities, classroom observations did not seem to be a standardized practice at all four of the institutions participating in the study. This may be the result of the loose ties to central administration and the autonomy that campuses are afforded—an issue that will be discussed in the final section of this case study.

A Temporary Stopover

In speaking with participants it became clear that many faculty members teaching at Miller, do so only for a brief period of time. This factor may contribute to the apathetic feelings among faculty members with regard to their at-will status. Participants mentioned that it is common for faculty members to spend only a few years teaching before returning to their main profession. "Some of them will [teach] for awhile and then they'll go back into the field, because it is difficult doing the days and doing the nights, especially if you're a family person too." A faculty member who attended Miller College as a student commented that in the past, the typical instructor spent less than two years at Miller. "An interesting thing that I think you would probably like to know about for your study is the frequency of instructors, the in and out . . . When I was in school, if an instructor lasted a year and a half, that was a pretty long time."

The participant continued, adding that the tenure of faculty members tends to be short because Miller hires professionals rather than educators.

Faculty members view their teaching posts as a short-term hiatus from their high stress jobs. The revolving door approach within the faculty ranks presents a challenge for the institution.

> The frequency of instructors coming and going—that's the hardest thing that a school like ours has to deal with is the fact that really, what you need are not professional teachers. [Our faculty] are professionals that are working in the industry. They need to get away from the stress, you know, 12 hours a day, beeper on their hip, getting called on Saturday kind of stuff. And they just need a break from that. They come in and they take a cut in pay, and typically would work anywhere from nine months to a year and a half. And I guess, get refreshed, get a good offer, and out the door, and they move on. And that's always been a great challenge.

Miller College strives to hire quality faculty with professional experience. Since most of the faculty positions are full-time, individuals who fill those posts are only able to teach if they are not employed elsewhere. In other words, the institution's focus on hiring individuals with professional experience, and the nature of their teaching posts as full-time positions, contributes to the revolving door effect of faculty.

CAMPUS AUTONOMY

Miller College's seventeen campuses operate with a great deal of autonomy from the central administration. This results in both positive and negative consequences for the institution as a whole. For example, a number of participants argued that the lack of standardization leads to disparities in student knowledge. Conversely, campus autonomy allows individual campuses to tailor academic programs that fit the needs of the local community.

Standardization

Unlike DLU and PAU, Miller College does not standardize courses or academic programs across campuses; each campus designs their own courses and programs. All curricula must meet certain requirements and accreditation standards, but individual campuses are granted the freedom to design programs that accommodate the needs of their local community. "The health care programs here at our campus are probably our biggest programs, because the [city name] area is a very big medical community. So, we have medical assisting, we have medical office assisting, we have pharmacy technician programs, and we have dental assisting." While most participants appreciate the freedom to design their courses, one faculty member has been advocating for a more standardized curriculum in his program. He pointed out the negative effect of not having a standardized curriculum and set of courses, and emphasized that students enrolled in similar academic programs at different campuses should receive a similar education and possess equivalent skills.

> Almost every school has [an] introductory visual basic class. That's one of the core languages that everybody needs to learn. My suggestion was to have a basic competency test on visual basic, and that everybody had to pass that test. I mean, the teacher could get there anyway they wanted to get there. They could use their own teaching style, they can use their own books. However they want to teach it is fine, but the basic competencies should be there, and when you say that you got a 95 at Campus X that should be equal to a 95 at Campus Y or Campus Z.

He argued that standardized final exams could be used to indicate problems within a specific course.

> I had advocated having consistent final exams in the classes . . . If the students at Campus X are scoring 95's and students in Campus Y are scoring 80's. Well, maybe that's an indication that something is not right at Campus Y. Maybe it's the book, maybe it's the way that the person is teaching, or maybe it's the teacher but you know it would be a unit of measurement.

Awareness of Accreditation Standards

Faculty members are very knowledgeable about accreditation standards, more so than faculty at traditional institutions as well as the other institutions participating in the study. Participants often spoke about the need to follow ACCSCT (Accrediting Commission of Career Schools and Colleges of Technology) standards when modifying or designing courses and when choosing textbooks. In fact, faculty members are taught the accrediting commission's guidelines before they begin working on the curriculum.

> Normally what happens is that [our compliance officer] would come to the people that are going to be involved with the program with the technical jargon as to what we have to do to meet the accrediting commission's requirements. And with that in mind, then we are able to design a program that is going to fit the guidelines that she has announced for us.

Many of the participants already were familiar with specific accreditation policies. For example, most participants were aware that they could change only a small portion of a course without having to send it back for re-approval. "The accreditation process, the way it works is that we are allowed to change up to 25% of our curriculum, and if we do any more than that than they have to go back to the accreditation board to get it approved. So, we usually don't change more than 25%, but up to 25%, we can change." Another faculty member explained that the accrediting commission requires that faculty members have a minimum number of years of professional experience before they can be hired to teach at Miller. "Our accrediting commission requires at least three years [of] experience in whatever field they are teaching."

Faculty members at Miller have a thorough knowledge of ACCSCT accreditation rules and regulations because they have greater authority in designing curriculum than their counterparts at Distance Learning and Pacific-Atlantic Universities. Miller faculty are obligated to become familiar with accreditation standards to participate in curriculum development activities.

Faculty Training and Evaluation

The lack of a standardized curriculum presents challenges to the institution as a whole, especially as it relates to providing students with comparable training and education from one campus to the next. Consistent faculty training is another important element that influences whether students are receiving a similar education across campuses. A participant mentioned its importance stating that "I need to make sure that teachers have the tools they need to be successful in the classroom, that they have proper training upfront as an instructor on how to instruct, how to be a teacher at Miller College." Yet, faculty training is not consistent throughout the institution.

A participant from Campus A who is responsible for training new faculty members in his department explained that the training he provides his faculty is of his own design. "It's just something that I put together over the years. I thought about the things that faculty members need to know before they get started in the classroom." His training process is unique to his campus,

> [As for] the training that I put my faculty members through—well they go through some classroom management skills—seminars for lack of a better word; some multimedia presentations, some computer stuff . . . We talk about different philosophies, educational philosophies; we talk about different learning styles. We talk about testing styles and strategies; we talk about retention, because that's important to us. We talk

> about how to be a good educator, those kinds of things. They do a cou-
> ple practice teachings. They teach 20 or 30 minute lessons and I'll
> observe them and talk about that and critique them. And they prepare
> a couple of lesson plans. . . .

Moreover, this participant commented that prior to his arrival at Miller College Campus A, his campus did not have a formal training process. "Before I put this together, there really was no training that I saw or that I could get my hands on. So, there needed to be something. So, in just remembering my educational background and my first month or so at Miller, the training has evolved, and it continues to evolve."

A faculty member at Campus C who is responsible for training faculty in her department described her training process as follows: "We have a CD disc, they sit and watch it. It tells [them] all about Miller and what we expect and then I work with them usually for about a week just going over everything." In addition to the training she offers at her campus, her faculty members attend additional in-depth training at the central headquarters.

> We also have a training center that we have up [at headquarters], that
> they send the teachers up to. They are there for about three days, and
> they go through a training, a new teacher training. It's everything you
> need to know about Miller, and what we expect and that type of thing.
> They go through the policies and stuff. They have the instructor's man-
> ual, they have the employee manual, and they go through all that to
> make sure that everything is crystal clear on what we expect.

It is clear that faculty training has not been formalized across the institution. Similarly, in-class observations and peer evaluations of faculty are not performed on every campus.

Faculty members at Campus A are observed by other faculty on a regular basis. A faculty member/program head at Campus A explained "I do the performance reviews . . . we review [faculty] once a year." In contrast, faculty members at Campus C are not reviewed on a regular basis. Although one participant from Campus C would welcome regular peer evaluations, he has not received an in-class assessment during his 5-year tenure at Miller. "I've been in the Miller system since 1999. I can tell you that since the time I've been here, I have not had a single classroom evaluation. Nobody has come in and sat in my class to evaluate what I was doing." The faculty member suggested to his campus co-directors the need for faculty to be evaluated regularly. "And that was another one of my suggestions, is that we need somebody to do that. Every [year] there should be somebody sitting in the class, unannounced by the way. I think that's really important. And it doesn't have to be negative. It's not about ripping somebody. It could be a variety of things, but we don't do that." He explained that his campus co-directors replied to his suggestions with, in his words, "No we're not going to do that. We have student critiques." He speculated that in-class observations of faculty are not part of his campus' culture and would not be instituted for fear of losing faculty.

> I think there's just resistance and I think that they are concerned that some of the older teachers that have been around for a while are used to the old way of doing things; they would run into a lot of resistance from [faculty] if they tried to institute this, and they would lose instructors. That's my guess, you know, the [co-directors] never told me that. I'm just speculating that that might be the deterrent.

Miller College does not appear to have fundamental policies and procedures in place, such as those on faculty training and in-class evaluation. Individual campuses are free to create and implement such policies, and are provided with a great deal of autonomy to govern themselves. As was argued by participants, the autonomous governance structure of this multi-campus institution can have both positive and negative effects on the quality and consistency of the curriculum and on the faculty.

CONCLUSION

Miller College is an institution in transition. As new campus administrators are appointed by the new ownership, many of the institution's policies and guidelines are evolving. The institution has its roots in vocational education, with most of its program offerings below the baccalaureate level. Faculty members are not required to hold a graduate level degree. Unlike DLU and Pacific-Atlantic, Miller College hires predominantly full-time faculty members. As a result, faculty members have an increased level of authority over the courses they develop and the curriculum as a whole. Participants seem less concerned with their at-will employment status, and more concerned with the future direction of their individual campuses. The loose ties between the individual campuses and the central administration have created a degree of autonomy that allows each campus to tailor degree offerings that fit the needs of their local communities. However, unlike DLU and PAU, there remain unresolved issues with regard to standardized faculty evaluations and training.

Chapter Seven
Southeastern College

"A few years ago our president, who is a great guy, wanted to be on the best 100 places to work in [the state]. It came at a particularly bad time when he made us fill out the survey. And he did not expect the result that he got."

Southeastern College (SC) is a single-campus, for-profit institution located in a small town in the Eastern United States with a population of about 1,000 residents. The campus is modest in size, about 35 acres, with approximately 850 students. The institution traces its roots to 1881, although the current incarnation of the institution was established in 1970 by the Harris family, a pseudonym for the current owners of the institution. Prior to 1999, the institution was previously known as Southeastern Business School. After the state authorized it to award associates degrees, and more recently bachelors degrees, the institution became known as a college. Southeastern College is regionally accredited by the Middle States Association on Higher Education, and is a privately owned college. John Harris, Sr. was the president of the college until his son, John Harris, Jr. took over as president and CEO.

On the surface, the college appears to be a traditional, non-profit institution. It offers on-campus student housing with many amenities such as cable TV and high speed Internet access. The college offers opportunities for students to participate in organizations and clubs, study abroad programs, and intercollegiate athletics; Southeastern is a member of the National Junior College Athletic Association (NJCAA). There is a student-operated restaurant, student newspaper, and a school mascot. The majority of the students attend school full-time, with courses offered during the day. The majority of the faculty members also are full-time. The college offers degrees in the following areas: Business, Healthcare, Information Technology, Legal, and

Office & Administration. The college also offers continuing education courses in the evening for part-time students, many of which are working professionals and are designated as a separate student population. Students that attend the evening courses are labeled 'continuing education' students, although full-time students are allowed to enroll in evening courses. According to faculty members, the distinction is made "to facilitate the tracking of students in order to maintain standards for accreditation."

The institution's identity is based on what is known as "The Big Eight Philosophies" which include: Appearance, Attendance, Conduct, Drug and Alcohol Use, Grades, Hands-on Education, Service/Community Service, and Technology. These philosophies are unique in that they are not only meant to provide a set of values that guide the institution, but are also meant to prepare students for real world expectations. Take, for example, the first philosophy—appearance. Students are required to dress in business attire, which was defined by faculty members as: "Men wear a coat and tie, and women wear slacks or long skirts." The rationale behind this philosophy is stated in the college catalog as follows: "By maintaining an appearance policy in academic buildings on class days, [students] will develop good habits and build a professional wardrobe for career success." Other philosophies also speak in terms of enhancing the campus community and preparing students to be successful in the workplace. The eight fundamental philosophies provide a context from which to understand the working environment for faculty members at Southeastern College.

Table 10: Distribution of Faculty Participants from *Southeastern College* by Discipline, Status, and Length of Service

Discipline	Full-time	Part-time	Number of Years at Institution		
			0–2 years	*3–5 years*	*Over 5 years*
Business	4	1	0	1	4
Education	No program	No program	No program	No program	No program
IT/Comm.	2	0	1	1	0
Health Sciences	1	0	0	0	1
Social Sciences	1	1	1	1	0
General Education	1	0	0	1	0
Totals	9	2	2	4	5

In what follows, I examine faculty work life at SC, focusing on the major responsibilities that define faculty work. I turn to a discussion of faculty participation in governance activities before exploring what many faculty members referred to as "right to work" or contingent status and its effect on faculty work life. I conclude by exploring issues related to the consolidation of authority between four individuals, focusing on the expressed need for open communication between the administration and faculty. Table 10 provides background information on faculty employment status by discipline. Before beginning, it is important to note that all but two of the faculty participants are full-time faculty members. Therefore, data from participants overwhelmingly reflects the experiences of full-time faculty.

PARAMETERS OF FACULTY WORK

Faculty work life at Southeastern College, as with Miller College, is dominated by teaching. A full teaching load consists of four courses per quarter, i.e. every 11 weeks, for a total of 16 courses per year. Full-time faculty members spend 16 hours a week in the classroom, 4 hours a day Monday-Thursday. In addition they have daily office hours on teaching days. "Basically we have 20 hours a week of classroom activities."

Practical Training

Faculty members define their classroom work within the context of the institution's career-focus. Given the history of the institution as a business college, SC takes a hands-on approach to teaching. A faculty member in business administration explained, "We do lots of hands-on here which is a competitive advantage of Southeastern College . . . We incorporate student discussions, case studies, lectures, and a lot of hands-on projects. For example, when I teach a class in planning and marketing communications [students] do a complete promotional plan."

The hands-on experience extends beyond the classroom for many students. Faculty participants spoke about how the practical experience students receive is as valuable as their classroom studies. In addition to a mock jail program, a faculty participant teaching in the legal studies division explained that students in his department also have the opportunity to participate in a mock trial program. "They have a mock trial program here that is every bit as intense as what you find in law school. It's usually done by [our] law students [who are] beyond their first year. They do it here and they do it very, very well. Sometimes it just astonishes me that they reach that level of competence while they are here. They are only here for 18 months."

Similarly, students in the travel and tourism program are provided with the opportunity to hone their skills at the campus' student-run travel agency. "We have a live travel agency here on campus—and it's student run. They actually run it and I oversee it. I manage it, as they call it. And basically what it's for is for the students to get, you know, a hands-on feel for working for a travel agency. Getting some experience. Doing what they're taught in the classroom."

A faculty member teaching in the general studies department, with teaching experience at traditional 4-year institutions, commented on the difference between teaching at Southeastern College versus at a traditional university. After teaching his first course at SC, he quickly became cognizant that students attend the institution to gain practical knowledge they can use in the workplace, even if they are enrolled in a general education course such as ethics.

> The first time you teach a class here, you are evaluated at midterm and at the end of the term. On my midterm evaluations the students literally wrote 'dumb it down, this is not the University of—,' because they knew it's where I came from. I said 'No, I'm not going to do that.' I was supplementing the book with what I thought was real ethics, theory in how to solve problems, and that type [of] stuff. So, I had to adjust and find middle ground. I realized they need to face problems they see themselves. It is going to be the stuff that's going to help them in their career. So they are not interested in knowing what utilitarianism is, the ontology. I kind of sneak that stuff in the back, and focus on the issues. So now I talk about pornography, euthanasia, and that stuff. I give them the philosophical stuff, but don't emphasize it as much.

While hands-on practical experience is "what Southeastern is about," faculty members expressed the need to offer more than just training. "My role is providing the foundation skills, especially critical thinking, reading analysis, and writing skills that they are going to need regardless of what their job is." A faculty member in the Information Technology division felt that Southeastern students received a well-rounded education compared to students attending other career-oriented institutions.

> I have been to only a few other career schools; I have not been in too many. The other schools I have been to, I really feel like they are short-changing the students. We give them their liberal arts education. For example, I was at a private school just this weekend, looking at their

curriculum . . . Where are their English comp I and II [courses]? Where are their statistics and their pre-cal courses? I'm comparing this private education to [Southeastern College] and I am going 'No, I would not want my kid here.'

Advising

In addition to their teaching responsibilities, faculty members are required to act as academic advisors to students in their department. Participants regarded the academic advising function of their job as equally important to their teaching responsibilities and many participants spent as much time teaching as they did advising students.

> Some students are really low maintenance, they basically look after themselves and there isn't a whole lot we have to do. Other students need more guidance. It really varies. Some weeks you barely have advisees other weeks it seems like I'm spending more time with my advisees than I am with my students in class. So, it all kind of evens out to me—50/50 [teaching vs. advising].

The responsibilities of a faculty member in the 'academic advisor' role are similar to those of an academic advisor at a traditional college or university. That is to say, faculty members are responsible for making sure their advisees are making satisfactory progress in their academic programs and are able to manage their course loads. Faculty members also assist students in scheduling the proper courses to ensure that they graduate in a timely manner. "Academic advisors help students solve problems with their credits and make sure they are on track, and if they have problems in their courses I can address that with them, [and] whatever else they come into my office with."

Faculty members also provide academic support to students, but the type and degree of support differs from one faculty member to another. In other words, faculty participants approach academic advising in various ways. A number of participants maintained a strictly professional relationship with their students. "There is a professional line that they can't cross. I will be their advisor, I'll be their teacher, but they do not need me as a friend. I will support them 120% and they know that." Other faculty members believed their advisory role calls for them to be much more involved in a student's personal life in addition to performing the functional task of academic advising. Several participants saw themselves as mentors and felt a responsibility to help students overcome external obstacles to their success.

> We have had students with so many various situations where a faculty
> member stepped in and got them the help they needed, and they were
> able to make it through their degree. I also see the faculty member as a
> friend, and as an advisor for scheduling decisions. Getting the students
> to manage and balance all the forces in their life, as well as balancing
> them in areas of weakness such as time management, test preparation
> and note taking—things of that nature.

Although participants viewed their advisory roles differently, all were dedicated to helping students complete their programs of study. Each viewed
the advisory role as critical to a student's success inside and outside of the
classroom.

Dress Code, Attendance, and Internships

Faculty members also spoke about the secondary responsibilities of their
job, including coordinating internships and enforcing the institution's
attendance and dress code policies. Each of these elements seem to be unrelated to one another yet when viewed as a whole, they provide a unique
perspective into the institution's culture and the nature of faculty work. For
example, the internship component of the curriculum reinforces the practical training and hands-on approach to education, while the attendance and
dress code policies offer a distinct view into the conservative nature of the
institution. While only a select number of faculty members are responsible
for coordinating internships, all faculty are responsible for maintaining
attendance records and enforcing the dress code policy.

To begin, students in associates and bachelors degree programs participate in internships, ideally after they have completed their coursework. Every
student is required to complete an internship for credit. "It is a four credit
course, with 180 hours of work experience over a quarter, which is 10 weeks.
[Students] have to find a job that will allow them to do 15 to 18 hours per
week, because they do it after they finish their coursework. Some do it during
the summer between their junior or senior year, but we have classes over the
summer." Although faculty are granted relief from one course per year for
coordinating internships, many described the process as somewhat time consuming. "Not everybody [in the department] does it, just selected faculty.
They are selected by [their] expertise. There are two accounting professors so
only one does internship." She continued, "During the year, you get one
opportunity to teach an internship course. Those of us that do the internship's
every quarter have like six classes . . . It is sometimes very difficult."

The attendance and dress code policies are a tradition of the institution dating back to when Southeastern College was strictly a business

school that did not grant degrees. It has remained in place as the institution continues to grow. "These are two items that are very, very important to our president." The policies are in place to simulate the work environment for students, in a similar vein to the internship experience.

> When you come onto the Southeastern campus our men will be in suits, our girls will be in dress slacks or skirts. During the summer, July 1- October 1, men could have their sport coats and they don't have to have a tie. They are allowed to wear short-sleeves. Women have to wear panty hose year-round. It is to prepare them for that career that they're going to be embarking on shortly.

The attendance policy is strictly enforced. Even if students are performing well in a course, they can automatically fail a course based on poor attendance.

> Some of our courses require a 73 to pass. So, if you had a B and you miss [classes], I automatically fail you because of your attendance. Not so much because of your performance in the class when you were there, it's about your attendance. That is there for them to realize that you are only given so many sick days and vacation days at work. When you use them all up they are going to dock your paycheck. We're docking your grades, because we can't dock your paycheck.

Although all faculty members understand the rationale behind the attendance and dress code policies, a number of participants felt reluctant to enforce them.

> I have mixed feelings about it. I don't see any problem with shorts in the evening classes so when they change the strict guidelines of what evening students can wear, to me that is one of the main problems . . . I do think the [dress code] is important for internships except that sometimes some of our time that is taken for [enforcing] dress code could be used as a better method. I'd say the best way to describe it is mixed feelings.

The aforementioned policies offer a view into the working environment for faculty. In the words of one participant "We are a very conservative, business oriented, proprietary school. Someone who has never worn a suit and has a ponytail would probably not fit in." As a result, the institution seeks faculty "that fit that mold, that are not going to come in a tie-dye

T-shirt, cut off jeans and a tie and say 'Well, I'm in dress code, because I have a tie on.'"

PARAMETERS OF GOVERNANCE

Faculty governance at Southeastern College, like the other for-profit institutions in the study, is limited mostly to areas of curriculum development. As one faculty member explained "In curriculum we have some say, otherwise none. [Everything else] is all taken care of by the dean." The governance structure is hierarchical in nature with the majority of decision-making authority resting atop the hypothetical organizational pyramid. The concentration of power is the cause of several faculty issues, which will be discussed in the final section of this case study.

Course Development

The course development and curriculum review process involve a great deal of faculty input. All courses are developed by faculty members with some input from administrators as well as external parties from the business community. Ideas for developing courses can come from administrators who are aware of the current needs of employers or can be initiated by individual faculty members who perceive a void in the curriculum.

> It could go bottom-up or top-down. It has been both cases for me. Two days ago, the dean saw the need for a program that was called Accounting Information Systems and she wanted us to write a curriculum . . . That came from the top-down. A few years ago I saw the need for a few math classes we should throw in and I said, 'I'm going to write this class.' So it works both ways.

The process of creating a course is similar to that of Miller College. Faculty members are provided with guidelines to follow when developing a course, most of which pertain to accreditation standards, but are given plenty of latitude in determining course content. A participant responsible for reviewing curricula explained, "I give them aspects that they need to focus on for accreditation. However, if they want to bring up new courses it's up to them what it's about," adding that courses need approval from the Registrar before they can be offered to students.

The process by which courses are developed is not standardized, which gives faculty the freedom to develop courses of interest to them.

In the past year, we did make some courses at the 300 or 400 levels in our general studies. [Faculty] were tasked with developing so many courses in social sciences and humanities at the 300–400 level. They didn't tell [faculty] it had to be a history of jobs or African-American literature or Renaissance literature. [Faculty] decided what they wanted to teach, and they gave a request to the registrar saying, 'I need a humanities class at this level, and this is what I'd like the theme to be' . . .

Another participant explained, "We don't have a formal process. We see a need for a class and we write one. Anyone can write a class if they want to."

Faculty members often are charged with developing new academic programs and have the flexibility to decide what courses to include. Participants felt the administration treated faculty members as experts in their respective fields and allowed them to use their expertise to develop courses and curriculum.

We have a lot of latitude in that area. For example, I wrote a class called Strategic Planning and Marketing Communications. You have to develop a course syllabus, get a book, write an outline about how the 44 hours will be spread out, and then it goes to curriculum review committee. They treat us as the experts; usually it is no problem getting a new class written into the curriculum.

Another faculty member described her experience developing a new curriculum for business administration students. Adding,

I just re-developed their human resource concentration here at Southeastern and it was a group of three of us. The chair of my division and another professor and I sat down and we decided by looking at other curriculums [sic] from other colleges what we would include in ours. Then we went to individuals and universities, we chose six, and we talked to them about the success and the failures and what they were teaching. And we came back and we decided on the number of courses that we were going to offer.

Curriculum Review

In addition to developing courses and designing academic programs, faculty members are involved in reviewing the curriculum on an annual basis.

The curriculum review committee at Southeastern College is made up of both faculty and administrators, however faculty comprise the majority of the committee. The committee is charged with keeping the curriculum current and making sure it meets the standards set forth by the state and Southeastern's accrediting body.

> Our curriculum review is mostly run by our faculty. However, [because of] an accrediting body such as Middle States or recommendations from our State Department of Education—faculty may be asked to focus on something. For example, the hands-on learning and information literacy & technology are two, and lately the rigor of courses. There are also things that are going to come from [the dean] regarding curriculum.

As well, the committee approves new courses proposed by faculty and evaluates the curriculum to remove courses that are no longer viable. "Our faculty also decides when to not offer a course any more. I think we reviewed 200 courses this year; I can actually give you numbers . . . A total of 200 courses were reviewed this year, 78 new courses were developed, and 20 courses were deleted."

Faculty involvement in governance is centered on curricular decision-making, and faculty members are as influential in shaping the curriculum as faculty at Miller College. Yet, faculty participants expressed dissatisfaction with their inability to impact other areas of institutional governance even with the presence of faculty committees and a faculty governance body.

Committee Work and Faculty Forum

Committee work is a requirement for all faculty members at SC. Participants described committee work as a tertiary function of faculty work. Moreover, faculty committees were described as ancillary to the decision-making process, i.e. faculty provide input rather than make decisions. "We all work on committees to a certain extent, but it's nothing you would compare to teaching, in the level of importance. I think that [committee work] is more of just providing constructive input, rather than making it an integral part of our jobs. Our jobs are to teach students."

To foster greater discussions across the institution, both faculty and administrators comprise many of the institutional committees. "I have someone from faculty, I have someone from staff, and I have someone from administration sitting on a committee. So everybody's input can be heard. We can have cross-college discussions." A number of participants explained that while committees can provide substantial input, implementing ideas rests with the executive administrators that comprise the Ways and Means Committee. "The Ways and Means Committee meets every other week, and they make sure that [committees] are working in line with the college's goals, our strategic direction, [and] everything else from capital expenditures to hiring decisions."

Southeastern College also has a faculty governing body known as Faculty Forum. Ideally the faculty forum represents the voice of the faculty body as a whole. It has yet to produce promising results, partly because it is a relatively new entity and because its previous incarnation was unsuccessful. "Our faculty forum is what other colleges might see as a faculty senate, but it is not well developed and our faculties don't really participate in it. I think that has to do a lot with the length of stay for some of our faculty, [also] because they've seen it under a different administration, and it failed so I think there was an attempt to try it again."

Numerous participants described the current faculty forum as ineffective. Faculty members expressed frustration with their lack of decision-making authority outside of the curriculum and felt further discouraged that decisions made in the faculty forum reaped little or no results. We have what is called faculty forum, which is supposed to be our governing body, but it hasn't really been successful very quickly. It has been implemented off and on. We do things and see things shot down, and the faculty becomes frustrated. Another faculty member offered his view on the faculty forum. "[Faculty] participation didn't reap any results . . . it was a useless endeavor."

The administration is making an effort to include faculty in the governance process of the institution. However, because of faculty members' major responsibilities—teaching, advising, curriculum development—they have little time to devote to other duties. An administrative faculty member remarked,

> [Faculty] time is taken up with teaching, their time is taken up with advising, and we do ask a lot of our faculty . . . right now we're trying to get them involved in caring with what's going on at the institution at a higher level and involving them. I think the current administration is working to see [that faculty] have results for their work on faculty forum, to see some changes go into effect that they are part of.

With a minimal amount of decision-making authority, faculty members are faced with working conditions that they cannot control. Their contingent status discourages them from calling for change without fear of reprisal from the president, and has negative effects on faculty work life.

PARAMETERS OF EMPLOYMENT

In speaking with faculty participants, two issues consistently arose—unionization and tenure. Southeastern College does not have either, and both topics elicited compelling remarks regarding the merits and probability of creating such systems. In addition, participants repeatedly mentioned the number of additional hours they spent working with students and preparing assignments without pay. Many faculty felt overburdened with their considerable workloads and made clear that, while they enjoyed teaching and working with their students, they also worked long hours with no additional compensation. "I think [the administration] is just afraid they're not getting their money's worth because we work four days a week, but if I charged them hourly for how many hours I put in, they would be shocked. For every hour in the classroom, I'm researching 4 hours easily. That doesn't even include grading . . . It's the students that motivate me to be here." Moreover, Southeastern College does not differentiate between its senior faculty and junior faculty, resulting in the inability for faculty to advance in the workplace.

Faculty Status

Southeastern College does not utilize faculty titles. "There is no designation between me, who has been here for six years, and someone who has just started." At the time of the interviews the institution was planning to implement a faculty seniority system, but plans were still under discussion. The lack of a faculty hierarchy has had negative effects on faculty work life at the college. Namely, faculty who had been teaching at the institution for many years expressed dissatisfaction with their stagnant status. A 'senior' faculty member who has been with the college for many years explained, "Well, they don't have a lot of promotions here. You are either faculty or you're not faculty. There is a chair position, but there's only one of those. There's no level of professor . . . I think it's very difficult for faculty, because you really have to love what you do because there is nowhere to go here. There's nowhere to move."

Other faculty participants felt that a faculty seniority system was long overdue after teaching at the institution for many years without a promotion. "As far as my colleagues, I think they need some sort of advancement here, some sort of [faculty] track." A senior faculty member explained that although the institution is implementing a faculty seniority system, faculty members are still at-will employees who can be fired without notice. "Yeah, I don't think it's really what would be called tenure because we're like in a right to work [status] so they can say 'See you' any time they want." Moreover, faculty members were generally unhappy with the working conditions at the institution, prompting changes by the administration.

A few years ago our president, who is a great guy, wanted to be on the best 100 places to work in [the state]. It came at a particularly bad time when he made us fill out the survey. And he did not expect the result that he got. It was bad, it was really bad. So, he brought in a consultant, who is still in the process. He basically came in to forward every-thing, and asked what are our problems.

Although the institution is making an effort to respond to the needs of their faculty members, participants are very cognizant of their right to work status and the institution's ability to dismiss them at any time. A participant who sits on a committee created in response to the aforementioned survey results described a situation that provides insight into the working environment for faculty at SC. "There were groups that addressed those major areas [of the survey]. For example, the area that I was on was Performance Appraisals and Process. The day I saw I was on that committee I said, 'I have to start looking for a job, because I'm going to get fired,' because it is a hot topic." This quote exemplifies how faculty members at the college—constrained by the fear of reprisal and/or dismissal—may be unable to express their opinions to help improve their working conditions. Without the protection of tenure or a union, faculty members' contingent status can prohibit frank dialogue with the institution's executive administration. Furthermore, the mention of the words *union* or *tenure* revealed the nature of the relationship between the administration and the faculty, and the constraints associated with contingent status.

Unionization

Another example that demonstrates the deficient working environment for faculty is related to the idea of creating a faculty union. After listening to faculty speak about their long hours and limited compensation, I inquired about the creation of a faculty union. It was difficult to gauge whether faculty members were in favor of establishing a union or not. However, it was clear that participants were extremely uneasy discussing the subject of unionization. "That is something we do not use here. We have a term called faculty forum. You don't want to use those other types of label words. That is part of our culture." After inquiring why the institution's culture does not allow faculty to have such discussions the participant responded, "I do not want to answer that because other people can hear my answer. We are not in a private office . . . faculty do not have private offices."

Another faculty member provided additional insight into why participants were reluctant to discuss the issue. "We are not allowed to say union . . . If you discuss it you can be fired." She added, "Well, let's just say that most of us would not push that because we know what would happen. People have tried in the past and were fired." The atmosphere of apprehension and uneasiness regarding employment stability has had its consequences. The most evident to participants was low faculty morale. "Relating to their morale, right now it is pretty low."

Participants opined that the reason Southeastern does not allow for discussions of a faculty union is due to the conservative nature of the institution, its private ownership, and profit-seeking motive. "Southeastern is a very conservative institution. Organized labor opportunities are unlikely to succeed in our environment. . . . While the administration has never addressed this issue, I would imagine that our executive management would not be receptive to organized labor activities any more than the college's conservative faculty and staff." Another added, "I also understand that we'll never have [a union] here because it's private ownership and it's for-profit. [But] it would be nice to have a little backup once in a while."

A number of participants candidly shared their views about the faculty work environment with regard to their employment status. "Our employment status is solely at the whim of the owner/president. If [a faculty union] were to be implanted, there would be a mass dismissal." Another participant agreed, stating that because ultimate authority is vested with one individual—the president and owner of Southeastern College—a faculty union will never materialize. "One person owns the school. He doesn't want it, so therefore, it doesn't happen."

Tenure

Similar to faculty unionization, the idea of tenure is frowned upon by the administration. Faculty members also are not aware of the rationale behind this decision. "Tenure is off the table . . . I don't know if that's ever been clearly explained to faculty but at the top level I guess there's a rational reason for that." Other participants were aware of the tenure issue and commented on why it is not a component of the organization's tradition. "It is a cultural aspect of the institution."

As with unionization, participants were reluctant to speak about the idea of implementing a tenure system; discussions regarding tenure are discouraged by the administration. A faculty member remarked, "We are not allowed to say the word tenure out loud so if we disconnect, you understand me [laughs]." Formal conversations among faculty members regarding the issue of tenure have taken place in the past. However, faculty acknowledged that discussions were brief, yielded no results, and do not occur frequently. "[Tenure] has come up in faculty forum, that kind of deal. It's come up but it's been dropped pretty quickly."

One participant speculated that tenure is not part of the institution's culture because of the profit-seeking nature of the college, pointing out that faculty members determined to perform well in the classroom do not need the protection of tenure. In other words, the institution benefits financially when its faculty members perform well in the classroom. In turn, faculty members have job security when the college is financially secure. "I cannot imagine that my executive management has any more appreciation for tenure than our performance-driven faculty. Simply put, my long term financial well-being is directly tied to the financial well-being of the college. Ergo, it is crucial that every employee performs at 150% of their potential."

Other faculty members offered a different perspective on the absence of tenure, assuming that it is not an option because research is not a component of faculty work. "We are not a research institution so it's not typically like other places where you get tenure based upon research for so many years. So how would they set up tenure for a non-research academic environment"? Moreover, a number of participants believed that tenure promotes the status quo and diminishes educational quality. Simply put, faculty should not rely upon the protection of tenure to protect their positions.

> Tenured positions are often viewed as a panacea by those who seek to rest upon their accomplishments of yesteryear. As a for-profit institution enjoying the ESOP [Employee Stock Ownership Plan] benefits; our faculty does not welcome 'dead wood.' As such, it seems to be the attitude of my colleagues and I, that we should earn our right to be employed each day—every day.

Clearly, topics such as faculty unionization and tenure are not up for debate at Southeastern College. The institution's president/owner, along with members of the executive administration clearly disapprove of any efforts to initiate such discussions among the faculty. The president of Southeastern College, along with three other individuals, hold the majority of the decision-making authority.

CONSOLIDATED AUTHORITY

Given that faculty members are ancillary to the decision-making process outside of the curricular realm, a number of faculty participants felt excluded from the governance process. Participants agreed that the president of the institution holds the greatest amount of influence and has input into all types of decisions regarding the institution. "He [the president] is involved in really every decision as far as I know. I really don't know personally what he does

[but] I am going to say he was, up 'til about a year ago, involved in all the salaries, the raises and promotions, and hiring and firing." Southeastern College has a board of directors, but faculty participants were not familiar with the board's function, i.e. whether it possesses final authority or serves in an advisory capacity to the president. However, most participants were aware of the institution's powerful Ways and Means Committee (WMC) and its role in governing the institution.

The institution's chief administrative officers, referred to by one participant as "the big 4," comprise the Ways & Means Committee. "The big 4 are our president, the dean, the [chief] financial officer, and the [chief] enrollment officer—the head of each of the three branches and the president." The committee is charged with maintaining the college's mission and vision. A faculty member explained their role.

> They are kind of the 'go to' committee prior to going to the board. They handle the decisions at the level below the board. So once the strategic direction and goals for the year are approved by the board, the Ways and Means Committee meets every other week and they make sure that we are working in line with those goals. Everything from capital expenditures to hiring decisions.

The composition of the WMC provides insight into the institution's foci and priorities. Academics are a priority as evidence with the inclusion of the institution's Chief Academic Officer, i.e. the dean. Additionally, issues of finance and student enrollment are considered as important as academics, which should come to no surprise due to the profit-seeking nature of the institution.

Problematic Communication

Of note is the absence of faculty representation on the Ways and Means Committee. Since faculty members neither have a voice nor an 'emissary' on the WMC, they are unaware of the institution's major decisions or strategic plans. One participant speculated that faculty members are not informed of certain decisions because they do not involve academic issues. "Sometimes [decisions] are done for business reasons, you know. And sometimes it's 'Well, why did they do that'? Well, there's a reason, you know." Yet, the majority of the participants felt that the lack of open communication between the administration and faculty was problematic. When participants were asked about changes faculty would make to improve their relationship with the administration most participants responded,

> One of my biggest problems is communication. I really am bothered
> when people don't open up and communicate with one another . . .
> Two faculty members were hired for two different divisions with the
> same course. People do not communicate. They need to open those
> doors, they need to communicate and they need to sit back and think
> about 'To whom do I need to communicate with and why do I need to
> communicate with them? What part are they going to play, and how
> does this affect them'?

In a similar vein, another participant commented, "I would have open communication number one, where everyone is treated in the exact same way
. . . [The administration] has some major issues with communication. I
don't know if it is a power trip or what it is, but there are major issues."

Many of the faculty members' concerns have not been addressed
because of the lack of communication. One participant shared her perspective. "I think [the administration] could listen. Listen and hear what some
people have to say . . . not just 'we're going to do it and it's too bad.'" She
added, "I think it's getting better, but there could be more. . . . Maybe to
the point of, 'Well, we'd like to pursue this' and telling us that this is what's
happening and maybe stick to it a little more."

Faculty Discontent

The consolidation of decision-making authority has led to problematic
communication and faculty discontent. Participants expressed displeasure
when the administration implements changes that affect faculty. One example involved the decision by the administration to restructure the institution's administrative posts. A participant explained that faculty members
were unaware of this decision and, in addition, were not offered the opportunity to apply for the new positions.

> We just had an organizational change and none of the positions that
> were changed were posted for [faculty] to have the opportunity to
> apply. They were just done. [The college] was changing management
> and upper management and there were new positions that were opened
> up and created, but none of the faculty or staff were invited to apply. I
> said to the dean 'How was that person appointed'? and she said 'I
> thought that was the best person for the job.' So, what do you say to
> that?

Many participants felt the limited amount of communication
between the administration and faculty has caused faculty to doubt the

administration's intent. "I think open communication would lead to more credibility and trust. We would have to start with some more open communication." One participant expressed some concern with the future of her program. While she felt confident that her job was secure, she also felt apprehensive not knowing the direction in which the institution was taking her program. "Like I said, it's really like 'OK, which way are we going'? And sometimes you get a little nervous like 'OK, what's going to happen'? But I think what's going to happen is, you know, there's going to be a good change, you know. We've had good changes so far."

There were a small number of faculty members who felt their relationship with the administration did not need improving. "I really don't have any complaints about them. I don't think that I want to change anything . . . I don't think there's any way to improve [our relationship]." A faculty member explained that he and members of his department "are in decent shape. We are not a bunch of grippers and complainers." He explained that "There are some folks that have no problem with [the administration], and yet there's a vocal minority."

After conducting the interviews, it became apparent that the majority of participants were unhappy with the relationship between the administration and the faculty. A number of participants went so far as to imply that the administration favors certain individuals and academic divisions over others, and that access to information is problematic. "Certain people have communication and others don't. So, there is limited communication depending on what division you are in and there is more communication depending on divisions." Another participant added, "We work in a 'cloak and dagger' type of thing where everything is a secret, and you tell a few people and wait a couple of days and you tell a few more. That breeds contempt and anger." A faculty member who has taught at Southeastern for a number of years was very blunt. After asking whether communication between the administration and faculty differs depending on academic divisions, she proclaimed "Oh yes. No question," and believed these differences are based on "friendships outside of the school."

Whether or not favoritism plays a role in the ability for faculty to access information about the college is beside the point. The lack of open communication and perceived favoritism is problematic and has had negative consequences on faculty work life and the institution's overall environment. The problem has influenced the attitudes of faculty members and has shaped the perceptions of faculty members towards the institution. The consolidation of authority has resulted in poor communication and low faculty morale.

CONCLUSION

Southeastern College is a unique institution that distinguishes itself from the other institutions represented in this study in a number of ways. First, it is a single-campus, residential college that caters mostly to full-time students. Part-time students are the minority and attend classes in the evening, whereas the rest of the student population attends during the day. Second, Southeastern is a residential college; it offers student housing, intercollegiate sporting teams, and a school mascot. While faculty members at DLU most closely resemble faculty at traditional 4-year IHEs with regard to education and training, Southeastern College most closely resembles a traditional college or university. However, upon closer examination there are stark differences. Institutional authority primarily rests with a handful of individuals—"the big four." Although faculty members have a great amount of latitude in designing their own courses and developing the curriculum, participation in governance activities ends there. Moreover, faculty members felt confined by their working conditions and the institutional culture, and were powerless to affect change. Given that the majority of participants were uneasy discussing issues of unionization and tenure, it is fair to say that strong tensions exist between faculty members and the administration with regard to conditions of employment. By and large, the institution is taking steps to address faculty members' concerns as exemplified by the reincarnation of the faculty forum. However, the lack of open communication seemed to be a systemic issue that is causing serious problems amongst particular faculty groups and between the faculty and the administration.

Chapter Eight
Looking Beyond Each Institution

"The real decisions are going to be made on strictly a marketing basis, and that's ultimately, where a decision is made."

Until now, I have presented data using four different case studies that focus on three institutional parameters—faculty work, governance, and employment. These areas provide insight into the nature of each institution with regard to faculty culture. Data from each case study were presented within the context of a particular institution. Specific subtopics within each institutional parameter were derivative of common beliefs and opinions that arose during conversations with faculty members regarding the nature of their work as a function of their institution.

In what follows, I offer additional data that extend beyond institutional borders. Data are organized into five themes and are not bound by an institutional perspective. Rather, data examine the whole of faculty participants' experiences and perspectives regarding their work life via themes that reach outside the context of any single university. The themes offered here are common to all participating institutions and are meant to foster a broader understanding of the universal issues faculty members face at for-profit colleges and universities. Table 11 outlines the major elements of each theme. The themes in no way attempt to represent a comprehensive analysis of faculty work life at for-profit higher education institutions in the US. Instead, they reflect the major elements of institutional culture and faculty work as expressed by study participants.

Table 11: Common Elements across all Four Institutions Represented in the Study

Characteristic	Defined as . . .
Parameters of entry	Difficulties in gaining access to participants and institutions
Parameters of evaluation	Methods used to evaluate the effectiveness of each organization
Parameters of disciplinary ties	Faculty members' links to their respective disciplines
Parameters of the market	The influence of the market on the institution's programs and curricula
Parameters of academic freedom	Academic freedom not extending beyond the context of the classroom

PARAMETERS OF ENTRY

Initially, my aim was to recruit faculty members via the Internet using email addresses obtained through institutional websites available to the public. My intent was to contact faculty members directly; the assumption being that it was unnecessary to inform institutions of my intention to speak with members of their faculty body. Faculty members, I assumed, would decide for themselves whether or not to speak with me without the need to inform their superiors. Because participants would remain anonymous, a direct recruitment strategy—without the assistance of the institutions—would result in a group of interested participants whom could speak freely about their work and their institution with no inhibitions or constraints. It had not occurred to me to seek external permission to conduct the study from anyone other than potential faculty participants and the institution I represent.

My incorrect assumption was that faculty members interested in participating in the study would not need to obtain permission from their superiors. However, it is important not to neglect that for-profit IHEs are, by nature, proprietary organizations. Unlike traditional colleges and universities who are accustomed to sharing information about how they create effective and efficient institutions, such information is proprietary in the business arena and goes against the character of a profit-seeking entity. It is easy to overlook their profit-motives because for-profit IHEs operate within the academic realm where the culture is to share rather than safeguard information.

The following scenario illustrates the protective nature of for-profit institutions and the difficulties associated with obtaining access to potential faculty participants. The institution that is discussed, XYZ University, was initially chosen as a potential participant, but was subsequently dropped from the study. However, the factors that led to its removal offer valuable insight and contribute to an improved understanding of the for-profit higher education sector.

After XYZ University was identified as a possible institution from which to recruit participants, I obtained a list of faculty members from the university's website. As stated earlier, faculty members were to receive an initial email invitation directly from me asking whether they would be interested in participating in the study. A number of faculty members agreed to participate without hesitation. "Hi Vince, no problem, glad to help." However, a small minority did not want to participate and responded as such by email. Some of the faculty members responded decorously. "Sorry Vince, but I would not be comfortable disclosing the information to you that you are seeking. Best of luck." Others believed it was improper for me to ask for their participation. "Dear Mr. Lechuga, With all due respect, I do not feel it appropriate to cooperate with your suggestion." A number of faculty members who felt it was improper for me to contact them directly also believed it was necessary for me to request permission from the institution and their superiors before speaking with me. "Dear Mr. Lechuga, officially and in writing request approval through the president's office." Rather than responding solely to me, two potential participants forwarded their email invitations to their superiors who then forwarded my request to members of the executive administration.

The individuals who forwarded my request to their superiors triggered a chain of events that concluded with the following email being sent to all faculty members teaching at the three Southern California campuses of XYZ University.

> Some of you may have received a survey request from a USC doctoral student by the name of Vicente Lechuga. We should not respond to such inquiries without OBT legal and PR's approval. Debbie G. coordinates this kind of approval process. This person is directly contacting lots of our faculty at the three campuses. The proper protocol for doctoral candidates when seeking to use members of an organization in their research is to get permission from the organization's leadership first. Mr. Lechuga has not done so, consequently his request should be viewed as being bogus. Officials at USC have been notified of this breach in research protocol.
>
> Please do not respond to Mr. Lechuga's request.
>
> Dean of Academic Affairs
> [XYZ University]

The institution and the faculty members were subsequently dropped from the study to avert further complications to the project and to the institution I represent. After this incident, I modified my recruitment process, as outlined in Chapter Three, to make certain that the remaining participants and the institutions they represented would not ask to be removed from the study. Nevertheless, the account illustrates the nature of for-profit institutions as proprietary organizations. Although they are academic institutions, they also are profit-seeking entities who protect themselves and their organization from individuals and groups not associated with the institution. As businesses they seek to maximize profits and monitor the quality of their product in an effort to maintain efficiency and achieve a high level of effectiveness. As a result, for-profit institutions also utilize methods to assess both faculty and students regularly as an established organizational practice.

PARAMETERS OF EVALUATION

Another common feature across the four institutions participating in the study involves the need to regularly evaluate the activities of the organization. For-profit institutions frequently assess student learning, and more importantly, evaluate the classroom success of instructional staff. While it is not a common practice for administrators or faculty peers to monitor the classroom activities of tenure-track faculty members at traditional colleges and universities, assessment is a yearly if not bi-yearly occurrence at the for-profit institutions represented in the study. Classroom assessments of faculty members at traditional IHEs tend to consist of student evaluations. However, end-of-course student evaluations are only part of the tools used to assess faculty members at for-profit college and universities.

Faculty Success

Although the methods used to evaluate faculty differ at each institution, each has some mechanism in place to assess whether faculty members are effective classroom instructors. By far the most rigorous faculty assessment process occurs at Pacific-Atlantic University. The evaluation process begins during the initial interview; a committee of senior faculty members evaluate whether applicants have the potential and skills to utilize the PAU teaching model. "You go to a faculty assessment and the assessment means that you come in for one night . . . [After] you've gone through this assessment, and [the committee] all agrees that you would make a good faculty member, then you go through a six-week [training] period."

After completing the mandatory training course, new faculty members also undergo an evaluation during the first course they teach.

Although this process was described as mentoring rather than evaluation, faculty members are removed from the classroom if their skills do not meet with the approval of the senior faculty mentor.

> You get assigned to your first class and during that first class you are mentored by a senior faculty mentor who meets with you before your class, and comes to at least two classes to monitor you and meets with you at the end of the class. And at that point, your faculty mentor can decide that you're not going to cut it and you can be dropped from teaching.

Additionally, senior faculty members evaluate all instructional staff annually to maintain consistent instructional quality and classroom effectiveness.

> Each year, every faculty member has a QAV, a quality assurance visit and at that point a senior faculty member can enter your class and fills out a very detailed form on your teaching technique or your handouts or your feedback to the students and whether or not you followed your syllabus and whether or not you covered the course content for the night. Then those QAVs are reviewed annually with each faculty member.

Each of the institutions represented in the study also utilized end of course student evaluations to assess a faculty member's classroom success. Many participants felt that course evaluations did not always provide a true picture of a faculty member's effectiveness. Nevertheless, participants explained that they do provide a measure of the faculty member's ability to connect with the students and communicate information and ideas clearly. Moreover, consistently poor student evaluations can warrant additional mentoring and more frequent faculty assessments. The following quote illustrates how the institutions represented in the study use student evaluations to determine a faculty member's teaching ability.

> And at the end of every class students are handed out an evaluation on the class. We understand that sometimes you have clashes with your class, and they think that it's going to be a piece of cake and you're not a piece of cake teacher, and so they will write some bad negative things. But, if we get instructors that continually get negative feedback from the students, then that's another quality assurance issue that we can use to determine that [this university] is not for you.

With the exception of Miller College, the institutions represented in the study rely equally on student evaluations and classroom visits as tools to assess instructional staff. Moreover, the institutions utilize feedback from student evaluations in a manner that can have deleterious consequences for faculty members who are no longer effective educators. Participants from all four institutions remarked that many traditional colleges and universities do not utilize student evaluations in a similar manner. Moreover, peer evaluations of classroom teaching are not a customary practice at many traditional institutions. Although Miller College did not seem to have a peer evaluation system in place at all of their campuses, it was not a foreign concept to faculty who taught at the institution.

Student Learning

There are similarities in the method that courses are developed. Courses are designed to measure student learning and faculty members are charged with ensuring that students learn the pertinent material. For example, courses at DLU are designed with a set of predetermined learning outcomes. "We develop a course so that you can measure the outcomes you established—to say 'yes, they learned what they should . . . '." The outcomes-based approach to course design enables faculty to shape the assignments and learning activities to meet the requisite learning outcomes. A participant from PAU explained, "We have to look at each course, you know, [and decide] where are we going to provide content and learning activities and assignments that will meet the overall outcomes of the program objectives. So then of course, you have your course objectives that support [the learning outcomes]." In addition to course development, a broad set of learning outcomes are created and utilized by faculty members who design academic degree programs. Faculty members use the program outcomes to shape the content and design of academic programs. "[Faculty] need to understand what your learning outcomes are before developing a whole curriculum."

Similarly faculty members teach courses that have predetermined learning objectives for each class session. Faculty members use the learning objectives to guide their class discussions and must be able to assess whether students have met those objectives. A faculty member from PAU explained, "So, each week those objectives are outlined. How you meet them, the point value you give them, how you assign that for an assessment for that objective, is up to you."

Pacific-Atlantic University demonstrates its commitment to student assessment and learning by offering a workshop on assessment to its faculty members. During the workshop faculty with little to no teaching experience are taught how to evaluate student learning. A faculty member who teaches the seminar explained its purpose. "I also lead a workshop on assessment for the faculty members who are here. . . . teaching them how to assess. When you're teaching, how do you know that the students have learned what you're trying to help them [learn]? That is basically what the workshop is."

The remaining institutions represented in the study did not offer a similar seminar. Instead, they used other measures to assess successful student learning. A faculty member from Southeastern College explained that students in her Travel and Tourism program are given a proficiency exam that tests their knowledge of the industry.

> They take a—it's called a proficiency test, and it's put out through the Institute of Certified Travel Agents, or Travel Institute as they're called now. Actually it's called the Travel Agent Proficiency Test, but it's not all about being a travel agent . . . It breaks [our curriculum] all down so for outcomes and that kind of deal. So, like 'where do I need to beef my curriculum up'? . . . [It covers] pretty much a lot of the topics that, you know, we cover in our curriculum, as well as business management.

While this exam is not a mandatory requirement of the college, the results are used to provide the faculty and the administration with a measure of student learning and the program's success. The exam also provides an assessment of the program's strengths and weaknesses, and serves as a foundation from which faculty members can modify the curriculum.

Miller College also gauges student achievement using external professional exams as a measure. Two of the health programs offered at the college—medical and dental assisting—use exams proctored by their respective professional associations to monitor the success of students completing associates degree programs.

> Our accreditation is from the American Medical Technologists in Park Ridge, Illinois. That's where we do our certifications for medical and dental [students]. And what it is, it's an accrediting board that gives the test [to students], and it's a written test. So when the students have completed their diploma, they're allowed to sit for this test. If they pass the medical assistance exam, they are RMAs [registered medical assistants], and if dental assistants pass the exam, they are RDA's [registered dental assistants].

Taken as a whole, the for-profit institutions represented in the study use various methods to measure and monitor faculty success and student learning. Both internal and external measures are used to determine the effectiveness of the organization as a whole. Although the methods employed by each institution differ, each school has structures and processes they use to assess the overall performance of the institution.

PARAMETERS OF DISCIPLINARY ACTIVITY

Participants from each institution had similar characteristics, most notably their ties to the professional world. Consequently, professional development activities are directly linked to their jobs and disciplinary ties are professional, not academic in nature.

Academic Activities

With the exception of faculty members from Distance Learning University—who are current or former academicians—most participants are linked to their respective disciplines via professional development activities. In contrast, faculty members at DLU interpreted disciplinary ties as research and publishing activities related to their fields of interest. A number of DLU faculty members maintain such ties. "Many of us do continue to read and write and publish and get grants." However, their disciplinary ties are a result of their work outside of DLU. Their research and publishing activities are not related to their work responsibilities and are linked to their work activities outside of the institution. "Many [faculty members] do have affiliations at other institutions and so if publications and grants are rewarded then they are rewarded to those other institutions or they are rewarded simply because faculty members in academe are rewarded for doing that kind of thing. . . . They don't get rewarded at DLU; it is not part of the process at DLU."

Across all institutions, faculty members who were interested in these types of disciplinary activities expressed the need for additional time because their current workloads precluded them from participating. In addition, many expressed that while their institutions did not discourage academic pursuits such as research and publishing, they also did not accommodate faculty members' schedules in order to accomplish these activities.

Professional Development Activities

The majority of the participants were practitioner-faculty with professional experience. Accordingly, faculty participants defined disciplinary ties as connections to their respective professions, including membership and participation in professional organizations. For example, after inquiring about how faculty members at Pacific-Atlantic University stay connected to their discipline one participant remarked, "Pick a discipline. If you're finance person, and you work in the finance industry, and you have a DBA or a Doctorate of Business Finance, you might be a business analyst, or you might be a CFO. You may regularly participate in your specific area, and you may belong to organizations. Or you contribute, or you write. All of those kinds of things."

A faculty member from Southeastern College kept current by attending professional conferences. "I stay abreast of the trends. I am fortunate that they allow me to be a member of the American Marketing Association, and I've been able to attend educator conferences. That is one area that they have been very gracious about, paying my dues and my conference attendance." Faculty members from Southeastern College "are required to go to two [professional development activities] per year." One faculty member explained, "I would do that anyway because that's the way you learn." She added, "I am involved with the Society for Human Resources Management or SHRM [and] I am an active member of that."

At Miller College, faculty members also are expected to attend professional development activities, partly because it is a required by the institution's accrediting commission.

> Our accrediting commission says that you have to document that you have a system of continuing ed [education], professional development. You have to document either what association meetings you went to, whether they were in-house, whether faculty members were to take classes at some university or something. That is part of the accrediting standard.

I inquired whether participants had opportunities to present at conferences. The majority of them replied with a similar response: "I really don't, but I haven't made time. I could if I wanted to. I could still have an interest in that right now. I think about writing a text, [but] that's not what I want to do right now." Although participants defined disciplinary ties within the context of their professions, faculty members provide but one link between for-profit IHEs and the marketplace; the curriculum provides another.

PARAMETERS OF THE MARKET

As previously mentioned, for-profit institutions base their academic program offerings on the needs of the market. The institutions represented in the study use standardized processes to identify employers' needs and determine the types of skills they desire from graduates. The institutions create curricula using methods that are foreign to most traditional colleges and universities. The use of advisory boards, who guide curriculum development, was common among the institutions in the study. In addition, it was common for the institutions to carry out market research to identify the needs of the business community before developing new courses and academic programs.

Market-based Research

The influence of 'corporate' practices results in an innovative approach to developing new courses and academic programs. Before deciding whether to offer new curricula, the faculty and the institution perform extensive research to make certain the curriculum is relevant to the needs of employers. A Southeastern College faculty member explained, "Before building a new program—like we just got approved to give a bachelors degree in Corporate Communications—we did some research. We decided this is a good bachelors degree for us to offer." Another Southeastern College faculty member and division chair provided additional insight. "I am responsible for keeping the curriculum up-to-date with current trends in the market. I am responsible to make sure their degree is marketable that [students] can actually do something with it once they graduate . . . I make decisions based on my personal experience and what I see the market doing."

For-profit institutions gather data to ensure that the institution does not misappropriate financial resources developing programs that will not flourish. A faculty member from Pacific-Atlantic University explained how market research is used to help formulate curricular decisions. Academic programs are developed only after data from market research is evaluated.

> The real decisions are going to be made on strictly a marketing basis, and that's ultimately, where a decision is made. We do marketing studies in the area, and contacts with both potential students and businesses. Then we determine what is needed for the community, and generally something will or will not be offered based basically on the idea of whether it is going to fly or not.

Feedback from individuals in the business community is an essential element from which decisions are based. Another common feature among the institutions represented in the study is their use of advisory groups to shape academic program offerings.

Advisory Boards

All four institutions represented in the study utilize program advisory boards to assist in the development of curricula. The boards ensure that program offerings are relevant to the business community. They also provide input into the decision-making process concerning the modification or development of the curriculum. The advisory boards performed similar roles across participating institutions. A faculty member at Pacific-Atlantic University offered insight into how the advisory board functions at her institution. "The meaning in our program and the deliverables in our program are set by a focus group that is put together by the dean and the curriculum development team. And they put together a career path for the particular program that meets the needs of the employers for graduates."

Advisory groups are created for specific academic programs and/or fields of study. Faculty members asserted that the advisory boards are a primary link between the institution and the employers. The boards are a critical component that sustains the real-world education for-profit institutions offer. At Southeastern College a faculty member explained:

> When you get into the major courses or the programs of study the faculty also drive that but they consult with their advisory board. They decide who is on their advisory and they consult with those professionals who are out working in the field to find out what we should be doing about keeping up to date to be state-of-the-art, and that will guide curriculum . . . I have an advisory board for childcare, an advisory board for optometry technician, there's an advisory board for physical therapy, for paralegal, for criminal justice.

Faculty members also consult with their advisory boards for input on how to improve the quality of the students graduating from specific academic programs.

> There is a whole infrastructure tied to making certain that our programs meet [employers] needs because we have a national curriculum not a state curriculum, which is now world wide. And we need to be certain that the curriculum we are delivering is what is expected . . . We meet with the [advisory group] and the opening question is 'What would a graduate with a degree in blank need to have, from your perspective, coupled with the academic preparation that we know'?

As a result of their close ties to the business community, participants contend that students at their respective institutions are highly sought after. The advisory boards help shape a student's education to fit the needs of potential employers. Employers affiliated with particular for-profit institutions are aware that students are consistently well-prepared by their respective institutions to enter the workplace with the necessary skills and requisite training.

PARAMETERS OF ACADEMIC FREEDOM

The institutions participating in the study espouse academic freedom. However, its meaning differs due to non-academic factors that relate to profit-seeking motives. In other words, the decision-making structures associated with for-profit IHEs hinder faculty members' freedom. Academic freedom at for-profit IHEs has its limitations and was defined by participants within a specific institutional context.

Contextual Freedom

With few exceptions, all participants felt that their respective institutions placed a priority on maintaining an environment that promotes academic freedom for faculty members. However, the majority of the participants defined academic freedom within the context of the classroom, i.e. the freedom to deliver course material in the manner in which they saw fit. For example, a faculty member from Pacific-Atlantic University offered her opinion on academic freedom, which mirrored the opinions of most participants. "The curriculum that [the institution] outlines is just that: an outline. The objectives must be met by the instructor, [but] they have the freedom to meet those objectives any way they see fit." Another faculty member from PAU who teaches marketing courses echoed the previous remarks. "Each instructor has the academic freedom to modify assignments and to do things differently in their own expertise, but you will cover the four P's of marketing and quality and what is a market plan. You get the basics, it would just be delivered slightly differently [sic]."

Faculty members at Southeastern College understood that academic freedom meant the freedom to design courses and academic programs as well as the freedom to deliver course content to students. Still, many participants from SC were cognizant that academic freedom had its boundaries, even within the classroom. A faculty member at Southeastern College offered his views on academic freedom at the college.

> As a professor there are certain things that I need to do. There are certain [accreditation] standards I need to measure up to. Within those bounds I do have a great deal of intellectual creative freedom. I don't want someone looking over my shoulder saying you have to teach this class a certain way . . . I think that this school has recognized that when it comes to running the classroom the professors really are the

professionals. And you have to trust them to do with they need to do. I'm told what to teach, but I am not to how to teach it. With very few exceptions, I think that is the process and policy throughout the school.

A participant from PAU asserted that faculty members are afforded considerably more freedom than faculty at most traditional colleges and universities. He believed that academic freedom was more prevalent at PAU because dissenting and unpopular faculty perspectives are encouraged rather than restrained, in part because of the institution's historic roots.

> Pacific-Atlantic University [has] a culture that came into being in some-what of a defiance of the education establishment. So, they embrace the alternative ways of thinking, because the university emerged from alter-native ways of thinking. The odd thing is that at the traditional univer-sity . . . the idea of free speech, at worst, has been decapitated and, at best, it has been distorted to mean that your speech is free as long as you are taking a more liberal perspective to your thoughts and your discussions. And that is tragic . . . That was the culture from which Pacific-Atlantic University emerged. For that reason the discourse here is much more 'liberal' than it is in many other colleges and universities that I experienced.

He added that students at PAU benefit when faculty members with oppos-ing viewpoints are afforded the opportunity to speak openly about their beliefs. "Because of that freedom, our students experience a wider variety of viewpoints, as opposed to having a more narrow orientation . . . It allows for a richer discussion within the classroom [and] that can only serve to improve student thinking in a variety of subjects, which they might not have an opportunity to do at too many other places."

Admissions Standards and Decisions

Faculty members at traditional IHEs establish admissions criteria and admit students into their programs. Conversely, faculty members at the for-profit institutions represented in the study do not determine admissions standards and do not make decisions about whom to admit. Those decisions are made by other individuals within the institution. Many of these individuals have little or no academic background in postsecondary education.

Surprisingly, none of the participants were aware of the criteria used to determine admissions at their respective institutions. Moreover, numerous participants were unaware of the extent to which faculty members were involved in admissions decisions. When queried about faculty involvement in admissions decisions, most responses were similar to that of a part-time faculty member from Distance Learning University.

> I don't know, that is a good question and it is one that I have been wanting to ask. I don't know how much faculty are involved in admissions. I know before they never were, that was kind of a marketing thing that at least the founder of the university wanting faculty involved. I don't know how that works . . . I mean I am not familiar with even if faculty have a role in it.

Faculty members from Miller College also were unclear about the criteria the institution uses to determine admissions decisions. After inquiring about the standards for admission at Miller College one participant responded,

> Well, I'm not an expert in the admissions area so I'm not sure that I can answer that for you, or be on target. My understanding is that there is an assessment profile of some type that the individual goes through and they have to have had some knowledge, I think, of the field that they're interested in. And [they] need to know what to expect from the field they're trying to pursue. I suppose that those are the general requirements. Again, I'm not in that area and I don't know exactly how to answer your question.

Another participant from Miller explained that the institution has individuals who are not only responsible for recruiting students; they also have the authority to admit students into the college.

> Natalie is our high school rep. and she goes to all the high schools throughout the wintertime. That's her job. She goes to all the high schools and then she gets what we call lead cards, and they say 'I want to come' or 'I don't want to come.' That type of thing. Then the students start coming in here. And in the summertime, she is here most of the time. But as far as criteria, she would have to answer that. I really don't know. Like I said, she goes to the high schools and then they start coming in here for enrollment, and she's the one that determines all of that. I really don't know.

As previously discussed, full-time faculty members at Distance Learning University perform administrative duties. While decisions regarding admissions constitute a portion of their responsibilities, such decisions are not made exclusively by faculty members. Instead, admissions decisions are made in conjunction with individuals at the corporate offices. "I deal with the enrollment and admission teams that work out of [the corporate office]."

Although the majority of the faculty members at DLU are not involved in the admissions process, many remarked that they were satisfied with the quality of their students. "The only lens I would have [into admissions] would be the end results. And to that end, I have been very satisfied with the students in the program."

CONCLUSION

This chapter provided an in-depth view of faculty work life at for-profit institutions. The four case studies offered in Chapters Four–Seven provided detailed insights into the roles and responsibilities of faculty members by focusing on three distinct areas—faculty work, governance, and employment status. Each institution has unique characteristics that differentiate them from one another. DLU has a distinctive and highly trained faculty body made up of current and former educators, whereas faculty members from Pacific-Atlantic University have extensive professional backgrounds in the fields in which they teach. Miller and Southeastern College faculty are predominantly full-time employees whose major responsibilities lay in the classroom, yet both groups have relatively more influence over the curriculum than their counterparts at DLU and PAU. Faculty members generally do not have final authority in the decision-making process, even with regard to academic programs and course development. In other words, a system of shared governance is all but absent.

All four institutions share other commonalities. They are protective of 'outsiders' because of the proprietary nature of their organizations. Also, they regularly evaluate the effectiveness of their organizations and closely align themselves with the needs of the marketplace via program advisory boards. Participants defined academic freedom as contextual, residing in the classroom, and most were unaware of their institution's admissions standards.

In the following Chapter I discuss the findings and provide a cross-institutional analysis of the data within the context of the faculty culture model discussed in Chapter Two. In the final chapter I examine how the absence of the conventional paradigm of teaching, research, and service affects faculty work life, and explore the factors that shape faculty culture at for-profit IHEs. I also offer alternative subcultures from which one can examine faculty culture at for-profit colleges and universities. I suggest implications for policy and conclude the study by offering areas for future research.

Part III

A Distinct Perspective of Faculty Work Life

For-profit colleges and universities challenge fundamental tenets of the academy such as shared governance, tenure, and academic freedom, and alter the familiar paradigm that defines faculty work at many traditional colleges and universities, i.e. teaching, research, and service. By examining the attitudes, perceptions, and working environments of faculty participants, this study provides an in-depth understanding of the factors that shape faculty culture at for-profit degree-granting institutions. At issue are the roles and responsibilities of this new faculty workforce, and the effects that institutional cultures—which are influenced by external forces such as employers and the marketplace—have on faculty work and faculty culture.

Recall the purpose of this study as stated in Chapter One:

- *To gain insight into the issues confronting faculty members at for-profit IHEs by exploring faculty culture*
- *To explore the challenges, roles, and responsibilities associated with faculty work at for-profit colleges and universities*

With these goals in mind, I offer an analysis of the data presented in the previous chapters. Data are analyzed within the context of traditional colleges and universities. While this study is not intended to be a comparative study of traditional vs. for-profit higher education, it is necessary to discuss faculty work at traditional colleges and university to contrast the similarities and differences that shape faculty culture at for-profit IHEs. For that reason, the context in which data are offered utilize traditional IHEs as a point of reference. I focus the analysis around six themes: 1) Diverse faculty bodies; 2) Increased administrative authority; 3) Institutional adaptability;

4) Performance-based employment; 5) Academic constraints; and 6) Learning-centered organizations, which are summarized in Table 12.

The themes underscore the aspects of culture that are specific to for-profit institutions. The roles and responsibilities of faculty members at for-profit institutions are explored within the context of the themes outlined here. In effect, the analysis examines how faculty work at for-profit institutions shapes faculty culture with regard to specific and fundamental principles such as shared governance, tenure, and academic freedom. Following the cross-institutional analysis, I conclude with a discussion of the merits of for-profit higher education before moving into the final chapter of the study. Chapter Ten revisits the cultural framework within the context of faculty roles and responsibilities at for-profit IHEs. I conclude the chapter with policy implications, areas for future research.

Table 12: A Summary of the Six Major Themes Emerging from the Data

Theme	Characterized by . . .
Diverse faculty bodies	Level of education and types of degree programs differ by institution
Increased administrative authority	Contingent employment status, decreased level of participation in governance activities
Institutional adaptability	Quick decision-making, responding to the needs of employers and the market
Performance-based employment	Good performance is rewarded, poor performance is not
Academic constraints	Inability to address working conditions, and limits on faculty input into the curriculum
Teaching/Learning-centered institutions	Faculty are expert instructors, student-centered, and are responsible for student learning

Chapter Nine
A Cross-Institutional Analysis

What should now be apparent to readers is that for-profit colleges and universities are not all alike. Each institution in the study has its own unique characteristics that define it as an organization. For instance, DLU focuses on graduate education offering masters and doctoral degrees. The majority of PAU's faculty are part-time, and the institution seeks faculty with professional, rather academic, backgrounds. PAU also offers graduate degrees but a large proportion of their academic programs are at the baccalaureate level. Miller and Southeastern College hire only a handful of part-time faculty. Moreover, full-time faculty at those institutions have much more influence in the curriculum than their counterparts at DLU and PAU. All four institutions have a distinctive culture that is a product of its history, mission, and most importantly its people. In what follows, I examine in more detail several factors that contribute to the development of faculty culture, paying special attention to the attributes that distinguish each institution.

DIVERSE FACULTY BODIES

One of the most apparent distinctions between institutions participating in the study relates to the make-up of their faculty. The most obvious difference pertains to the type of faculty each institutions hires. As previously mentioned, part-time faculty members make up over 90% of the instructional staffs at DLU and PAU. At Miller and Southeastern Colleges, full-time faculty are the majority. Different types of institutions also require different types of faculty. An associates degree program in travel and tourism will require a different type of faculty than a masters degree in educational administration.

Table 13 provides an overview of faculty members at each institution, by highest level of education. For instance, because of its focus on graduate

Table 13: Highest Degrees Held by Faculty Participants, by Institution

Institution	Associate	Bachelor	Master	Doctorate*	Doctorate in progress**
Distance Learning University	0	0	1	17	1
Pacific-Atlantic University	0	0	10	5	2
Miller College	1	6	0	1	0
Southeastern College	0	2	8	1	0

*Juris Doctorate included
**These individuals also are included in the masters degree category

education, DLU requires that faculty members hold doctorial degrees. In addition, the institution seeks faculty with extensive research and/or professional backgrounds in higher education. One way to examine this phenomenon is by comparing the educational backgrounds of participants at different institutions.

Level of Education
Faculty members at traditional colleges and universities typically will have similar levels of training and education. At the community college level, faculty are required to have a masters degree, but it is not uncommon to see many with a Ph.D. By and large, traditional 4-year institutions require full-time faculty to have a doctorate and part-time faculty at least a masters degree, if not a doctorate. The composition of the DLU faculty body most closely resembled the faculty structure at a traditional 4-year college or university with regard to training and level of education. Consider that 17 of the 18 participants held doctorates, while the 18th participant currently was pursuing a doctorate. Consider also that 13 participants had achieved or currently were pursuing tenure at a traditional institution. DLU makes an effort to hire individuals from the traditional higher education ranks. "Over the last two or three years, DLU has been hiring more academic type of people . . . because at the doctoral level you have the research requirement. So, DLU is sort of strengthening the faculty with respect to their background."

Conversely, faculty members from the remaining three institutions were recruited from outside the education arena. "In order to teach at PAU you have to be working in the area you are going to teach . . . that is one of

Table 14: Number of Undergraduate and Graduate Degrees Offered, by Level and
         Institution

Institution	Associate	Bachelor	Master	Doctorate
Distance Learning University	0	2	6	7
Pacific-Atlantic University	1	15	26	4
Miller College	22	2	0	0
Southeastern College	17	18	0	0

the things we push pretty heavily at Pacific-Atlantic University." PAU
seemed the most reluctant to hire individuals from the traditional higher
education world. The institution provides a specialized teacher training
program designed to meet the needs of the adult student population; prior
teaching and/or research experience was not necessary. PAU's educational
focus was on undergraduate and graduate training, with the majority of
graduate programs at the masters degree level, as shown in Table 14. Faculty members were required to hold at least a masters degree. Nevertheless,
five participants held doctorates (including a J.D.) and two currently were
enrolled in doctoral programs. What's more, of the 7 participants who held
a doctorate or were currently enrolled in a doctoral program, 6 were full-
time faculty members of the institution, otherwise known as Campus College Chairs.

Types of Programs

Differences with regard to highest level of education also were evident
when comparing the two privately held institutions, Miller and Southeastern Colleges. As with DLU and PAU, the level of degree programs offered
was directly linked to the type of faculty members hired. In other words,
the number of bachelors, masters, and/or doctoral degrees offered by the
institution determined the level of education required of faculty. For example, both Miller and Southeastern College offered associates and bachelors
degree programs. On the one hand, Miller College offered only two bachelors degrees; they focused mainly on training at the diploma (vocational)
through associates degree level. Thus, faculty members typically were not
required to hold a degree above the baccalaureate level. On the other hand,
Southeastern College offered nearly the same number of bachelors degrees
as associates—18 programs vs. 17 programs, respectively. The majority of

participants from Southeastern College, 9, held at least a masters degree, which was required to teach at the baccalaureate level.

INCREASED ADMINISTRATIVE AUTHORITY

Since faculty members at for-profit institutions are employed on a contingent basis, administrators retain much of the employment discretion. Specifically, they have greater latitude in hiring and dismissing faculty members than do their counterparts at traditional IHEs. Faculty authority is minimized, which also gives administrators greater discretion in dealing with the policy. For example, executive administrators are able to implement new practices that affect the classroom without consulting with their faculty. Such was the case when administrators at Pacific-Atlantic University decided to make all course readings and textbooks available only online, referred to as "resource." "I am sure if my faculty had a vote, they would not have us going to resource because faculty, for the most part, like books. There are some decisions that are simply corporate decisions, and faculty won't have even a vote in that."

Full-time vs. Part-time

Full-time faculty at DLU and PAU hold more decision-making authority than do part-time faculty. At both institutions, however, full-time faculty consisted of less than 5% of the faculty body, and much of their responsibilities were administrative in nature. Take, for example, full-time faculty at PAU who are otherwise known as Campus College Chairs. They have a variety of administrative responsibilities which include hiring, training, and evaluating practitioner-faculty members within their college. A number of participants explained that full-time faculty, in essence, do not exist at PAU. Many stated, "There really are no full-time faculty. There are full-time employees that also teach, but there are no full-time faculty." While it is fair to say that full-time faculty members at PAU and DLU are involved in some decision-making activities, one also can argue that these individuals hold positions that are comparable to administrative posts at traditional IHEs.

As illustrated in Table 3, Chapter Six, Miller and Southeastern Colleges had a greater percentage of full-time faculty. Yet with the exception of curricular decisions, full-time faculty at both institutions held relatively little authority. The majority of the decision-making authority at Southeastern College rested with the owner/president. As a result, he was able to pressure the faculty not to establish a faculty union by creating the impression that faculty would risk losing their jobs. "Our employment status is solely at the whim of the owner/president. If [a faculty union] were to be implemented, there would be a mass dismissal." With regard to creating a faculty union, another participant from SC added, "One person owns the school. He doesn't want it, so therefore, it doesn't happen."

Business Decisions

Increased administrative authority at for-profit IHEs can be attributed to the profit-seeking nature of the institutions. Participants described much of the administrative decision-making activities as "business decisions." For-profit institutions were described by numerous participants as "corporate" in nature. Recall the remarks of a faculty member from DLU regarding the institution's decision-making activities. They often "take a top-down approach [because] that's the way corporations are." In some instances, faculty asserted that the corporate decision-making model was dominant, as illustrated by a quote from a DLU faculty member. "Everything is a business decision."

Administrative decisions take into account both the academic and profit-seeking characteristics of the institution. "Business decisions" are not meant to suggest that academic quality is overlooked or compromised in favor of profits. Rather, business decisions strive to maintain a balance between quality and profits. For-profit IHEs attempt to maximize profits while maintaining a desired level of educational quality. The repeated use of the phrase "ensuring quality in the classroom" by faculty members at PAU illustrates my point. While profits are obviously important to the institution, quality is also an entrenched value of the institution's culture.

When business decisions are the norm, business-oriented individuals make the majority of the decisions at for-profit institutions. Faculty members at for-profit institutions are not necessarily the most qualified individuals within the organization to make business decisions; therefore they are often excluded from the process. The remarks from a faculty member from PAU illustrate the point. "It's pretty easy on my level, I do not have any voice on the business side of things, and it's just that simple. I am aware that it exists." The comments previously made by a participant from Miller College also illustrate how faculty members are excluded from decision-making activities. "Sometimes [decisions] are done for business reasons, you know. And sometimes it's 'Well, why did they do that?' Well, there's a reason, you know."

Faculty members at for-profit institutions are excluded from much of the institution's decision-making activities because their expertise lies in the academic rather than the business realm. They are given a certain amount of authority to make curricular decisions, and in most cases faculty members make decisions about course content. A full-time faculty member from PAU

Table 15: Faculty Participation in Various Types of Governance Activities at
Traditional vs. For-profit Colleges and Universities

Governance Activities	Traditional IHEs	For-profit IHEs
Develop their own courses	Yes	Varies by institution
Design the curriculum/ programs	Yes	Limited participation
Admissions decisions	Yes	No
Faculty hiring/firing decisions	Yes	Limited input
Faculty promotion decisions	Yes	No

stated, "I really trust [faculty] input because they have become experts in their content area so when a question comes up about something in their content area I really work very closely with them and I trust their input on what might be most effective in those issues."

The differences between faculty participation in governance activities at for-profit as opposed to traditional institutions are evident as summarized in Table 15. Administrators at for-profit institutions do not favor a system of shared governance. Although decision-making activities are shared between faculty members and administrators, a large proportion of the decision-making authority resides outside the faculty domain. Faculty participation in governance activities is minimized at for-profit IHEs, resulting in increased administrative authority.

INSTITUTIONAL ADAPTABILITY

Conventional notions of shared governance maintain that faculty members and administrators share decision-making responsibilities. It has been argued that faculty involvement in shared decision-making is connected to the (traditional) university's unique mission of creating and disseminating knowledge (AAUP, 2001). For-profit IHEs are not research institutions, and knowledge production is not a function of these institutions. Nevertheless, when faculty members are limited in their ability to govern, questions arise about the motives that drive institutional decisions and their effect on educational quality.

Centralized Decision-making

Within the for-profit institutions represented in the study, a large amount of authority was vested in relatively few individuals. Pacific-Atlantic University and Distance Learning University both had centralized management, with a relatively small number of individuals holding the preponderance of authority. Centralized decision-making allows an institution to make quick decisions because fewer individuals are involved in the process. For example, PAU and DLU are publicly traded institutions—meaning that individuals can buy and sell shares of the institution—but are managed by a board of directors who oversee operations via each institution's president and national deans. Miller College also has a centralized decision-making body. All four institutions promote faculty participation in decision-making activities, but their governance structures are such that only a few individuals make decisions, including those that directly affect academic quality. Many of these decision-makers have corporate backgrounds. For example, the decision to offer new degree programs at DLU is often made outside the faculty realm. "To get a program approved, there are many different people looking at it. And in the end, it's truly a business decision." Governance and decision-making structures diverge from what is common at traditional colleges and universities, as another faculty member from DLU explained. "If your profits go down to an unacceptable level you are going to do something about it and that is still a little bit different than the kind of bottom line discussions that happen, I think, in [traditional] private and public institutions."

Southeastern College provides another example of a system of governance that deviates from the norms of traditional IHEs. Southeastern is owned by John Harris, Jr., who acts as the institution's president. Consider how one faculty member described Harris' role in governing the institution. "He is involved in really every decision as far as I know. I really don't know personally what he does [but] I am going to say he was, up 'til about a year ago, involved in all the salaries, the raises and promotions, and hiring and firing." Southeastern College refers to its decision-making body as the "big four." "The big four are our president, the dean, the [chief] financial officer, and the [chief] enrollment officer—the head of each of the three branches and the president."

Flexible Organizations

The governance structures of for-profit institutions are intended to promote swift decision-making. Decisions regarding the institution can be made quickly because fewer individuals are involved in the process. In addition, decision-making involves external constituencies, such as program advisory boards. This type of governance structure has both positive and negative consequences.

On the positive side, for-profit IHEs are able to quickly adapt to the external environment and the changing needs of the market. With input from advisory boards, for-profit IHEs are able to assess the needs of employers and students and design courses and programs that fit those needs. Since fewer individuals are involved in the process, for-profit IHEs are able to make decisions about which academic programs to offer and which to close. A faculty member from PAU offered the following comments regarding the institution's ability to make relatively quick decisions compared to traditional colleges and universities.

> In my conversations with my friends at [Traditional University], they just sit there and say, 'you know we can't get anything off the ground. You have to go through academic council, and yada, yada, yada, the bureaucracy is just a killer. We've got unions and everything else we have to deal with.' What I say is, 'what you've got is a situation where you're aiming at this target, and you go ready, ready, ready, ready, ready, aim, aim, aim, aim, aim, fire.' See what we do is just go 'fire!, ready, aim.'

Other participants commented that while the decision-making process at traditional institutions favors inclusion, it is cumbersome and unable to respond as quickly to the needs of the market. "My colleagues and friends that I have in more traditional educational institutions get very frustrated sometimes with the pace of change. It just crawls. By the time it gets to where it needs to, some things have passed." A participant from PAU provided an additional example that demonstrates the difference in decision-making abilities between for-profit and traditional IHEs.

> X University, here in [the city], is a great institution. There are some marvelous people there. They've been putting together the Management College, probably for about five years. It still hasn't started. They have a dean, they have funding, and they've done a fabulous job raising money. But they haven't taught one student. I mean, we would have changed it five times in that length of time.

For-profit institutions are able to adapt to meet the needs of the changing educational environment, but to do so requires decreased levels of faculty involvement in the decision-making process. Consequently, when faculty involvement in the decision-making process is minimized, decision-making activities can be regarded negatively by individuals who are accustomed to faculty involvement in the process—in other words, those in the traditional academy. Critics of for-profit education often point to the tension between education and profit as an element that can damage the quality of an education.

Institutional Tensions

The tension between the academic and business divisions of for-profit institutions and the consequences that result when faculty authority is minimized in favor of quick decision-making also must be considered when examining the governance structures at for-profit IHEs. The goals of the administration become the institution's goals, and faculty members tend to have little influence in the process. A participant from DLU shared his perspective pertaining to how the institution planned to accommodate increasing enrollments. He explained, "The push from corporate is to conduct [a class] with twenty-five students whereas in the past we definitely would have split the class . . . I believe it has changed to meet the corporate goals. [To meet] the budget goals, and revenues and profits, we are finding that we need to increase the caps of our classes."

He also commented, "Faculty really have issues with corporate influencing, [or] trying to influence the academic side of the business." While faculty members at DLU believe "quality is very, very important and most faculty won't sacrifice quality for numbers," faculty members also are unlikely to change corporate goals. This type of governance structure raises questions about educational quality. A participant from PAU explained that the institution's ability to make quick decisions can sometimes go amiss, but its ability to rebound quickly minimizes the harm resulting from a poor decision. "It is true, sometimes we try to do it too fast, but we're fluid enough that we can change quickly. So I think that that's one of the things I like about it. I like the change of pace." On the one hand, centralized decision-making leads to quick decisions, and on the other, it also leads to a loss of shared governance. Faculty authority is diminished.

PERFORMANCE-BASED EMPLOYMENT SECURITY

Without the protection of tenure or a faculty union, job security was viewed differently. Yet, with the exception of faculty members from DLU, participants came from professional backgrounds and were accustomed to the notion of job security as a function of one's ability to perform well. Not surprisingly, a number of the participants' perceptions of tenure were cynical. "Tenured positions are often viewed as a panacea by those who seek to rest upon their accomplishments of yesteryear." In other cases, the lack of tenure was not a factor for faculty members who chose to teach at a for-profit institution. "I don't think tenure is an issue. If tenure were important to you, you wouldn't come to work at a place that doesn't have tenure." Whether an institution offered tenure was irrelevant because participants viewed job security within the context of job performance, as a faculty member from Southeastern College explained, "It seems to be the attitude of my colleagues and I, that we should earn our right to be employed each day—every day." A faculty member from Miller College also commented, "I cannot imagine that my executive management has any more appreciation for tenure than our performance-driven faculty. Simply put, my long term financial well-being is directly tied to the financial well-being of the college. Ergo, it is crucial that every employee performs at 150% of their potential."

Measuring Job Performance

The for-profit institutions represented in the study relied heavily on student evaluations and in-class peer evaluations to determine the performance levels of their faculty members. A full-time faculty member from Miller explained, "I try to sit in on classes and talk to students in the hall during the breaks and get an idea of what's going on in the classroom." Student and faculty evaluations help to maintain quality, and also provide administrators with feedback regarding faculty members' classroom performance. For example, at PAU student evaluations play a major role in measuring whether faculty members are successful in the classroom. The evaluations are used to make judgments regarding a faculty member's future. A faculty member commented, "We look at what our students are saying about the facilitator." Another added, "If we have indications in student evaluations that we have a specific problem, we may either run a quality assurance visit to take a look at the facilitator in the classroom, or we might go in and do some mentoring and try to correct some minor difficulties."

Although traditional institutions also utilize course evaluations to assess course quality and faculty success, the culture of the traditional academic profession allows each faculty member to determine course quality. Course evaluations often serve as a forum for students to make suggestions to faculty on how to improve the course. Conversely, faculty members at for-profit institution whose student and/or peer evaluations are substandard either are placed on probationary status or are removed from the classroom. "If there are major difficulties then normally that faculty member is pulled off the line and is probably going to be placed in an 'observe' status . . ." Moreover, those who continually receive negative feedback from student evaluations risk losing their job. "If we get instructors that continually get negative feedback from students, then that's another quality assurance issue that we can use to determine that Pacific-Atlantic University is not for you."

Adhering to Guidelines

Connecting job security to job performance appears to be a clear and sensible method to determine a faculty member's employment security; excellent performance is rewarded, poor performance is not. As such, faculty evaluations can be a valuable, if not a necessary, tool used to maintain quality and measure success. However, when evaluations take into account whether a faculty member follows a prescribed set of guidelines, the value of an assessment becomes arbitrary and subjective. Evaluations become meaningless when faculty members are not evaluated on their ability to convey relevant information to students in a dynamic or meaningful way, and instead are judged on their ability to follow course instructions and proper procedure. A faculty member described the peer review visit at PAU.

> Each year, every year [a] faculty member has a QAV, a quality assurance visit. And at that point, a senior faculty member can enter your class and fills out a very detailed form on clear teaching technique, or your handouts, or your feedback to the students and whether or not you followed your syllabus and whether or not you covered the course content for the night.

This is to say that a faculty member who covers the course material for the day, as conveyed in the syllabus, and answers students' questions courteously may receive good marks on their peer evaluation with less attention being paid to whether the students were able to grasp the material or whether the material was even relevant.

Moreover, a faculty member who deviates from the prescribed curriculum also will receive a poor performance evaluation. Recall that faculty members from Pacific-Atlantic are required to "teach to the objectives" or risk an unfavorable evaluation. A faculty member provided an example that illustrates this point.

> I do feel an allegiance to teach the curriculum here because it's there, and that's my job, and so I would present that to students. But I would also do a little thing I would say 'OK. Now I have taught you their curriculum.

But let me share with you my personal experience,' and I would say that to them. 'This is in not necessarily what PAU is saying I should teach you, but I think that as an educator in the field, you will benefit from knowing my experience.'

While many participants felt obligated to teach what was outlined in the syllabus, they also felt it necessary to justify deviating from the fixed learning objectives, if and when this occurred.

No Compromises

An argument that critics of for-profit higher education often make is that the fixed curriculum and customer-service approach to education compromises academic quality. However, participants unambiguously indicated that all students must earn their grades. Grading was a serious matter and grade inflation was not a common practice among the participants. "I've had classes where there were no A's, and I've had classes, where there were all A's. It just depends on the class. And we really evaluate [students] on the basis of performance, it's not on the basis of effort. If they don't produce, they don't get the grade."

Yet, because student and peer evaluations are such valuable assessment tools, and because evaluations are based in part on whether a faculty member provides a level of service to their students, a perceived conflict of interest may exist. A faculty member from SC explained, "Somebody that has been here for 10 years has to continue to perform [well] to remain employed. So, I think that affects how they interact in the classroom . . ." The assessment process coupled with the pressure to perform well places certain demands on a faculty member's activities with regard to student interactions. The number of full-time non-tenure-track appointments is growing at a faster rate than the number of part-time appointments, and more than half of all appointments today are off the tenure-track (Schuster, 2003). Without the protection of tenure or a union, a contingent faculty member's ability to perform their work can be compromised.

ACADEMIC CONSTRAINTS

Outside the Classroom

As previously illustrated, faculty members from DLU and PAU work within a set of guidelines that restrict their freedom in the classroom. In addition, restrictions on their personal behaviors places limits on their actions outside of the classroom. For instance, faculty members from Miller and

Southeastern College were discouraged from speaking about tenure and were fearful of forming a union. Consider the comments from an SC faculty member, "[Tenure] is something we do not use here. We have a term called faculty forum. You don't want to use those other types of label words. That is part of our culture." In the case of Southeastern College, the very mention of a faculty union could cost an individual their job as was illustrated in this quote, "We are not allowed to say union . . . If you discuss it you can be fired."

The atmosphere of anxiety and fear regarding employment security results in negative consequences on the faculty. One of the most noticeable effects of the restrictions placed on personal and intellectual freedom manifests itself through low faculty morale. Participants from Miller and Southeastern College explained that the low levels of morale on their campus are a direct result of the increased administrative authority that imposes said restrictions. "Well, let's just say that most of us would not push [for a union] because we know what would happen. People have tried in the past and were fired . . . Relating to the morale, right now it is pretty low."

Inside the Classroom

When faculty members do not feel protected because of the absence of a union and tenure, limits on academic freedom are foreseeable. Faculty members who are unable to speak freely about ideas pertaining to their work life will feel less free to speak about intellectual ideas that may or may not conflict with those of the institution. As a result, boundaries on academic freedom are created, as illustrated by a previous quote from a PAU faculty member. "We are told, you know, 'This is a guideline, there are objectives you have to meet,' but if you've taught the course before and you've found some things that you would like to tweak. Go for it. Go ahead and make the tweak . . ."

Curricular Decisions

For-profits limit faculty members' authority over academic decisions for a number of reasons: to maintain quality, to standardize the courses and the curriculum, or both. Although, faculty members at Miller and Southeastern College can design their own courses and in some cases choose their own textbooks, the administration and the external advisory boards play a major role in determining course content and the direction of academic programs. "The meaning in our program and the deliverables in our program are set by a focus group that is put together by the dean and the curriculum development team. And they put together a career path for the particular program that meets the needs of the employers for graduates."

Faculty members at DLU and PAU do not have the option to design their own courses. Courses are standardized and academic programs, while designed by faculty, are chosen by administrators, advisory groups, and the market. All four institutions seek to maintain standards to preserve the quality of their product, i.e., the quality of the students graduating from the institution. They make use of external parties to keep current with the needs of employers, a practice foreign to many traditional colleges and universities. DLU and PAU go one step further; they maintain quality through standardization as well. Although for-profit institutions may or may not be serving their students well by standardizing the curriculum, their motives are not without merit. For-profit IHEs aspire to graduate high quality students, which is no different than traditional colleges and universities.

Corporate thinking assumes that academic quality is best maintained via standardization; standardization also creates efficiency. While this may be the case with certain organizations that produce products such as automobiles or hamburgers, education as a product is intangible and hard to define. The notion of academic freedom assumes that faculty members are best able to determine what constitutes a quality education. DLU and Pacific-Atlantic recognize this concept, and faculty members participate in curriculum development. They help to design the courses that other faculty will teach. Still, since education is an intangible product, what one faculty member considers relevant knowledge, another may consider inconsequential. The underlying premise of academic freedom asserts that faculty members should determine knowledge and content with regard to the courses they teach.

Although standardization is part of the institutional culture at PAU and DLU, the need for efficiency, in essence, infringes upon the academic freedom of faculty members. Consider the role of lead faculty members, who are appointed by the administration. "[The] lead faculty decides on the textbook, sets up all the assignments, the syllabus. And everyone who instructs must follow that." What's more, faculty members from PAU seemed content with not having to design their own courses; the standardized curriculum was not cause for concern. "One of the things I like about PAU is that you're not creating something from nothing. It is standardized, 'Here's what you're going to do now and how you get there . . . ' It would be a mess if everyone just taught whatever they wanted."

The profit-seeking nature of for-profit IHEs places limits on personal and intellectual freedoms and diminishes faculty authority in favor of revenue generation. The role of the faculty member becomes that of an instructor. Students benefit from this in that faculty members become expert teachers. Yet the academic profession, as has been previously defined, entails more than teaching.

TEACHING/LEARNING-CENTERED INSTITUTIONS

For-profit colleges and universities focus on teaching as their major responsibility. This is reflected in the mission statements of the institutions represented in the study. PAU's focus is on assisting adult learners to "develop the knowledge and skills that will enable them to achieve their professional goals" through active learning and collaboration. Miller College provides "training designed to get you a job faster." DLU's mission is framed within a scholarly context, but focuses on preparing students "to be leaders in making positive social change in their areas of influence."

Student-centered Approach

The focus on teaching also is evident in the characteristics that are required of faculty members. DLU "look[s] for faculty who can create good student relationships." PAU recruits faculty that are "experts in their field" who know "how to communicate that information." Recall the quote from a DLU faculty member, "What makes DLU unique is that fact that it is very much student-centered. I'm not sure if this is true of other places as much as it is with DLU." For-profit institutions recruit faculty members that will focus on the needs of their students. A faculty member referred to this skill as "student relationship management."

A faculty member's responsibility to the student does not end once class has concluded for the evening. Instructors must ensure that students learn the course materials. Faculty work equally centers on the ideas of teaching and learning; for-profit institutions have both a learning as well as a teaching focus. The focus on learning was summarized by a prior quote from a full-time faculty member at DLU.

> If you take the traditional university as research, service, and teaching, I would say that at DLU we are reversed. The primary purpose at DLU is learning, which was never part of the triad at research universities. Ten years ago [people] never talked about learning. It was always number one-research, number two-probably teaching, and number three was service. At DLU, student learning is number one. Some [part-time] faculty have, I think, a modicum role in service and some might have a modest role in research, but it is almost probably 95% teaching and learning.

The student-centric approach is part of the institutional culture at for-profit institutions. It is fair to say that faculty and administrators at for-profit IHEs are more cognizant of students' needs than their counterparts at traditional universities. Yet, the lines between academic freedom and customer service can sometimes be obscured. For example, the customer service approach may infringe upon a faculty member's ability to prepare coursework. The quote by a faculty member from DLU illustrates my point. "Recently, I had someone who included four textbooks [in his course], and I said 'No, we don't want to do that to our students, do you really need all those textbooks'? And, of course, he came back with one textbook and one little handbook. I look at that because we do have to be considerate of [students'] money."

This is not to say that the education students receive is incomplete. The student-centered culture and the focus on customer service, though a positive attribute of for-profit colleges and universities, may limit the type of information and education students acquire.

Practical Knowledge

Faculty members at for-profit IHEs approach teaching in a very different manner than faculty at the traditional institutions. Participants make certain that what they are teaching their students is directly applicable to what employers are looking for. Consider the previous remarks from a professor at Miller College. "From the business perspective, employers would like for [students] to be better prepared to communicate with others in their organization and others outside of the organization such as customers, clients, etcetera. So, that gives us the focus on how [and] as to what direction we want to go educationally."

Participants also spoke about how the focus on teaching practical skills calls for an approach to teaching that differs from traditional colleges and universities. Pacific-Atlantic faculty recruitment materials stated, "Faculty must show a willingness to utilize Pacific-Atlantic University's teaching and learning model." Their teaching model is grounded in adult learning theory, with a curriculum that contains relevant and applicable knowledge. Faculty not only must be skilled instructors, they also must possess the skills to teach in a way that meets the needs of their clientele, i.e. working adults. Faculty members that are unfamiliar with the teaching methods at for-profit institutions may not succeed. This brings to mind the incident in which a faculty member from Southeastern College, whose prior teaching experience was at a traditional research institution, was compelled by his students to modify his approach to teaching. "On my midterm evaluations the students literally wrote 'dumb it down, this is not the University of XXX,' because they knew it's where I came from . . . So, I had to adjust and find middle ground. I realized they need to face problems they see themselves. It is going to be the stuff that's going to help them in their career." By modifying his teaching methods, students were able to receive the type of education they expect from the institution—the type of education articulated by the institution's mission statement.

As this study shows, for-profit IHEs share some similarities but also have distinct features that make them unique. Part-time instructors make up over 90% of the instructional faculty at the two publicly traded institutions, DLU and PAU. Conversely, full-time faculty members constitute the majority of instructors at the two privately held institutions, Miller and Southeastern College. Some for-profit institutions, such as DLU, focus primarily on graduate education, while others focus on education at or below the baccalaureate level. The types of degrees they offer typically indicate the types of faculty members they hire. Faculty members teaching at one institution may not qualify to each at another institution because, unlike many traditional IHEs, academic degree programs are not similar across for-profit colleges and universities.

The responsibilities associated with faculty work also differ by institution and faculty status. Full-time faculty members at the two publicly traded institutions spend much of their time outside of the classroom performing administrative tasks. The full-time faculty members from the two privately held institutions, in contrast, spend the majority of their time teaching. Their level of involvement in curriculum development also varies. Unlike faculty members from Miller and Southeastern Colleges, DLU and PAU faculty are not allowed to design their own courses; courses are standardized to ensure quality and consistency. One characteristic the institutions represented in the study share is a centralized decision-making body. At all four institutions, the administration had final authority over most decisions, including those regarding the types of courses and degree programs to offer. In short, not all for-profit institutions are alike.

In the final chapter, I re-examine the cultural framework proposed in Chapter Two. I provide an alternative view into the prominent subcultures that influence the development of faculty culture. The elements that define faculty culture at traditional colleges and universities differ from those that contribute to faculty culture at for-profit IHEs due to differing roles and responsibilities that shape faculty work life at each institutional type. Many of these differences can be attributed to the close links between for-profit institutions and business and industry.

Chapter Ten
Re-Evaluating Faculty Culture

The education that for-profit IHEs provide can be described as market-based teaching and learning; educational activities are based on the needs of the market. Knowledge is skill-oriented and applicable to the workplace. The influence of advisory boards and corporate administrators—who are involved in academic decisions—creates a culture that orients teaching and learning within the domain of employers and businesses.

The primary responsibilities of faculty members at traditional colleges and universities—teaching, research, and service—contribute to the development of faculty culture at these institutions and serve to define the academic profession (Campbell, 2003). For-profit institutions do not use the traditional paradigm of teaching, research, and service to define faculty work. They are learning-centered institutions whose goals are twofold: to prepare students to enter the workforce with the skills necessary to succeed in their jobs; and to generate profits. The culture of these institutions reflects three major functions of for-profit colleges and universities:

- *Offer a practical, hands-on learning experience*
- *Furnish an applied curriculum that is relevant to the job market*
- *Provide a body of faculty who have considerable field experience*

This chapter revisits the cultural framework presented in Chapter 2 and offers a different interpretation of faculty culture based on data previously presented. I then move to a discussion of how the needs of employers and the market influence the development of an additional culture—the culture of the industry. I conclude the chapter by discussing possible policy implications and offering areas for future research.

Current notions of faculty culture have been constructed with the assumption that faculty members are full-time, tenure-track employees who are engaged in varying degrees of teaching, research, and service, depending on their institution. Faculty culture also has been framed within the context of traditional, non-profit higher education institutions where shared governance is the norm and faculty members have input and decision-making authority into several areas of the university. Faculty culture and its subcultures as previously defined in the literature (Austin, 1990; Becher, 1987 Clark, 1983; Tierney & Rhoades, 1993) do not fully explain the work environments for faculty members participating in the study. While the subcultures themselves remain the same and are applicable to for-profit institutions, the manner in which they are defined differs. To be clear, cultures are distinct at each type of institution. Just as faculty members and faculty work is impacted by traditional institutions, faculty are impacted when they work at for-profit institutions.

A logical question stemming from a re-evaluation of faculty culture pertains to its impact on faculty work life at for-profit IHEs. Table 16 compares faculty culture at traditional, non-profit institutions with that of the for-profit institutions represented in this study. In what follows, I revisit the cultural framework using the roles and responsibilities of faculty members at for-profit IHEs as a basis from which to reconsider faculty culture. I provide alternative perspectives on each of the subcultures that contribute to the overall development of faculty culture at for-profit colleges and universities.

Table 16: A Comparison of Faculty Culture at Traditional vs. For-profit IHEs

Cultural component	Traditional IHEs	For-profit IHEs
Institution	Policies are based on the norms of the academy— shared governance	Policies based on the norms of business— centralized governance
Discipline	Defined by area of expertise, i.e. Sociology, History, Physics, etc.	Defined by profession, i.e. computer programmer, financial analyst, travel agent, etc.
Academic Profession	Focus on teaching, research, and service to the university	Focus on teaching, learning, and service to the students
Individual	Belief in tenure, academic freedom	Job security linked to performance; academic freedom is contextual
National	Education as a public good	Education as a private commodity

Institutional Component

The institutional component of faculty culture refers to the manner in which colleges and universities operate, based on the norms of institutional type. Institutional culture impacts policies, methods of decision-making, and formal and informal rules. As a consequence, faculty work life is influenced in numerous ways. A major difference between traditional and for-profit institutions pertains to faculty participation in governance and decision-making activities.

Shared decision-making is common at traditional IHEs. Decision-making activities typically are shared between faculty, administrators, and other members of the university community, i.e. staff and students. A key difference between institutional cultures at for-profits vs. at traditional IHEs is that the policies that dictate the operation of for-profit institutions are based on the norms of the business sector. Decisions are made quickly and the institution is able to adapt to the needs of employers and the market. Nonetheless, decisions involve a relatively small number of individuals who hold a significant amount of authority. Shared governance is not a component of decision-making in the realm of business.

Administrators retain much of the decision-making authority at for-profit IHEs. Faculty members, in essence, become managed professionals (Rhoades, 1996). In other words, administrators have enormous control over the hiring, firing, evaluation, and working conditions of faculty members. Governance structures at for-profit IHEs shift a greater proportion of the decision-making to non-faculty professionals, i.e. business executives and full-time administrators. In addition, external constituencies have influence over curricular decisions. The method in which for-profit institutions are governed has a direct bearing on the development of faculty culture.

Disciplinary Component

The disciplinary component of culture focuses on a faculty member's primary specialization or area of expertise. It refers to the field in which individuals receive their educational training. Faculty members at traditional IHEs are defined by their discipline; it is a function of their research interests and educational background. With the rise of interdisciplinary inquiry, faculty members are finding new ways to look at problems and are creating new knowledge bases. At for-profit institutions, a faculty member's discipline—defined here as their prior educational training—is less relevant than their professional work experience. Moreover, faculty structures are such that different academic programs or curricula require faculty with varying levels of professional and educational training.

Faculty members at for-profits are linked to their discipline via their professional activities. Since research is not a function of their job, disciplinary activities such as writing articles, book reviews, or reviewing manuscripts are not as important as keeping current with the latest trends in their respective fields. A key difference between faculty members at traditional vs. for-profit IHEs is that faculty at for-profit institutions teach from a different knowledge base. Faculty members have formal training, i.e. they have degrees, but much of their knowledge is gained through professional experience rather than through academic or scholarly inquiry. In other words, 'real world' knowledge is rewarded as much, or more than, formal educational training.

Academic Profession

Faculty work life at for-profit colleges and universities centers around three components—teaching, learning, and service. Although faculty members at traditional and for-profit IHEs both have teaching responsibilities, teaching comprises the majority of work for instructional faculty at for-profits. Instructional faculty members also are responsible for ensuring that their students learn. The service component differs at each type of institution as well. For example, faculty members at traditional IHEs are required to serve the university community through committee work or participation in an academic senate. They also serve the at-large academic community through disciplinary activities such as reviewing manuscripts, presenting at conferences, etc. Faculty members at for-profit institutions are expected, to a much greater extent, to serve the needs of their students.

The unique characteristics that define the academic profession at for-profit IHEs are evident in the chief responsibilities of faculty members; different faculty members perform different functions. Part-time faculty members primarily serve as instructors and/or mentors and spend the majority of their time working with students. In contrast, some full-time faculty members spend little time teaching, while others spend most of their time in the classroom. The responsibilities of full-time administrative faculty focus on the teaching and learning components of the institution. They are responsible for hiring faculty members and maintaining the curriculum through the evaluation of faculty and the assessment of student learning. In addition, many full-time faculty members are responsible for evaluating new courses to ensure they satisfy the needs of students and employers.

Individual Component

The culture of the individual centers on the idea that the distinctive characteristics of individual faculty members contribute to the development of faculty culture. Simply put, faculty members' perspectives influence how they experience their working environment. Here, the *individual* component situates the faculty member within the context of the organization. For instance, in the context of this study the distinctive characteristics of faculty members at DLU influence how they viewed a number of issues, including tenure. Although faculty members were contingent employees, their contingent status had little bearing on how they perceived of themselves in relation to the institution. Put another way, faculty members participating in the study made the decision to teach at a for-profit knowing that tenure was not part of the institution's culture. Job security was viewed within the context of superior performance.

Faculty members at traditional IHEs view academic freedom as an intrinsic value of the profession that is fundamentally linked to tenure. Academic freedom is rooted in the belief that faculty members have a right to pursue 'truth'; both faculty and society benefit from such endeavors. Not all faculty members in traditional higher education settings are involved in research, and faculty work often consists of various activities unrelated to the pursuit of 'truth.' However, a faculty member's belief in that pursuit is essential to understanding the different perceptions of academic freedom between faculty from traditional and for-profit institutions. For-profit IHEs are not research oriented institutions; their focus is on teaching and learning. Faculty work at for-profits is rooted within the curriculum. In the view of participants, academic freedom does not extend beyond the limits of the classroom and the curriculum. And even within the curriculum, it has its limits.

National Component

The national component of culture defines national perspectives of higher education by for-profit and traditional institutions. Clark (1983) posits that there are basic features of higher education systems that are common throughout various higher education structures around the world. Knowledge-bearing groups are an essential component of higher education and tasks are organized around knowledge areas. For-profit institutions also are organized around knowledge-bearing groups—the faculty. However, tasks are organized not only around knowledge-bearing areas—academic departments or schools, but also are organized around 'corporate' departments of the institution, as well as external market forces. The academic and business divisions of the institution have distinctive priorities that often can conflict with one another. Numerous participants spoke about tension between the academic and business sides of their institution.

A fundamental difference in how higher education is organized at for-profit colleges and universities relates to whether higher education is considered a public or private good. Conventional notions of higher education maintain that education serves the public good through the pursuit of new ideas, the discovery of knowledge, and its dissemination via publications, presentations, and classroom instruction. For-profit IHEs are not research-focused institutions, yet one can argue that they serve the public good in several ways. For instance, they are able to educate students efficiently and cost-effectively. In addition, they provide educational opportunities to previously underserved student populations such as adult and minority students.

Although debates persist regarding the merits of higher education either as a public or private good, the for-profit higher education market is clear about their perceptions of higher education as a private commodity, as evidenced by the clear distinction between the academic and business sides of each institution. The former focuses on academic quality and the latter on generating profits. Balancing academic quality and profit generation places certain demands on for-profit institutions, creating a new and distinctive culture that is unique to for-profit colleges and universities.

CULTURE OF THE INDUSTRY

For-profit higher education institutions operate in two ostensibly dichotomous domains, the profit-generating/commerce sector and the traditional non-profit sector of higher education. Traditional IHEs utilize practices that are influenced by the business sector; they have increasingly become more customer-oriented and have focused their efforts on increasing revenues along with efficiency. A major difference between traditional and for-profit IHEs is that for-profits are required to meet the needs of their owners/investors as well as the needs of the student. Profits allow the institution to continue to operate, and to improve quality and service. The culture of the for-profit higher education industry impacts faculty work on a variety of fronts, and is a key component that influences faculty culture.

External factors, in particular demands from the marketplace, influence how for-profit institutions operate. Although faculty responsibilities can be linked to the culture of an institution, the impetus for implementing certain procedures, policies, and guidelines is a direct consequence of the demands from businesses and employers. In other words, the business sector expects for-profit institutions to take certain actions and to develop specific procedures that ensure that the institution meets the needs of the employers and the market (see Table 17). These expectations influence faculty work life and manifest themselves within three specific areas—assessment, knowledge, and service.

Table 17: Areas Influenced by the Culture of the Industry

Element	Characteristics
Assessment	A focus on organizational effectiveness and indicators of success
Knowledge	Education aligned with the needs of employers and the marketplace
Service	A commitment to students and a responsibility to employers

Assessment

The culture of the for-profit higher education industry concerns itself with indicators of success. For example job placement rates are closely monitored at for-profit institutions. Faculty and students place a high value on job placement rates and link them to the quality of the institution. Traditional institutions, such as community colleges, may focus on placing students into the job market, but placement rates are not used to measure the success of these institutions because community colleges concern themselves with more than job training.

The culture of the industry also places an emphasis on institutional assessment. For-profit IHEs regularly evaluate courses and teaching through the use of student evaluations and peer review. Traditional institutions also utilize student evaluations, but do so differently. For example, student evaluations at traditional IHEs serve as a tool for faculty members to improve their course content and teaching skills. They rarely are used to determine the future employment of a faculty member. Conversely, for-profit IHEs rely on student feedback to make critical decisions about the curriculum and instructional staff. Students complete end of course surveys that are used to determine whether the instructor successfully delivered the requisite information. Faculty members who are rated poorly will face scrutiny from the administration.

Faculty members at traditional IHEs also are evaluated by their peers. Tenure can be considered the definitive evaluation tool at traditional IHEs. It is a peer-reviewed process that assesses a faculty member's overall abilities. However, tenure is an evaluation tool used to assess the individual rather than the institution. For-profit institutions view the evaluation process as a means to assess the success of the organization. If faculty members at for-profit IHEs fail to perform to standards and students are unable to learn, the organization as a whole is not meeting its full potential.

Knowledge

Faculty members at traditional institutions possess a great deal of education and training related to their discipline. As knowledge-bearers (Clark, 1983), they are allowed to design their own courses and participate in the development of academic programs based on their considerable educational expertise and training. The knowledge base from which students at traditional IHEs learn is grounded in a faculty member's theoretical expertise. For-profit institutions regard knowledge differently. The knowledge and skill sets that students obtain are influenced by the needs of the market. The culture of the industry views knowledge as revolving around the needs of employers and businesses. As a result, courses are designed and academic programs are developed to fit those needs. Moreover, learning outcomes for courses and programs also reflect market needs. One can argue that faculty members at for-profit IHEs and their specific institutions have similar beliefs as to the type of knowledge students must acquire. Yet, at for-profit institutions, it is the marketplace rather than the faculty member that determines what students should and should not learn.

For-profit institutions rely on faculty members to convey their professional work experience to students as part of the educational process. Given that the knowledge faculty members impart is practical rather than theoretical in nature, an approach to teaching that focuses on applied learning activities is the preferred method of delivery. Although faculty members may utilize theoretical frameworks to support course content, their knowledge base is rooted in what they have experienced. As a consequence, knowledge—as defined by for-profit institutions—attracts a different type of faculty member. The culture of the industry expects for-profit IHEs to hire faculty members who have a wealth of professional experience as opposed to faculty whose knowledge is grounded in theoretical frameworks.

Service

The culture of for-profit IHEs can be described as customer service-oriented. For-profit institutions focus on the needs of the student in numerous ways. First, because they cater to working individuals, many institutions offer courses at times that are convenient to such students. Courses also are likely to be offered online to further meet the needs of students who are unable to enroll in courses offered on-ground. Second, courses and programs are designed to be relevant to the current job market and are offered in an accelerated format. Lastly, faculty members at for-profit IHEs must be cognizant of students' needs. Faculty members offer lectures that provide students with a hands-on, practical approach to learning. They share real-world knowledge in an effort to prepare students for the current job market. Service to the students is a large component of the culture at for-profit institutions.

As has been shown, faculty members work within the context of a customer-centered environment. However, it is important to recognize that the impetus for creating a culture that caters to customer's needs comes not only from internal institutional demands, but from external demands of business and industry. As such, for-profit IHEs meet the needs of an additional set of customers—employers. In seeking to educate members of their organization, employers turn to for-profit institutions because they provide practical knowledge and requisite skills sets, utilizing techniques and methods that are convenient to both employers and employees. To be clear, the culture of the industry compels for-profit institutions to meet the needs of two distinct sets of customers—students and employers.

LESSONS LEARNED

As this study has shown, faculty members at for-profit institutions live and work in an environment that differs in many ways from that of traditional non-profit institutions. There are numerous policy implications that will develop as the research base on for-profit higher education expands. The focus of this study is on faculty work life and its influence in the development of faculty culture. Accordingly, the lessons learned from this study and their implications on policy are highlighted here. I center the final conclusions around three broad themes: 1) Faculty work; 2) Engagement and; 3) Learning.

FACULTY WORK

Unbundling of Faculty Roles and Responsibilities

The manner in which for-profit institutions view the job responsibilities of their faculty differs. Full-time faculty responsibilities at traditional institutions require that faculty members be involved in numerous activities, each with its own set of responsibilities. Faculty members teach courses, are involved in some degree of research, chair dissertations, participate in committee work, etc. For-profit institutions view faculty work differently. Faculty responsibilities are unbundled, meaning that teaching, writing curriculum, chairing dissertations, and administrative duties are separate activities, and faculty members are hired to perform specific tasks. Moreover, faculty can choose their work activities, whether it is developing a new course, teaching a class, sitting on a curriculum committee, or a combination of all three. Each task is a separate responsibility, and faculty members are compensated on a 'per-task' basis.

Academic Freedom

Clarity in the types of responsibilities required of faculty members also has its disadvantages. More specifically, when faculty members are hired to teach, their role as an instructor limits their ability to determine course content and program goals. Many of those decisions already have been determined by others. An instructor's academic freedom is constrained. Academic freedom at for-profit institutions is contextual, and is interpreted to mean freedom within the classroom environment.

Yet, the concept of academic freedom provides faculty members with autonomy in their teaching and research, and also protects the individual from recrimination if they disagree with the institution, i.e. over lack of benefits or policies concerning dismissal. Faculty members at for-profit and traditional institutions do not work in environments where they persistently require the protection of academic freedom. Nevertheless, for-profit IHEs may consider extending the protection of academic freedom into other areas of the institution so as to allow faculty to have input into decisions that pertain to their working conditions, the evaluation process, and the promotion and release of other faculty members. Limits on academic freedom may reduce a faculty member's engagement with the institution. Yet, by extending the protection of academic freedom beyond the classroom realm, for-profit IHEs will help to develop an environment that promotes increased faculty engagement in the institution's academic community.

ENGAGEMENT

Faculty Involvement in Decision-Making

Faculty culture at for-profit colleges and universities is shaped in many ways by corporate culture. Decisions are made quickly, are data-driven, and reflect the needs of consumers. However, faculty members often are left out of the decision-making process. Faculty engagement in the university community is minimized when faculty members are unable to participate in governing their institution. One can argue that many faculty members from traditional institutions are not heavily engaged in their university community and are more focused on their own endeavors. The major difference, however, is that faculty from traditional IHEs can choose whether or not to be engaged. By increasing faculty engagement, for-profit IHEs could improve morale, increase job satisfaction, as well as close the gap between the business and academic divisions of the institution.

Student involvement

Unlike many traditional IHEs, for-profit institutions tend not to concern themselves with the development of the student as an individual. For-profit IHEs are concerned with a student's development outside of the classroom as it pertains to acquiring skills for the workplace. Yet, research shows that engaging in academic and social activities within the context of a university community produces positive outcomes for students (Astin, 1993; Tinto, 1993). For example, student involvement in campus activities has a positive effect on retention. For-profits may consider developing approaches by which students can engage in social and academic activities outside of the classroom to increase the likelihood that they will continue their education.

LEARNING

Considering Outputs as Well as Inputs

For-profit institutions concern themselves more with student outputs rather than inputs. Traditional colleges and universities typically measure the academic characteristics of students before making admissions decisions. It is quite common for traditional universities to consider an individual's SAT or GRE scores, as well as their high school or undergraduate grade point average. Rather than focusing on standardized test scores and prior academic performance, for-profit institutions place a higher value on what their students have learned once they are in the classroom. Although admissions standards are admittedly weak, I am not arguing for more stringent admissions criteria at for-profits. Instead, my point is to identify a critical difference in the way students are evaluated.

Teaching and learning at for-profit institutions focuses on mastering core competencies for each course, as well as for each degree program. Faculty members are required to cover predetermined content areas to assure that students receive a fundamental knowledge base. It is a very different approach than that of traditional IHEs. In the current climate of accountability, traditional institutions would be well served to establish learning outcomes and place more of a focus on measuring whether students have met certain competencies. Calls for increased accountability in higher education may place traditional colleges and universities in a position where they may be forced to measure specific outcomes, without the option of determining what those outcomes are.

Depth and Breadth of Knowledge

While assessment of student learning is not a common practice at traditional IHEs, students' educational experiences will differ by type of institution, with regard to their depth and breadth of knowledge. Students who attend for-profit IHEs will have a different, and in some respects narrower, intellectual experience than those who attend traditional colleges and universities. For example, professional schools at traditional institutions, such as those in engineering, business, and music, focus their curricula and teach courses specific to their fields. Undergraduate business students at both types of institutions will be required to take courses in marketing, finance, and organizational behavior. However, business students at traditional IHEs may be required to take a greater number of general education courses unrelated to business than students at for-profit IHEs. Students' education experiences, academic quality not withstanding, will differ by institutional type as a result of the tangential knowledge students acquire in their academic programs.

AREAS FOR FUTURE RESEARCH

Given what we know about faculty members and faculty culture at for-profit institutions, the next logical step could involve an examination of academic quality at for-profit institutions. A study of academic quality will require one to define the term quality. In addition, questions arise with regard to assessing the academic quality of an institution. For-profit institutions measure quality based on job placement rates as well as graduation and attrition rates. This may not be the optimal method of assessing quality because many students attending for-profit institutions already are employed at the time of enrollment. Graduation and attrition rates provide valuable information regarding the institution's ability to retain and graduate students, but do not necessarily offer a clear measure of academic quality.

Another area of inquiry could examine the academic quality of for-profit institutions by exploring faculty members' level of engagement in their professional communities. This will require the researcher to define faculty engagement. Faculty at traditional IHEs are engaged in the academic community through their research and publishing. Faculty engagement is also linked to other academic activities such as presentations, participation in professional associations, among others. Since the majority of faculty members at for-profit institutions are not engaged in the academic community in a manner akin to faculty at traditional colleges and universities, it would be important to explore the link between educational quality and involvement in a professional community. What effect does engagement in professional activities, including working in the field, have on the academic quality of for-profit institutions? This argument assumes that faculty engagement is tied to educational quality; therefore it would be important to establish whether there is a link between engagement in professional activities and academic quality. Based on what is now known about faculty work life and faculty culture at for-profit institutions, studies that focus on the impact that this new breed of faculty have on the educational quality of these institutions can provide further insight into this growing sector of higher education.

A final topic of particular concern that may influence areas for future research relates to the issue of academic freedom. Faculty members at for-profit IHEs are, by default, contingent employees; tenure is not an option. Faculty members are often constrained by a prescribed curriculum, choice of textbooks, and their inability to offer new courses and programs without prior approval from the administration. If for-profit colleges and universities say that they espouse the tenets of academic freedom, how are faculty members protected? What mechanisms are in place to protect faculty when issues regarding their academic freedom arise and threaten their employment? The answers to these questions are complex and are not the subject of this study. However, issues of academic freedom as well as educational quality are areas that may best be addressed in future research regarding for-profit colleges and universities. Such empirical research can help educators in the non-profit and for-profit sectors better understand one another, and can contribute to the growing body of literature on for-profit colleges and universities.

Appendix A
Interview Protocol

1) Describe your professional background in higher education.

2) How did you become a faculty member at this institution?

3) What are the greatest barriers you face in being effective in the classroom?

4) How do you define your role as a faculty member?

5) Please describe the classroom environment with regard to academic freedom.

6) What are the greatest strengths and weaknesses of teaching on-line? (if applicable)

7) How do you define your institution to others? What makes your institution unique?

8) Describe the types of decisions that involve faculty input. What role do faculty members play in the decision making process?

9) Describe the role of the faculty with regard to curriculum development?

10) What changes would you make to improve your relationship with members of the administration? With other colleagues?

11) What factors motivate you to continue working at your institution?

Appendix B
E-mail Invitation

Dear (Full Name),

My name is Vince Lechuga. I am a doctoral student and a research assistant in the Center for Higher Education Policy Analysis Center, at the University of Southern California. I am conducting research on for-profit colleges and universities for my dissertation project.

I am contacting you because I would like to understand the role of faculty within for-profit colleges and universities. You have been identified as someone who has taught courses for (Name of Institution). If at all possible, I would like to interview you over the telephone for approximately thirty minutes. A total of 60 subjects from several different for-profit colleges and universities will participate. I am primarily concerned with faculty work-life at for-profit postsecondary institutions, and am interested in two major issues: 1) Faculty members' roles/relationship with the institution, and 2) The organizational culture at (Name of institution).

Any information that is obtained in connection with this study and that can be identified with you or (Name of Institutions) will remain completely CONFIDENTIAL. Data gathered from the interviews will be used only for authorized research, and will not be used for competitive advantage or financial gain by anyone. I have attached a list of questions that will guide our conversation and am happy to send you a detailed description of my project.

Please let me know if you are free to speak with me next week (Dates). Feel free to suggest another day or week if you are not available next week. If you have any questions or concerns regarding this study, feel free to contact

William G. Tierney, Director, Center for Higher Education Policy Analysis using the link below. I look forward to speaking with you.

Regards,

Vince

Vicente M. Lechuga
Center for Higher Education Policy Analysis
University of Southern California
Rossier School of Education, WPH 703
Los Angeles, CA 90089–0031
(213) 740–3453
http://www.usc.edu/dept/chepa/

References

American Association of University Professors. (2001). Statement on government of colleges and universities. In *AAUP Policy Documents and Reports* (9th edition). Washington, DC: AAUP.

———. (2003). *Policy statement: Contingent appointments and the academic profession.* Retrieved on November 24, 2003, from http://www.aaup.org/statements/SpchState/contingent.htm

Astin, A.W. (1993). *What matters in college: Four critical years revisited.* San Francisco: Jossey-Bass.

Austin, A.E. (1990). Faculty cultures, faculty values. *New Directions for Institutional Research, 17*(4), 61–74.

Bailey, T., Badway, N., & Gumport, P.J. (2001). The contours of for-profit higher education. *Change, 33*(6), 47–50.

Baldridge, J.V. (1980). Organizational characteristics of colleges and universities. In J.V. Baldridge & T. Deal (Eds.), *The dynamics of organizational change in education* (pp. 38–59). Berkeley, CA: McCutchan Publishing Corporation.

Baldridge, J.V., Curtis, D.V., Ecker, G., & Riley, G. (1977). Alternative models of governance in higher education. In J.V. Baldridge & G. Riley (Eds.), *Governing academic organizations* (pp. 2–25). Berkeley, CA: McCutcham Publishing.

Baldwin, R.G., & Chronister, J.L. (2001). *Teaching without tenure: Policies and practices for a new era.* Baltimore, MD: Johns Hopkins University Press.

Becher, T. (1987). The disciplinary shaping of the profession. In B.R. Clark (Ed.), *The academic profession: National, disciplinary, and institutional settings* (pp. 271–303). Los Angeles: University of California Press.

———. (1989). *Academic tribes and territories: Intellectual inquiry and the culture of the disciplines.* Bristol, PA: Open University Press.

———. (1990). The counter-culture of specialization. *European Journal of Education, 25*(3), 333–347.

Benjamin, E. (2003). Editor's notes. *New Directions for Higher Education, 123,* 1–13.

Birnbaum, R. (1988). *How colleges work: The cybernetics of academic organization and leadership.* San Francisco: Jossey-Bass Publishers.

——. (1984). Introduction. In R. Birnbaum (Ed.), *ASHE Reader in Organization and governance in higher education* (pp.1–5). Lexington, MA: Gin Custom Publishing.

Bleak, J.L. (2004). For-profit subsidiaries of non-profit universities: A challenge to governance and culture? *Metropolitan Universities, 15*(4), 38–66.

Blumenstyk, G. (2003, March 14). For-profit colleges attract a gold rush of investors. *The Chronicle of Higher Education,* p. A25.

Bolman, L.G., & Deal, T. (1997). *Reframing organizations: Artistry, choice, and leadership.* San Francisco: Jossey-Bass Publishers.

Breneman, D. (2003). The University of Phoenix: Poster child of for-profit higher education. Paper presented at Columbia University Teachers College Conference: Markets, Profits, and the Future of Higher Education, New York, NY. Retrieved May 3, 2004 from http:// www.ncspe.org/publications_files/breneman.pdf.

Breneman, D. (1997). Alternatives to tenure for the next generation of academics. *New Pathways: Faculty Career and Employment for the 21st Century Working Paper Series, Inquiry #14.* American Association for the Advancement of Science. Washington, D.C.

Breneman, D., Pusser, B., & Turner, S. (2000). *The contemporary provision of for-profit higher education: Mapping the competitive market.* Unpublished manuscript, University of Virginia.

Buck, J. (2001). The president's report: Successes, setbacks, and contingent labor. *Academe, 87*(5), 18–21.

Campbell, C.D. (2003). Leadership and academic culture in the senate presidency: An interpretive view. *American Behavioral Scientist, 46*(7), 946–959.

Chaffee, E. E. (1998). Listening to the people we serve. In W.G. Tierney (Ed.), *The responsive university* (pp. 13–37). Baltimore, MD: Johns Hopkins Press.

Clark, B.R. (1963). Faculty organization and authority. In T. Lunsford (Ed.), *The study of academic administration* (pp. 37–51). Boulder, CO: Western Interstate Commission for Higher Education.

——. (1983). *The higher education system: Academic organizations in cross-national perspective.* Los Angeles: University of California Press.

——. (1987a). *The academic life: Small worlds, different worlds.* Princeton, NJ: The Carnegie Foundation.

——. (Ed.).(1987b). *The academic profession: National, disciplinary, and institutional settings.* Los Angeles: University of California Press.

——. (1996). The ties of association. In D.E. Finnegan, D. Webster, & Z.F. Gamson (Eds.), *Faculty and faculty issues in colleges and universities* (2nd ed.). Needham Heights, MA: Simon & Schuster.

Cohen, M. D., & March, J.G. (1974). Leadership in an organized anarchy. In M.D. Cohen & J.G. March (Eds.), *Leadership and ambiguity: The American college president* (pp. 195–229). New York: McGraw-Hill.

Collis, D. (2000). "When industries change" revisited: New scenarios for higher education. In M. Devlin & J. Meyerson (Eds.), *Forum futures: Exploring the future of higher education* (pp. 103–126). San Francisco: Jossey-Bass.

Collison, M.N. (1998). Proprietary preference: For-profit colleges gain momentum in producing graduates of color. *Black Issues in Higher Education, 15*(10), 31–32.

Cook, C.A., & Fennell, M. (2001). Capital gains: Surviving in an increasingly for-profit-world. *The Presidency, 4*(1), 28–33.

Dandridge, T.C., Mitroff, I., & Joyce, W.F. (1980). Organizational symbolism: A topic to expand organizational analysis. *Academy of Management Review, 5*(1), 77–82.

De Alva, J.K (1999/2000). Remaking the academy in the age of information. *Issues in Science and Technology, Winter, 52–58.*

Deal, T. E., & Kennedy, A. A. (1982). *Corporate cultures: The rites and rituals of corporate life.* Reading, MA: Addison-Wesley Publishing Company.

Dever, K.A. (1999). A comparative analysis of leadership styles of executives in higher education and for-profit corporations: A study of context and gender (Doctoral Dissertation, The Claremont Graduate University, 1999). *Dissertation Abstracts International, 60,* 234.

Dill, D.D. (1982). The management of academic culture: Notes on the management of meaning and social integration. *Higher Education, 11,* 303–320.

Duderstadt, J.J. (2000). *A university for the 21st Century.* Ann Arbor, MI: University of Michigan Press.

Education Commission of the States. (2000a). *Report from the regions: Accreditors' perceptions of the role and impact of for-profit institutions in higher education* (Report No. PS-00–01W). Denver, CO: Peter Ewell & Paula Schild.

———. (2000b). *Survey analysis: State statutes and regulations governing the operation of degree-granting for-profit institutions of higher education* (Report No. PS-00–02). Denver, CO: Tunde Brimah.

———. (2001). *Meeting the needs and making profits: The rise of the for-profit degree-granting institutions* (Report No. FP-01–01W). Denver, CO: Kathleen F. Kelly.

Ehrenberg, R.G. (2002). *Tuition rising: Why college costs so much.* Cambridge, MA: Harvard University Press.

Farrell, E.F. (2003a, April 18). Signer beware: For-profit colleges increasingly use arbitration agreements to prevent lawsuits. *The Chronicle of Higher Education,* p. A33.

———. (2003b, August 15). A common yardstick? *The Chronicle of Higher Education,* p. A25.

———. (2004, February 11). Deeper pockets, different tactics. *The Chronicle of Higher Education,* p. A26.

Finkelstein, M.J. (1984). *The American academic profession.* Columbus, OH: Ohio State University Press.

Finkelstein, M.J., & Schuster J.H. (In press). *The American faculty: The restructuring of the academic profession.* Baltimore, MD: Johns Hopkins University Press.

Foster, D., & Foster, E. (1998). It's a buyer's market: "Disposable professors," grade inflation, and other problems. *Academe, 84*(1), 28–32.

Freedman, M. (1979). *Academic culture and faculty development.* Berkeley, CA: Montaigne Press.

Gallagher, S., & Newman, A. (2002). *Distance learning at the tipping point: Critical success factors to growing fully online distance-learning programs*. Eduventures Report, September 2002. Retrieved September 10, 2003 from, http://www.eduventures.com/research/research-home.cfm

Gappa, J.M., & Leslie, D.W. (1993). *The invisible faculty: Improving the status of part-timers in higher education*. San Francisco: Jossey-Bass.

Garber, M.P., & Steiger, F. (1996). Wall Street PhD: For-profit education can be good for business and for education. *National Review, 48*(18), 57–59.

Gardner, H. (1999). *The disciplined mind*. New York: Simon and Schuster.

Geertz, C. (1973). Thick Description: Toward an interpretive theory of culture. In C. Geertz (ed.), *The interpretation of cultures* (p.3–30). New York: Basic Books.

Glassman, R.B. (1973). Persistence and loose coupling in living systems. *Behavioral Science, 18,* 83–98.

Goldstein, M.B. (2000). To be (for-profit) or not to be: What is the question? *Change, 33*(5), 24–31.

Hamilton, N. (2000). The academic profession's leadership role in shared governance. *Liberal Education, 86*(3), 12–19.

Hebel, S. (2004, March 26). Led by Colorado, states weigh new approaches to financing colleges. *The Chronicle of Higher Education,* p. A26.

Horvat, E.M., & Antonio, A.L. (1999). "Hey those shoes are out of uniform": African American girls in an elite high school and the importance of habitus. *Anthropology & Education Quarterly, 30(3),* 317–342.

Kahn, R., & Cannell, C. (1957). *The dynamics of interviewing*. New York: John Wiley.

Kinser, K. (2003). A profile of regionally-accredited for profit institutions in higher education. Paper presented at the meeting of the Association for the Study of Higher Education, Portland, OR.

———. (2004). What is for-profit higher education? Paper presented at the meeting of the Association for the Study of Higher Education, Kansas City, MO.

Kirp, D.L. (2003). Education for profit. *Public Interest, 152,* 100–106.

Kolb, C.E.M. (1995). Accountability in postsecondary education. In *Financing postsecondary education: The federal role*. Washington, D.C.: U.S. Department of Education Retrieved on September 13, 2003 from http://www.ed.gov/offices/OPE/PPI/FinPostSecEd/kolb.html

Kuh, G.D., & Whitt, E.J. (1988). *The invisible tapestry: Culture in American colleges and universities* (ASHE-ERIC Higher Education Report No. 1). Washington, D.C.: ERIC Clearinghouse on Higher Education.

Ladd, E.C., & Lipset, S.M. (1975). *The divided academy*. New York: McGraw-Hill.

Leatherman, C. (1997, October 10). Growing use of part-time professors prompts debate and calls for action. *The Chronicle of Higher Education,* p. A14.

Leslie, D.W., & Gappa, J.M. (2002). Part-time faculty: Competent and committed. *New Directions for Community Colleges, 101*(3), 59–67.

Levine, A.E. (2000, October 27). The future of colleges: Nine inevitable changes. *The Chronicle of Higher Education, 47*(9), B10.

Longin, T.C. (2002). Institutional governance: A call for collaborative decision-making in American higher education. In W.G. Berberet & L.A. McMillin (Eds.), *A New Academic Compact: Revisioning the Relationship between Faculty and their Institutions*. Bolton, MA: Anker Publishing.

Marshall, C., & Rossman, G.B. (1999). *Designing qualitative research* (3rd ed.). Thousand Oaks, CA: Sage Publications.

Martin, H.J. (1985). Managing specialized corporate cultures. In R.H. Kilman, M.J. Saxton, & R. Serpa (Eds.), *Gaining control of the corporate culture* (pp. 148–162). San Francisco: Jossey-Bass Publishers.

Masland, A. (1991). Organizational culture in the study of higher education. In M. Peterson (Ed.), *Organization and governance in higher education* (4th ed.) (pp. 118–125). Needham Heights, MA: Simon & Schuster Custom Publishing.

Mason, J. (1996). *Qualitative researching*. Thousand Oaks, CA: Sage Publications.

Mathison, S. (1988). Why triangulate? *Educational Researcher, 17*(2), 13–17.

Miller, M.A. (2000). The marketplace and the village green. *Change, 32*(4), 4–5.

Millett, J.D. (1962). *The academic community*. New York: McGraw-Hill.

Morey, A. (2001). The growth of for-profit higher education. *Journal of Teacher Education, 52*(4), 300–316.

Morgan, R. (2002, October 11). Lawmakers call for more accountability from accreditation system. *The Chronicle of Higher Education*, p. A28.

Morphew, C.C. (1999). Challenges facing governance within the college. *New Directions for Higher Education, 27*(1), 71–79.

Munitz, B. (2000). Changing landscape: From cottage industry to competitive industry. *Educause Review, January/February,* 12–18.

Myers, D., Park, J., & Hacegaba, N. (2000). *Reversing the shrinking middle in California's labor force*. Los Angeles, CA: University of Southern California.

National Association of State Universities and Land Grant Colleges, American Association of State Colleges and Universities. (2002). Student charges & financial aid, 2001–2002. Washington, D.C.: National Association of State Universities and Land Grant Colleges, American Association of State Colleges and Universities.

National Center for Education Statistics. (1998). *Faculty staff in postsecondary institutions*. Washington, DC: U.S. Department of Education.

———. (1999). *Students at private, for-profit institutions*. Washington, DC: U.S. Department of Education.

———. (2000). *Enrollment Survey*. Washington, DC: U.S. Department of Education.

———. (2001). *Postsecondary institutions in the United States: Fall 2000 and degrees and other awards conferred: 1999–2000*. Washington, DC: U.S. Department of Education.

———. (2002). *Findings from the Condition of Education 2002: Nontraditional undergraduates*. Washington, DC: U.S. Department of Education.

———. (2003a). *Enrollment in postsecondary institutions, Fall 2001 and financial statistics, fiscal year 2001*. Washington, DC: U.S. Department of Education.

———. (2003b). *Postsecondary institutions in the U.S.: Fall 2002 and degrees and other awards conferred*. Washington, DC: U.S. Department of Education.

Newman, F., & Couturier, L.K. (2002). The new competitive arena: Market forces invade the academy. *Change, 33*(5), 11–17.

Nuss, E.M. (1996). The development of student affairs. In S.R. Komives, D. B. Woodward Jr., & Associates (Eds.), *Student services: A handbook for the profession*, (3rd ed.). (pp. 22–42). San Francisco, CA: Jossey-Bass Publications.

Patton, M.Q. (1987). *How to use qualitative methods in evaluation.* Thousand Oaks: Sage Publications.

Pusser, B. (2005). *What are those data worth? The problems of conducting research on for-profit colleges and universities.* Unpublished manuscript, University of Virginia.

Pusser, B., & Turner, S.T. (2004). Non-profit and for-profit governance in higher education. In R.G. Ehrenberg (Ed.), *Governing academia* (pp. 235–257). Ithaca, NY: Cornell University Press.

Pusser, B., & Doane, D.J. (2001, January/February). Public purpose and private enterprise: The contemporary organization of postsecondary education. *Change, 33*(1), 18–22.

Rhoades, G. (1996). Reorganizing the faculty workforce flexibility: Part-time professional labor. *Journal of Higher Education, 67*(6), 626–659.

Rodenhouse, M.P. (Ed.). (2000). *2000 Higher education directory.* Fall Church, VA: Higher Education Publications, Inc.

Rosovsky, H. (1990). *The University: An owner's manual.* New York: W.W. Norton & Company, Inc.

Roueche, J.E., Roueche, S.D., & Milliron, D. (1996). Identifying the strangers: Exploring part-time faculty integration in American community colleges. *Community College Review, 23,* 33–48.

Rubin, H.R., & Rubin, I.S. (1995). *Qualitative interviewing: The art of hearing data.* Thousand Oaks, CA: Sage Publications.

Ruch, R.S. (2001). *Higher Ed, Inc.: The rise of the for-profit university.* Baltimore, MD: Johns Hopkins University Press.

Schneider, A. (1999, December 10). To many adjunct professors, academic freedom is a myth. *The Chronicle of Higher Education,* p. A18.

Schrage, M. (1998). Brave new world for higher education. *Technology Review, 101*(5), 90–91.

Schuster, J.H. (2003). The faculty makeover: What does it mean for students? In E. Benjamin (Ed.), *Exploring the role of contingent instructional staff in undergraduate learning. New Directions in Higher Education, 123,* 15–22.

Schwandt, T.A. (2001). *Dictionary of qualitative inquiry* (2nd ed.). Thousand Oaks, CA: Sage Publications.

Selingo, J. (2003, January 25). California's public universities adopt steep tuition increases. *The Chronicle of Higher Education,* p. A20.

Sessa, D. (2001, March 12). Business plan. *Wall Street Journal,* p. R8.

Soley, L. (1998). Higher education or higher profit; For-profit universities sell free-enterprise. *In These Times, 22*(21), 14–17.

Sperling, J., & Tucker, R.W. (1997). *For-profit higher education: Developing a world-class workforce.* New Brunswick, NJ: Transaction Publishers.

Strauss, A., & Corbin, J. (1998). *Basics of qualitative research: Techniques and procedures for developing grounded theory* (2nd ed.). Thousand Oaks, CA: Sage Publications.

Symonds, W.C. (2003, April 28). Colleges in crisis. *Business Week, 74–79.*

Tierney, W.G. (1988). Organizational culture in higher education: Defining the essentials. *Journal of Higher Education, 59*(1), 2–21.

———. (1991). Utilizing ethnographic interviews to enhance academic decision making. *New directions in Institutional Research, 71*(Winter), 7–22.

———. (Ed.). (1998). *The responsive university.* Baltimore, MD: Johns Hopkins Press.

Tierney, W.G., & Rhoads, R.A. (1993). *Faculty socialization as cultural process: A mirror of institutional commitment.* ASHE-ERIC Higher Education Report No. 93-6. Washington, D.C.: The George Washington University, School of Education and Human Development.

Tinto, V. (1993). *Leaving college: Rethinking the causes and cures of student attrition* (2nd Ed.). Chicago: University of Chicago Press.

Traub, J. (1997, October 20). Drive-thru u.: Higher education for people who mean business. *New Yorker,* 117–123.

Ward, D. (January/February 2000). Panel on the future of American higher education. *Educause Review, 35*(1), 32–35.

Weick, K.E. (1979). Educational organizations as loosely coupled systems. *Administrative Science Quarterly, 21*(1), 1–19.

Winston, G.C. (1999). For-profit higher education: Godzilla or Chicken Little? *Change, 102*(1), 12–19.

Wolfe, A. (1998, December 4). How a for-profit university can be invaluable to the traditional liberal arts. *The Chronicle of Higher Education,* p. B4.

Yin, R. K. (1984). *Case study research: Design and methods.* Beverly Hills, CA: Sage Publications.

Index

Printed in the USA/Agawam, MA
February 15, 2013

572884.024